MW00914631

DAILY SPIRITUAL REFLECTIONS

VIMA DASAN SJ

Daily
Spiritual Reflections

(ROOTS & FRUITS)

*How to live a grace-filled life
on your journey of faith*

ST PAULS

ST PAULS Publishing
187 Battersea Bridge Road, London SW11 3AS

Copyright © ST PAULS 2000

ISBN 085439 580 6

Set by TuKan, Fareham, Hampshire
Produced in the EC
Printed by Società San Paolo, Roma, Italy

ST PAULS is an activity of the priests and brothers
of the Society of St Paul who proclaim the Gospel
through the media of social communication

CONTENTS

January – JUBILEE

Week 1:	Fullness of Time	12
Week 2:	Year of the Lord	20
Week 3:	Year of Liberty	28
Week 4:	Year of Joy	36

February – CREATION

Week 1:	Creator	44
Week 2:	Creatures	51
Week 3:	Human Person	58
Week 4:	New Creation	66

March – THE FATHER

Week 1:	The Father's Face	74
Week 2:	The Father's Children	82
Week 3:	Divine Providence	89
Week 4:	Abba, Father	97

April – JESUS CHRIST

Week 1:	The Incarnation	106
Week 2:	The Good News	113
Week 3:	The Universal Saviour	121
Week 4:	The Sole Mediator	129

May – CROSS AND RESURRECTION

Week 1:	Suffering	138
Week 2:	Dying	146
Week 3:	Rising	154
Week 4:	Living	162

June – HOLY SPIRIT

Week 1:	The Spirit in the Trinity	170
Week 2:	The Spirit in Creation	177
Week 3:	The Spirit in the Church	184
Week 4:	Life in the Spirit	192

July – VIRGIN MARY

Week 1:	Mary our Model	202
Week 2:	Highly Favoured	210
Week 3:	Marian Devotions	217
Week 4:	Guiding Star	225

August – THE CHURCH

Week 1:	Attributes	234
Week 2:	Symbols	242
Week 3:	Sacraments	250
Week 4:	Vocation	257

September – THE KINGDOM OF GOD

Week 1:	Mysteries of the Kingdom	266
Week 2:	Glad Tidings of the Kingdom	274
Week 3:	Signs of the Kingdom	282
Week 4:	Proclamation of the Kingdom	289

October – THE CRISIS OF CIVILISATION

Week 1:	The Crisis	298
Week 2:	Religious Indifference	306
Week 3:	Loss of Higher Values	313
Week 4:	The Return	321

November – BACK TO BASICS

Week 1:	Faith	330
Week 2:	Scriptures	337
Week 3:	Prayer	344
Week 4:	Family	352

December – CIVILISATION OF LOVE

Week 1:	Love	362
Week 2:	Solidarity	370
Week 3:	Liberty	378
Week 4:	Peace	385

ABBREVIATIONS

TMA	Tertio Millennio Adveniente
MD	Mulieris Dignitatem
GS	Gaudium et Spes
VS	Veritatis Splendor
RP	Reconciliatio et Penitentiae
CCC	Catechism of the Catholic Church
CTH	Crossing the Threshold of Hope
DV	Dei Verbum
AG	Ad Gentes
AMi	Redemptoris Missio
LG	Lumen Gentium
DeV	Dominum et Vivificantem
PO	Presbyterorum Ordinis
OL	Orientale Lumen
ChL	Christifideles Laici
VR	Veritas Redintegratio
EV	Enchiridion Vaticanum
CDF	Congregation for the Doctrine of Faith
LF	Letter to the Families
DH	Dignitatis Humanae
RM	Redemptoris Mater
AHM	Addresses, Homilies, Messages
	AHM (1) Address to Italian Servicemen, 1 March 1979
	AHM (2) Homily, Cotonous Benin, 4 February 1993
	AHM (3) Address to Bishops of Latin America, 21 October 1992
	AHM (4) Address to the Diplomatic Corps, 16 January 1993
	AHM (5) Homily, Dublin, 29 September 1979
	AHM (6) Homily for Young People, Munich, 19 November 1980
	AHM (7) Address in the Sanctuary of the Madonna della Grazie, Benevento, 2 July 1990
	AHM (8) Address to the Slmo Collegio Capranica, Rome, 21 January 1980
	AHM (9) Address to the Young, Paris, 1 June 1980
	AHM (10) Apostolic Letter to World Youth, Op. cit.

AHM (11) Homily for University students, Vatican Basilica,
          5 April 1979

AHM (12) Address to Young people. Santiago de
          Compostla, 19 August 1989

AHM (13) Address in the Sanctuary of Madonna delle
          Grazie, Benevento, 2 July 1990

AHM (14) Address to Scientists and Students, Cologne,
          15 November 1980

AHM (15) Address to Salesian youth, Rome, 5 May 1979

AHM (16) Audience to Young People, 14 March 1979

AHM (17) Ibid.

AHM (18) Ibid.

AHM (19) Ibid.

AHM (20) Homily for Holy Mass, Perth, Australia,
          30 November 1986

AHM (21) Address to the Young, Foggia, 24 May 1987

AHM (22) Address to the Families, Ibid.

AHM (23) Address to the Young, Ibid.

AHM (24) Solicitudo rei Socialis 39–40

AHM (25) Address to Workers, Sao Paolo, Brazil,
          3 July 1990

AHM (26) Homily, Kevealaer, Federal Germany,
          2 May 1987

AHM (27) Homily Punta Arenas, Chile, 4 April 1987

AHM (28) World Congress on Promotion of Human
          Rights, 1990

AHM (29) Message for World Peace day, 1996

AHM (30) Homily, Droghede, Ireland, 29 September 1979

All Scriptural Quotations are from New Jerusalem Bible.

January:
JUBILEE

Week 1
Fullness of Time

Week 2
Year of the Lord

Week 3
Year of Liberty

Week 4
Year of Joy

PRECIOUS TIME

Root > The creative act of God marked the absolute beginning of time, though at this time God already existed. What unrolled in time is God's plan for it, which first orders all creation with regard to man and then directs the destiny of man with regard to his eternal end. It is in time God set in motion humankind's salvation history culminating in the death and resurrection of Christ who will return to restore all humanity to their original destiny and with that time will end.

> *"In Christianity, time has a fundamental importance. Within the dimension of time, the world was created. Within it, the history of salvation unfolds, finding its culmination in the Fullness of Time, of the Incarnation and its goal in the glorious return of the Son of God at the end of time"* (John Paul II – TMA 9).

Fruit > Therefore time is a sacred creature. God worked everything for humankind in time and still does. We human beings are called to become aware of the spiritual demands required by the time in which we live. We will make the best use of our time, if we work towards the dawn of a new age, an age of peace and happiness which will restore here below the perfection of paradise. The rest is killing time and killing time is not murder, it is suicide. Time is like a circus always packing up and moving away; Let us not waste it.

A SINGLE RIVER

ROOT > History understood in its full sense is Christian history, for it begins with the birth of Jesus Christ who recapitulates everything and is at the same time the fulfilment of all things in God. The plan of God for humanity, of perfect happiness with him, runs from the beginning to the end uninterrupted. God who revealed his saving love to the people of Israel, finally and definitively revealed his universal plan of salvation for humanity in Jesus Christ who in his turn works out the salvation through his Church the extension of his Body, a work that will continue to the end of time when all will be restored to God in Christ.

> *"The whole of Christian history appears to us as a single river, into which many tributaries pour their waters. The year 2000 invites us to gather with renewed fidelity and ever deeper communion along the banks of the great river: the river of Revelation, of Christianity and of the Church"* *(John Paul II – TMA 26).*

FRUIT > Standing on the bank of Revelation, we recognise Christ as the supreme sacrament of history, for we see God through his body, eternity through his time and loving God in his person. Standing on the bank of Christianity, we realise that Christianity is either relevant all the time or useless any time, for it is not just a phase of life, but life itself. Standing on the bank of the Church, we come to understand that there is nothing credible in the Church apart from Christ who lives in it, and hence if the Church goes wrong on Christ, she goes wrong on everything.

FULLNESS OF TIME

ROOT > From the onset of his preaching, Jesus proclaimed that with his coming "The Time is fulfilled" (Mk 1;15), meaning that with him the last of the stages of God's plan had begun, when God brings to completion not only the Scriptures and the Law but also the whole purpose of the old Covenant. By "Fullness of Time", he also meant that he being the Son of God, eternity which is fullness of time, has entered on earth with him. As a result, those who believe in him will also share in his fullness, thus entering into eternity even while living on earth.

> *"Time is indirectly fulfilled by the very fact that God in the Incarnation came down into history. Eternity entered into time: what 'fulfilment' can be greater than this? To enter into the 'fullness of time', means to reach the end of time and to transcend its limits to find time fulfilment in the eternity of God" (John Paul II – TMA 9).*

FRUIT > What is fulfilling in life? To some it is a life given to prayer; to others it is given to social activism or caring of the poor. Some see it in terms of healing; others in terms of successful and important secular career, still others in terms of virtue. Clearly, we will measure fulfilment depending on the values we hold. But Jesus probes beyond these differences to ask the question: what constitutes fulfilment? And his answer is that fulfilling life is union with him as branches united with their vine, for he is the fullness of life which is eternal life and in him eternity entered into time.

A DIMENSION OF GOD

ROOT > A human being lives in time; God lives in eternity, a duration which surpasses human measurement and of which we have no experience. God lives for ever, in ages of ages: "A thousand years are to you like a yesterday which has passed, like a watch of the night" (Ps 90:4). And yet, through the Incarnation of the Son of God, human time which is like a declining shadow is assumed by the Second Person of the Holy Trinity. The Son of God was born in time, suffered and died in time. Thus time becomes a dimension of God and human history also becomes God's history.

> *"In Jesus Christ, the incarnate Word, time becomes a dimension of God, who in himself is eternal" (John Paul II – TMA 10).*

FRUIT > Time is holy because it has become a dimension of God when the Word of God took flesh. It is this unique event which the Church actualises now in the cycles of its liturgical calendar in order to sanctify human time. Each Sunday, the day of the Lord becomes within the framework of the week, a celebration of the resurrection of Jesus. The celebration takes on a more solemn character when the anniversary of the death and resurrection of the Lord makes its annual return. If time has become part of eternity, right 'now' counts for ever. Hence it is difficult for us to understand how an intelligent person can spend all of his or her time building for this world, and have no time for the future world.

THE LORD OF TIME

ROOT > All times belongs to Jesus Christ. The Past belongs to him: Jesus is closely associated with the Father in his creative activity and therefore is "the one Lord through whom all things exist and by whom we are" (1 Col 8:6). The Present belongs to Jesus. As a consequence of sin, humanity was destined to dissolve. But Christ redeemed the world and God has made him the head of the redeemed humanity (Col 1:18), giving him all power on earth (Mt 28:18). The Future belongs to Jesus: The expectation of Christ's return as judge of the living and the dead is part of the Christian belief (Mt 25:14-30). Every human person will appear before Christ to render an account of his or her action.

> *"Christ is the Lord of time: he is the beginning and its end; every year, every day and every moment are embraced by his Incarnation and Resurrection and thus become part of the 'fullness of time'" (John Paul II – TMA 10).*

FRUIT > If we recall our past mistakes we must do so to learn something from them, because the only complete mistake is the mistake from which we learn nothing. For the rest, we must surrender all our past mistakes to the Lord, for he is the Lord of the Past. Our present life is a paradox of tension and relief, of privilege and denial, of love and hatred. But if we surrender our present to the Lord, he can create heaven in this paradox, for he is the Lord of the Present. We fear for the future for we don't know what is in store for us. But entrust your future to the Lord, for he is the Lord of the Future. His grace that has brought us thus far through many dangers, toils and snares, will also lead us home.

IMMORTAL LIFE

ROOT > Human person created in the image of God, is endowed with a spiritual and immortal soul. Human person alone is called to share, by knowledge and love, in God's own life. It was for this end we were created. The human person is a being at once corporal and spiritual. But the human body too shares in the dignity of the image of God because it is animated by a spiritual soul, and it is the whole human person that is intended for immortal life.

> *"Some have thought in terms of certain mysterious cosmic cycles in which the history of the universe and of mankind in particular would constantly repeat itself. Yet in man there is an irrepressible longing to live for ever. Man rebels against the finality of death. He is convinced that his nature is essentially spiritual and immortal"* (John Paul II – TMA 9).

FRUIT > We feel and know that we are immortal. Take for example, our growing old. Year by year we are ageing; yes, but we are only ageing on the outside. Inside we feel the same as we did when we were young. We still love intensely and have a deep need to give and receive love. As our body is ageing, our real life that will live on, is developing. As we grow older, the love of every person and the music of creation penetrate our being more and more deeply. Yes. God is preparing us, for something that will go on for ever. That is why, the nearer we approach the end, the plainer we begin to hear around us the immortal symphonies of the world which invites us.

ONE EARTHLY EXISTENCE

ROOT > Hindus and Buddhists speak of man's rebirth or new fall into a new earthly existence through an unlimited series of passages or reincarnations of the soul from one body to the other. To them, human being's destiny is not confined to a single earth-life but is worked out in many. Jesus did not teach reincarnation. Christianity is pre-eminently a religion arising from and centred in a single life-pattern; and it thus raised the life-history of every person to a position of great importance.

> *"Christian revelation excludes reincarnation and speaks of a fulfilment which man is called to achieve in the course of a single earthly existence"* (John Paul II – TMA 9).

FRUIT > Our earthly existence being only one and not more than one, it stands to reason that we seize the present day and live it to the full. But strangely enough, many people have the feeling they are chasing after something but not catching it. To them, the real thing always seems to be happening somewhere else. When they are here, they think it is there, but when they get there, it has moved on to somewhere else. They are rarely satisfied with the present moment. But given the certainty that we pass through this life only once, we must consider each day as an invitation to achieve fullness wherever we are, whatever our circumstances. Seizing the day requires us to change gears from hurry to contentment, from worry to appreciation, from seeing life as one in many to recognising it as only one.

SANCTIFICATION OF TIME

ROOT > Christianity values time as a means which God uses to become incarnate, and to reveal and give his grace. From the beginning of his revelation, God manifested himself by means of history, and thus time became sacred. For Christianity, time is linear, not a cyclic repetition, and salvation is not an exodus from time. Time and salvation are destined to meet in history, thus history becomes salvation history. Because of this relationship of salvation with time, there arises a duty to sanctify time.

> *"Christian Revelation tells us that all human history is salvation history, progressing through three definite stages: Creation, Redemption and final Recompence. With incarnation, God himself entered history to redeem it. Human beings collaborate with God in the perfecting of human nature, that is, in the development and progress of history" (John Paul II – AHM [1]).*

FRUIT > If time is sacred, we are called to sanctify every moment of it. Time, of course, is not automatically sacred, so that all we have to do is sit tight and wait. As each day comes, it calls for us to get involved and choose how to use it, to make decision between what is good, healthy, and constructive, and what is unhealthy, evil and destructive. Time offers us the chance to be creative, to help create our authentic selves and work for the progress and development of humanity.

CUSTOM OF THE JUBILEE

ROOT > In the Old Testament the Jubilee was a time dedicated in a special way to God. It was celebrated every fifty years. A Jubilee implied restructuring of society which would bring with it freedom from whatever that divided the communities. This custom of the Jubilee, begun in the Old Testament, continues in the history of the Church until today.

> *"I invite the faithful to raise to the Lord fervent prayers to obtain the light and assistance necessary for the preparation and celebration of the forthcoming Jubilee, opening their hearts to the promptings of the Spirit. He will not fail to arouse enthusiasm and lead people to celebrate the Jubilee with renewed faith and generous participation" (John Paul II – TMA 59).*

FRUIT > We often hear and read about 'Millennium Bids'. There is constant debate about where Millennium Party should take place. Some people are even planning to fly around the world to see the dawn of the new Millennium in as many different locations as possible. But the Church calls upon all Catholics to celebrate the Millennium of the year 2000, in a spirit of prayer and meditation, on the wondrous works of the Incarnation and Redemption. She has especially asked us to remember the themes of God the Creator, God the Redeemer and God the Sanctifyer, so that we achieve a deeper and more vital spiritual life, leading us ever closer to eternal union with the living God.

OF LORD'S FAVOUR

Root > Since all Jubilees refer to the salvific dimension of 'time', they point to the Messianic mission of Christ. The Jubilee is not merely the recurrence of an anniversary in time, but characterises all the activities of Jesus. It is he who proclaims the Good News to the poor, who brings liberty to those deprived of it, who frees the oppressed and gives back sight to the blind. Thus, he ushers in a year of the Lord's favour not only with his words but, above all, with his actions.

> *"'The Spirit of the Lord is on me, for he has anointed me to bring the good news to the afflicted. He has sent me to proclaim liberty to captives, sight to the blind, to let the oppressed to go free, to proclaim a year of favour from the Lord.' He then rolled up the scroll, gave it back to the assistant and spoke to them: 'This text is being fulfilled today even while you are listening'"* (Lk 4: 16-22).

Fruit > How much we wish, that the Spirit who anointed Jesus on that day in the Synagogue, also falls on us today and daily, during the Jubilee year, even as the first drops of rain on a parched and barren land, awakening us like seeds in the desert, to flower and carry on the same ministry which Jesus inaugurated! Yes, May the spirit fall on us like the ripples in the lake, reaching out through our minds, bodies and souls to renew the face of the earth.

CHRIST THE FOCUS

ROOT > All Jubilees point to Jesus Christ, for in him the fullness of time had arrived and through whom we fulfil ourselves in God who comes to meet us through his eternal Son. With the coming of Christ, there began 'the last days'(Heb. 1:2), 'the last hour'(1 Jn 2:18), and the time of the Church which will last until the Parousia. Hence Christ's words and actions are even today efficacious saving actions, for those who celebrate them especially through the Liturgical Year, which in a certain way reproduces the whole mystery of the Incarnation and Redemption.

> *"The Liturgical Year is not a cold and lifeless representation of events of the past nor a simple and bare record of a former age. It is rather Christ himself who is ever living in his Church. Here he continues the journey of immense mercy that he lovingly began with his mortal life" (Pius XII – MD 165).*

FRUIT > A beautiful resolution that all of us can make to mark the Jubilee year 2000, is to come daily closer to Christ, our light. If we are walking away from the sun, the shadows are before us. This is one of the reasons why many Christians are afflicted with every manner of psychosis and neurosis. As we walk away from Christ, the sun, the longer the shadows that appear before us: the resentments, fears and aggressiveness. If however, we walk towards Christ, the sun and intensify our focus on him, then all these shadows are behind us.

THE CENTRE OF CALENDAR

ROOT > Christ is the great central fact of the whole history. All lines of history converge upon him. All the great purposes of God culminate in him. Only for three years he preached his Gospel, but after two thousand years, he is the one central character of human history. All the armies that ever marched, all the navies that ever were built, all the parliaments that ever sat, and all the kings who ever reigned, put together, have not affected the life of humanity upon earth, as powerfully as has that one solitary life – the life of Christ.

> *"It is significant that the calculation of the passing years begins almost every where with the year of Christ's coming into the world, which is thus the centre of the Calendar most widely used today. Is this not another sign of the unparalleled effect of the birth of Jesus of Nazareth on the history of mankind?" (John Paul II – TMA 14).*

FRUIT > If Christ has become the centre of human history, when will he become the centre of our lives? To make Christ the centre of our lives, he must become the law of our lives. Some make their own self, the guide of everything; it is like looking into the pool where you see your own image and fall in love with it and become a thoroughbred egoist. Others follow the commandments and some rules of life. Though this is very commendable, it is very difficult to fall in love with an abstraction. But there is another way of living: to try to repay Christ's love for us by living his life. When Christ becomes the rule of life, then his life becomes ours.

INDIVIDUAL JUBILEES

ROOT > Individual Jubilee or Anniversary, is also a particular year of the Lord's favour. A wedding anniversary, for example, is a time to thank God for keeping the partners united in love, and to pray for continued grace of God to love one another ever more intensely. Likewise, Ordination jubilee is a time to praise the priest who has strived so far to live up to his priestly calling, and to pray for more grace to be showered on him in the year to come.

> *"In the lives of individuals, Jubilees are usually connected with the date of birth; but other anniversaries are also celebrated, such as those of Baptism, Confirmation, First Communion, Priesthood, and the Sacrament of Marriage. Some of these anniversaries have parallels in the secular world, but Christians always give them a religious character. In fact, in the Christian view, every Jubilee is a particular year of favour for the individual who has received one or other of the Sacraments" (John Paul II – TMA 15).*

FRUIT > On Sacramental anniversaries we are expected to recall the promises we made at the time of the reception of the Sacrament. For example, at our baptism we had our personal new beginning for in baptism we died with Christ to sin and rose to new life in him. But the process of death to self leading to a life for God and others must go on in our daily lives. Therefore, every Baptismal anniversary is a year of Lord's favour for it offers us an opportunity to recommit ourselves to the ongoing process of dying to self and rising to new life. So with other anniversaries.

COMMUNITY JUBILEE

ROOT > As individual Jubilees or anniversaries, there are community Jubilees and anniversaries too. For example, we celebrate Parish Anniversary. That too is a day of God's favour. On this day we thank God for what he has done in and through his people who are called his Church, we confess our failures to live up to our sacred duty to build up the Parish into a family of God, and pray that God forgives us and renews us as people of God.

> *"We celebrate the centenary or the millennium of the foundation of a town or city. In the Church, we celebrate the Jubilees of dioceses. All these personal and community Jubilees have an important and significant role in the lives of individuals and communities" (John Paul II – TMA 15).*

FRUIT > For a community celebration such as a Parish Anniversary to become a special year of God's favour, the members of the Parish have to ask themselves some soul-searching questions: Do I really belong to my parish? To belong to a parish is not to hang onto the parish by the membrane of an old childhood memory; I do not belong to my parish just because I pull off my hat every time I pass by my parish church. True belonging calls for developing close faith relationship with fellow parishioners.

A YEAR OF RECONCILIATION

ROOT > As followers of Christ we all have reasons to ask God and from one another forgiveness for the times we have departed from the spirit of Christ and the Gospel, for the times we have given counter witness and scandal, instead of offering the world the witness of a life inspired by the values of faith. This Jubilee Year urges us to seek penance and renewal. Jesus gave reconciliation and forgiveness of sins a very important place in his earthly ministry.

> *"For the Church, the Jubilee is precisely the year of the Lord's favour, a year of remissions of sins and of the punishments due to them, a year of reconciliation between disputing parties, a year of manifold conversions and of sacramental and extra-sacramental penance" (John Paul II – TMA 14).*

FRUIT > One fine morning, Pope John Paul II journeyed across the city of Rome to meet with Mehemet Ali Agca, the man who had shot the Pope at St Peter's Square in May 1981. The pictures of the Pope embracing the prisoner in his cell and the words, 'I forgive you', speak eloquently about the importance that the Church places on the event of reconciliation. The Sacrament of penance is one important way that the Church offers forgiveness of God. Communal celebrations of reconciliation is another way for Christians to admit their sinfulness and experience the Church's reconciliation with their brothers and sisters.

THE YEAR EXTRAORDINARY

ROOT > There has been no one in the history of humankind who has been seriously bidding for the heart of the world except Jesus Christ. Christianity has given humanity the most sublime and benevolent code of morals ever offered to humankind. Established by Christ as the fellowship of love, it has served the human race as light of the world and salt of the earth, promising a new world order based on justice and equality. Although its members are fewer than some of the other world religions, Christianity has had the greater influence on history, and is still the most influential faith in God.

> *"The two thousand years which have passed since the birth of Christ represent an extra-ordinary great Jubilee, not only for Christians but indirectly for the whole humanity, given the prominent role played by Christianity during these two millennia" (John Paul II – TMA 15).*

FRUIT > All those who are aware of the great power that Christianity has been down the centuries, face a challenge at the dawn of the third millennium. Christianity challenges them to continue to proclaim with new vigour the life of Christ, the holiest among the mighty and the mightiest among the holy. Christianity challenges the Christians to make their religion the way of life, and work towards a new world order permeated with Gospel values, and even be ready to sacrifice one's life for them. Christianity, indeed, is a demanding and serious religion. When it becomes easy and amusing, it is another kind of religion altogether.

THE SABBATICAL YEAR

ROOT > The liberation by God from the servitude in Egypt was the fundamental event marking the beginning of the Chosen People. However, Moses enjoined on his people that the Hebrew slaves should be let free after seven years, in honour of God's delivering them from Egypt. It was called the 'Sabbatical Year' during which, not only the earth was left fallow and slaves were set free, but the law also provided for the cancellation of all debts.

> *"At the end of every seven years, you must grant remission.*
> *The nature of remission is as follows: any creditor holding a*
> *personal pledge obtained from his fellow must release him*
> *from it" (Dt 15:1-6).*

FRUIT > The cancellation of debts enjoined by the Law of Moses to celebrate the Sabbatical Year would particularly be valid for the start of the third millennium, if such a cancellation takes place now. In the 1950's and 60's, Third World countries borrowed money from the richer North, but interest rate rose in 1970's and commodity prise fell, resulting in a massive burden of debt repayment on the poor countries. By 1996, poor countries were paying more than £10 billion per month to the rich countries. Every £1 donated in aid by the industrialised countries to the Third World, was matched by £3 paid by the Third World in interest to the rich countries.

FREEDOM FROM SLAVERY

ROOT > Slavery was practised in Israel. A good number of slaves were of a foreign origin: prisoners of war reduced to slavery or slaves brought from merchants who trafficked in them. But the code of the Covenant prescribed freedom from slavery after seven years. Levitical legislation on its part instituted a general liberation during the Jubilee Year wishing that one day the Hebrew slaves would rise to a salaried state. Therefore the custom of freeing slaves were celebrated with great solemnity in the Jubilee Year.

> *"You shall hallow the fiftieth year, and proclaim liberty throughout the land to all its inhabitants; it shall be a Jubilee for you when each of you shall return to his property and each of you shall return to his family" (Lev 25:10).*

FRUIT > As the people of Israel hallowed the Jubilee Year by allowing the slaves to return to their families and properties, can the present day Christian world do something to mark the Jubilee Year 2000, with regard to millions of refugees and asylum seekers, who are driven out from their homelands and properties by the selfish, the hateful, the violent, and the powerful? The refugees stream across our television screens balancing impossible burdens, the remnant of their lives tied up in bundles!

EMANCIPATION

ROOT > After the Exodus from Egypt and return from Babylonian captivity, which was understood as a punishment for people's sins, true liberation came to be understood as the purification of the remnant. That is why, the centuries immediately preceding the coming of the Messiah, were marked by an expectation of the definitive liberation from sin by Jesus Christ. By uniting us to the mystery of Christ's death and resurrection, baptism sets us free from sin and we are no longer under the Law but under grace.

> *"One of the most significant consequences of the Jubilee Year was the general emancipation of all the dwellers on the land in need of being freed. They thus became 'a prophetia futura' in so far as they foretold the freedom which would be won by the coming of the Messiah" (John Paul II – TMA 12,13).*

FRUIT > We have been definitively redeemed by Christ to live in his Spirit which is the spirit of charity We are free from our former slavery to sin in order to serve God and neighbour. We see many imprisoned behind brick walls and held by iron bars, but they are not so hopeless as those who are held captive by hate, and those encircled by envy and prejudice. The Jubilee year beckons us to join in the company of the Liberator. May we walk alongside him, who breaks the barriers of hate, and share in his pilgrimage towards peace and fellowship.

EQUALITY

ROOT > God's purpose in instituting the Jubilee Year was to guarantee equality, justice for all, and to keep the rich from accumulating wealth and land at the expense of the disadvantaged. The law was not always observed fully, however. Nevertheless, setting the oppressed free and breaking the yoke of inequality, was one of the forms of fast which was pleasing to God.

> *"Every Israelite could never be completely deprived of the land because it belonged to God. The Jubilee Year was thus meant to restore equality among all the children of Israel, offering new possibilities to families which had lost their property, even personal freedom" (John Paul II – TMA 12,13).*

FRUIT > It is our Christian belief that people are of inestimable value because they are the children of God, the concern of his love, created for an eternal destiny. We cannot dismiss any one as of no consequence; nor are we entitled to suppose that some are more important than others The consequences of accepting this basic truth are shattering, calling into question not only the discriminating way in which we often behave towards many of our fellow human beings, but the international, military, political, economic and social policies which have only strengthened the inequality among people, and yet considered reasonable.

THE RICH AND THE POOR

ROOT > In various ways God has revealed his great concern for the poor, the needy and the oppressed. In his law to the Israelites, he provided a number of ways to eliminate poverty among them. He forbade for example the charging of interests on loans to the poor; If the poor gave something as a pledge against a loan, the person loaning the money had to return that pledge by sunset. If the poor person was hired to work for a rich man he was to receive the pay every day. Thus God always sought to protect the poor against the exploitation of the rich.

> *"Yaweh, you have been a refuge for the weak, a refuge for the needy in distress, a shelter from the storm, shade from the heat, for the breath of the pitiless is like a winter storm" (Is 25:1,4).*

FRUIT > Not only the poor are always with us, but currently they are in the midst of a population explosion. The third millennium should heighten our Christian consciousness about our duty to care for the poor. Poverty is not just inconvenient to the poor, but insulting to the rich as well. All the natural and human resources and whatever riches we may possess come from God. Hence when we give to the poor even our best, we only return to God what is his. Let us not give like the sponge, which gives only when you squeeze it.

SOCIAL JUSTICE

ROOT > Social justice is to act with proper regard to others, giving what is due to them. It implies that common possession must be fairly distributed among all. It is social injustice for some people to accumulate wealth far beyond their needs, and leave others paupers. The Jubilee Year of the Israelites was meant to restore social justice. Justice according to the law of Israel consisted, above all, in the protection of the weak. The doctrine of the Church on social justice is rooted in the tradition of the Jubilee Year.

> *"In the midst of huge numbers deprived of the absolute necessities of life, there are others who live in riches and squander their wealth; and this happens in less developed areas as well. Luxury and misery exist side by side"* (GS 63).

FRUIT > We desperately need economists deeply sensitive to social justice, who will fundamentally rethink economics as if poor people mattered. At the heart of God's call for Jubilee is a divine demand for regular, fundamental redistribution of the means of producing wealth. We must discover new concrete models for applying the social teachings of the Church in our global village. How we wish, that a new generation of economists would devote their lives to developing and implementing a contemporary model of Jubilee!

HUMAN RIGHTS

Root > Created in the image of God and equally endowed with rational souls, every human person has the same nature and the same origin. The equality of human beings rests essentially on their dignity as persons. Respect for human dignity entails respect for the rights that flow from it. These rights are prior to society: right to have everything necessary for leading a life truly human. Social justice can be obtained only in respecting the basic dignity of every person.

> *"Every form of social and cultural discrimination in fundamental personal dignity on the grounds of sex, race colour, social conditions, language or religion must be curbed and eradicated as incompatible with God's design. Excessive social and economic disparity between individuals and the people of the human race militates against equity and human dignity" (GS 29).*

Fruit > How long, then, will the peasants still remain landless, and the workers remain displaced! How long the urban poor still remain homeless and the youth remain unschooled! How long the national minorities still remain ostracised and the women remain doubly burdened! How long will the countries be governed by manipulative, insensitive men with warped military and capitalist ideologies! What is at stake is the dignity of the human person.

THE RICHES OF CREATION

ROOT > God in his Providence has given the earth to humanity which means that he has given it to every one. It follows, then, that the riches of creation are to be considered as common good of the whole humanity. The early Christian community wanted to translate this basic belief into concrete action. All who owned land or houses sold them and brought the money to the apostles to give to others in need. They freely gave and shared eliminating poverty among them. They would not let a brother or sister suffer, when others had plenty.

> *"Whatever the forms of ownership may be, attention must always be paid to the universal purpose for which the created gifts are meant. In using them, a man should regard his lawful possessions not merely as his own but also as common property" (GS 69).*

FRUIT > That charity and justice begin at home is true; but they do not end there. While we provide for the needs of the home, let us not exaggerate these needs. We need not sell our possessions as early Christians did, but we need to use them well and wisely, so that we can give a helping hand to those who are in need of help. Have a look at your home, your way of dressing, your meals, your recreations and entertainments, and you may find many occasions for saving some money to give to relief-organisations.

PRAISE AND THANKSGIVING

ROOT > The glory of the Incarnation is that it presents to our adoring gaze, not a humanised God or a deified man, but a true God-man, one on whose almighty arms we all can rest and to whose redemptive sacrifice we can always appeal. If I had the wisdom of Solomon, the patience of Job, the meekness of Moses, the strength of Samson, the obedience of Abraham, the tears of Jeremiah, the enduring love of Paul, I would still need redemption through Christ's blood and forgiveness of sin.

> *"The Jubilee of the Year 2000 is meant to be a great prayer of praise and thanksgiving for the gift of the Incarnation of the Son of God and of the Redemption. Our thanksgiving will embrace the fruits of holiness which have matured in the lives of all those men and women who in every generation and every period of history have fully welcomed the gift of redemption"* (John Paul II – TMA 32).

FRUIT > At the death of Christ, the veil in the temple was rent open from top to bottom. But it was only a symbol of the heart of Christ which was opened on the hill of Calvary by means of a lance. When the curtain of his flesh was opened, the blood that poured from it has made us free, to enter into the sanctuary of God through a new living way. As we praise and thank the Lord for such a redemption, we must ask ourselves whether we have accepted this gift of redemption and if we have, we would have accepted the new living way of Christ.

INVISIBLE JOY

ROOT > Even after 2000 years, the birth of Christ, the Word made flesh, fills us with joy. It is that Word which is a lamp to our feet and a light unto our path, and if we take it out of our homes, the last glimmer of hope is gone. In him appeared the light of the world. It is that light for which restless millions waited. In him the glory of God appeared, and it is that glory which swallows up all the shining achievements of men and women, as the brightness of the sun swallows up the light of moon.

> *"I exult for joy in Yaweh, my soul rejoices in my God, for he has clothed me in garment of salvation, he has wrapped me in a cloak of saving justice, like a bridegroom wearing his garland, like a bride adorned in her jewels" (Is 61:10).*

FRUIT > Our joy in the birth of Christ is invisible, spiritual joy. It is not the fleeting joy that one gets when one has a good bank account, a good cook and a good digestion. It is deep, lasting and fulfilling joy, because it is the joy of salvation; it is the experience of peace and harmony, truth and goodness. Because it is the joy of salvation, there is nothing in affliction that can disturb it. It is a holy joy. No one can live without delight, and that is why a person deprived of spiritual joy goes over to carnal pleasures.

VISIBLE JOY

ROOT > The joy we experience at the birth of Christ is pierced with a lance of sadness when he dies on the cross. But, then, our joy is redoubled at his resurrection. Because of his resurrection, every healing hereafter is a partial resurrection, and every change is towards greater life: from the child leaving the womb up to the person's leaving this world at death, all move towards fuller life. All negative elements in our life, can be dealt with creatively. Death has been conquered by life and so we can continue to work for a better world with hope-filled visible joy.

> *"The term 'Jubilee' speaks of joy; not just an inner joy but a jubilation which is manifested outwardly for the coming of God is also an outward, visible, audible and tangible event" (John Paul II – TMA 16).*

FRUIT > The life of a Christian should be a perpetual jubilee, a prelude to the festival of eternity. The sin of the past is blotted out for a Christian, and the continued fellowship with risen Christ is offered for the present, and the future will reveal Christ as the conqueror over suffering and death. We must leave sadness to those in the world. We don't want long faced saints; a sad saint is a sorry saint. Melancholy is the poison of life. We must smile and laugh as we live our life of faith. Laughter adds richness, texture and colour to otherwise ordinary days.

JOY OF CONVERSION

ROOT > The journey home to God our Father is a journey of conversion, from brokenness to wholeness, that travels along the way of repentance. Authentic conversion includes a negative aspect, that of liberation from sin, and a positive aspect that of choosing good, accepting the ethical values expressed in the natural law, which is confirmed and deepened by the gospels. Authentic penance is inspired not by fear but by love, and consists in a serious effort to crucify the 'old man' so that the 'new' can be born by the power of Christ.

> *"No matter how many and great the obstacles put in God's way by human frailty, the Spirit who renews the face of the earth makes possible the miracle of perfect accomplishment of the good. This renewal which gives the ability to do what is noble offers liberation from the slavery of evil" (VS 118).*

FRUIT > An impression that pervades society is that nothing is really my fault. I am either a victim or a saint, never a sinner. Examination of conscience which is a honest personal examen of behaviour and how we responded to the voice of God as spoken through our own conscience, will disprove it. There is something honest and dignified and cathartic about owning up to my faults and my virtues. There is a dignity in saying, 'I did it, I was wrong, I am sorry.' Psychologically, it is also the best hope for forgiveness and growth.

JOY OF RECONCILIATION

ROOT > To acknowledge one's frailty, to recognise oneself being broken and inclined to fall away from God, is the essential first step in returning to God. In effect, to get reconciled with God presupposes and includes detaching oneself consciously and with determination, from the sin into which one has fallen. It presupposes and includes, therefore, doing penance, adopting a real attitude of repentance, which is the attitude of the person who starts on the road to the Father.

> *"God calls out persistently all the fallen-aways, to gather about his table in the joy of the feast of forgiveness and reconciliation. This initiative on God's part is made concrete and manifests in the redemptive act of Christ which radiates through the world by means of the ministry of the Church"* (RP 10).

FRUIT > Since all the faithful are in solidarity with the Christian community, reconciliation with God is to be also a reconciliation with the Church. For a Christian, the Sacrament of Penance is the ordinary way of making this reconciliation and obtaining forgiveness and remission of serious sins committed after Baptism. It does not mean that our Saviour is unable to work outside and above the sacraments. But the same Saviour desired that the simple and precious Sacraments of faith would ordinarily be the effective means through which the fruits of his redemption pass and operate.

THE JOY OF FULL COMMUNION

ROOT > Christ intended that his Church be visibly united in the profession of same faith, the celebration of the same sacraments, and in the unity of the one people of God. In order to bring about and maintain such a unity, Christ endowed his Church with threefold ministry of the Word, sacraments and leadership, first entrusted to the apostles with Christ as head, and then continued with the college of bishops under the Pope. Catholics pray for the restoration of this full communion with other Christians.

> *"The approaching end of the second millennium demands of everyone an examination of conscience and the promotion of fitting ecumenical initiatives, so that we can celebrate the Great Jubilee, if not completely united, at least much closer to overcoming the divisions of the second millennium" (John Paul II – TMA·34).*

FRUIT > The Church of Christ, of course, also exists in a certain way outside the visible boundaries of the Catholic Church. Other Christian communities also have means of sanctification and Christian truth. Through their belief in Christ and their baptism, Christians separated from us are already our brothers and sisters in imperfect union with the Catholic Church. In varying degrees, there exists either in doctrine, discipline or structure of the Church, obstacles to full communion, which can be overcome, through theological dialogue, mutual collaboration and prayer.

UNIVERSAL JOY

ROOT > Jesus Christ is the desire of all ages. When we speak about wisdom and virtue, we are speaking of Christ. When we speak about justice and peace, we are speaking of Christ. When we speak about truth and life, we are speaking of Christ. Christ is the light of the world and he shines for all humankind. It is in order to convey that he is the universal saviour, that God drew the gentile wise men from the east to the crib where Christ was born. Christianity is oceanic and you can't contain it in a tea-cup. The Jubilee celebration should therefore bring universal joy.

> *"The Church rejoices in salvation. She invites every one to rejoice and she tries to create conditions to ensure that the power of salvation may be shared by all. Everyone is asked to do as much as is possible to ensure the great challenge of the year 2000 is not overlooked" (John Paul II – TMA 16).*

FRUIT > The Jubilee Year challenges us to share the light of Christ with those who still grope their way from dark behind to dark before. It challenges us to offer Christ to those who are still searching for meaning in their lives, for Christ is the answer to the yearnings of every human heart. It challenges us to become channels of God's grace, because grace that cannot be seen is no grace at all. One wonders what God will say to those who manage to go to him without others!

February:

CREATION

Week 1
Creator

Week 2
Creatures

Week 3
Human Person

Week 4
New Creation

OUT OF NOTHING

ROOT > God is an infinite, eternal and self-existing Being who is the First cause of all that exists. Never was there a moment when God did not exist. God has created everything out of nothing. For God who is the totality of all that is, must include all things in his infinite Being. If God had drawn the world from pre-existent matter, what would be so extra-ordinary in that? A human artisan makes from a given material whatever he wants, while God shows his power by starting from nothing to make all he wants.

> *"We believe that God needs no pre-existent thing or any help in order to create, nor is creation any sort of necessary emanation from the divine substance. God creates freely 'out of nothing'"* (CCC 296).

FRUIT > The 'creation from nothing' was the beginning of the whole of God's plan of salvation. God is the Master of the world and history, precisely because he created everything from nothing. Because he created everything from nothing, he can give spiritual life to sinners through the Holy Spirit, bodily life through the resurrection, and light of faith to those who do not yet know him.

REASON COMMANDS

Root > The most common reason for belief in God is that there can be no adequate explanation of the universe and the order that maintains it, without a Creator. The formation of a human being in the womb and hundred other living things persuade us that there is a Supreme Spirit, the designer of all. We are strengthened in our belief in God by our knowledge of ourselves. We feel guilty when we have done evil and satisfied when we have done good. Moral goodness, therefore, suggests to us that there is a God who is infinitely good.

> *"Human intelligence is surely already capable of finding a response to the question of origins. Existence of God the Creator can be known with certainty through his works by the light of human reason, even if this knowledge is often obscured and disfigured by error" (CCC 286).*

Fruit > Nothing comes from nothing. Every 'why?' has a 'wherefore?' Hence, for all that we see and for all that we are, there must be reason, and that reason is God. Even some learned people do not believe in God, because they are too fixed in their opinion to bow their minds down before a Supreme Being. Many refuse to believe in spite of the evidence, because they are afraid of the consequences of believing, which may entail a change in their way of life. Yes, there is nothing harder to see a naked truth, but there is nothing so safe as accepting the truth.

REVELATION CONFIRMS

ROOT > Beyond the natural knowledge that every human being can have of the Creator, God progressively revealed himself in created realities, as the one to whom belongs all the people of the earth and the whole earth itself. Furthermore, he manifested himself to our first parents inviting them to intimate communion with him. Even after the fall, God buoyed them up with the hope of salvation. He then made a covenant with his people of Israel. Thus, creation was the only first step towards this covenant, a universal witness to God's all powerful love for human beings.

> *"Thus says Yahweh, he who created you and formed you. Do not be afraid, for I have redeemed you. I have called you by your name, you are mine. I regard you as precious; you are honoured and I love you" (Is 43:1-4).*

FRUIT > God who revealed himself to our ancestors in many ways, finally revealed himself in the person of his Son Jesus Christ. Why this revelation? Hidden as he is, God had become still more inaccessible by the sin of humanity, so that we by ourselves cannot discover him as he is. And yet, before humanity turned to him, God took the initiative and was the first to speak to us. But God's revelation is not only for our knowing it, but that through it, we may come into close loving union with God.

DIVINE ARTISAN

ROOT > In the beginning God drew the universe out of primeval chaos. Then he brought forth all that gives richness and beauty to the universe. He set a perfect order in the regular movement of the stars and in the laws of reproduction. The climax of God's work is the creation of human being in his own image. On the seventh day he rested. Thus the temporal order of creation by God, gave to the life of the human being the sacred rhythm of the week, a model of all human work.

> *"Human persons created in the image of God are called to prolong the work of creation by subduing the earth, both with and for one another. Work honours Creator's gifts and talents received from him. It can also be redemptive. Work can be a means of sanctification and a way of animating earthly realities with the Spirit of Christ" (CCC 2427).*

FRUIT > It is by work that we create even like God. God creates grass, we create gardens; God creates gold, we create wedding rings; God creates sounds, we create melodies. Our motivation for work cannot be just personal fulfilment or money, but to make the world a better place to live in, as God himself did his work of creation out of love for humanity. But human sin has made work more and more burdensome. However, if we endure the hardship of work in union with Jesus the carpenter of Nazareth, our work can become fulfilling and redemptive.

THE CREATOR TRINITY

ROOT > The Father created everything that exists through his Word in the power of the Holy Spirit. The entire Trinity, not just the Father, had a role in creation. The Son himself is the powerful Word through whom God created all things. "All things were made by him; and without him not anything was made that was made" (Jn 1:3). Likewise, the Holy Spirit had an active role in the work of creation. He is pictured in the Scriptures as moving over the creation, preserving and preparing it for God's further creative activity.

> *"The whole divine economy is the common work of the three divine persons. For, as the Trinity has only one and the same nature, so too does it have only one and the same operation. However, each divine person performs the common work according to his unique personal property" (CCC 258).*

FRUIT > Created in the image of the triune God who do things always together as a community, we the human beings would reflect that image more perfectly, if we too do things together for common good, in spite of our individual differences. If you had escaped from a shipwreck in a small boat in the middle of a storm, you certainly would not ask if the man beside you was a Christian or a Muslim or to what ethnic group he belonged, before you joined him at an oar. Joint action is needed for a common welfare and at times, joint action carried out for a period of time, helps us to forget the differences in order to live together in peace.

THE SUSTAINER

ROOT > Except for God who freely chose to create human beings, there would not be a human race. Nor is that all. God is in every thing which he gives us. The same Almighty that brought us and the rest of creation into existence, continues dwelling in them, sustaining them. Otherwise everything would lapse again into nothingness. Nor is this a passive exercise of divine power enabling creatures to continue into existence. He continually enables his creatures to live and act and exercise their power.

> *"With creation, God does not abandon his creatures to themselves. He not only gives them being and existence, but also, and at every moment, upholds and sustains them in being, enables them to act and brings them to their final end" (CCC 301).*

FRUIT > God is in everything sustaining them. Hence, everything created can be a channel of God's grace, and in everything we can encounter God. In the measure in which we use all created things according to their intended end, in that measure they become our saviours. Even in our pains and sorrows, including death, God is present and hence, in and through our suffering, we can come closer to God more purified and more loving. God sustains our existence even when we displease him through our frailties. Hence, when we repent and reform ourselves, even our wrong doing can become eye-openers into the mystery of God's love.

THE TRANSCENDENT

ROOT > Though God is present in every created thing, sustaining it, he transcends them all. What does it mean? It means that when we look at created things, it is in a sense like looking at some statues. A crucifix or a picture of Christ is not Christ himself. Their immediate function is to catch the eye and point to the reality they represent. Likewise, a created thing is not the Creator himself; It only points towards God who is sustaining it. The day when we attempt to identify it with its Creator, we are turning it into an idol.

> *"God is infinitely greater than all his works. Indeed, God's greatness is unsearchable. God is present to his creatures' inmost being. In the words of St Augustine, God is 'higher than my highest and more inward than my innermost self'"* (CCC 300).

FRUIT > Material things such as wealth, beautiful and pleasurable things are not bad just because they do not last for ever. They are still good for God sustains them. However, we cannot make them the end of our lives. Any group which journeys, may enjoy, but must not get attached to the landscapes through which it passes. We are only passing travellers through the material world. They can be enjoyed but cannot be held. They are only points of our encounter with God to take us beyond them, to himself.

'IT IS GOOD'

ROOT > Seven times God states that what he created was 'good' (Gen 1:10). Each part of God's creation completely fulfilled his will and its intended purpose. God created the world to reflect his glory and to be a place where humankind could share his joy and love. Thus, God's goodness surrounds us. We walk through it almost with difficulty, as through thick grass and flowers. We declare that God is good, not because we have comprehended him, but because we have seen his goodness in all of his creation.

> *"By the very nature of creation, material being is endowed with its own stability, truth and excellence, its own order and laws. Each of the various creatures, willed in its own being, reflects in its own way a ray of God's infinite wisdom and goodness" (CCC 339).*

FRUIT > Therefore, we human beings are urged to respect the particular goodness of each creature. By disrespectful use of things we would only treat God with contempt, and the consequences will be disastrous both for ourselves and our environment. Because everything in Nature is good, whatever is natural is graceful. It is the living, visible garment of God. Nature never breaks her own laws unless human beings break them. It is true, God has given humankind authority to govern over nature, but we cannot govern her, except by obeying her.

GLIMPSES OF GOD

ROOT > Through everything created, we get a glimpse of God. Through the perpetuity of rain and snow that make the earth fertile, we know God's concern for our basic necessities such as food. Majestic fountains and verdant valleys reveal God's beauty and charm. A little bee that builds ten thousands cells for honey reveal his wisdom. He fills the starlit nights since he is the Father of lights. The stormy billows shout that God is mightier than the seas. Something in each flower's face tells about God's love and grace. Yes, the heavens and skies declare God's glory and the earth takes up the chorus.

> *"Charmed by their beauty, those who have taken the creatures for gods, let them know how much the Master of these excels them"* (Wis 13:1).

FRUIT > Through God's wondrous creation, he has left his footprints. Those who in their blindness and unbelief refuse the evidences of the existence of an almighty God, would do well to recall what Rabindranath Tagore wrote as he stood before every created thing: "Day after day, O Lord of my life, I stand before thee face to face. With folded hands, O Lord of all worlds, I stand before thee face to face. And when my work shall be done in this world, alone and speechless shall I stand before thee face to face."

FOR OUR BENEFIT

Root > The lives of human beings depend completely on the riches which the earth conceals and on the fertility of the soil. It is God's providential framework for our life. It is not surprising therefore to see the earth and its material goods occupying an important place in God's care for us. The earth and its goods are thus a permanent reminder of God's faithful love for us. However, because God is the Creator of the earth, he has an absolute right over it, and he alone disposes of its goods, establishes its laws and causes it to bear fruit.

> *"House of Israel, may you be blessed by God who made heaven and earth. Heaven belongs to God, but earth he has given to the children of Adam. We the living, shall bless God for ever and ever" (Ps 115).*

Fruit > All material goods are placed at the disposal of human beings for our life and enjoyment. But we must keep in mind three important things in the use of them. First, remember who gave them to us – God our Creator to whom we owe all we are and have. Enjoy them according to God's plan. Second, be genuinely thankful. Appreciate the gifts, and let our hearts well up with gratitude to the One who loves us so much. Finally, do not forget to share these gifts with others. Be generous; Care for the poor and those in need. Do not hoard God's gifts.

JOY OF CREATION

ROOT > Concentrating on death and dread, existentialists call everything that exists as absurd. Absurdity means that there is no meaning in anything. It also implies that there is no meaning in everything put together as a whole. They deny that everything has a sufficient reason for what it is. According to them, our experience of reality points to the futility of life, and leaves us with feelings of anxiety and perplexity. But Christianity calls us to rejoice over human existence and over all existing creation.

> *"The Gospel, above all else, is the joy of creation. God, who in creating saw that his creation was good, is the source of joy for all creatures and above all for humankind. God the Creator seems to say of all creation, 'It is good that you exists!' And his joy spreads especially through the Good News that God is greater than all that is evil in the world"* (John Paul II – CTH p. 20).

FRUIT > The existentialist message of absurdity is itself absurd: (if everything is really meaningless, then, nothing of what existentialist-pessimists say is meaningful at all). It is clear that the final destination of the existentialists is the denial of the existence of God. The Christian affirmation is that God can be known explicitly through the revelation of Jesus Christ who by his own resurrection from the dead, proclaimed that evil that is in the world is neither fundamental nor definitive. There is therefore meaning to the world and our existence, and a reason to rejoice over it.

ORDER OF CREATION

ROOT > Because God creates through his infinite wisdom, his creation is ordered. The universe created in and by the eternal Word, is destined for and addressed to human being, himself created in the image of God, and called to a personal relationship with God. The order of creation is maintained, because God laid within creation fundamental laws that remain firm. In any orderly structure or movement, there is a hierarchy. We see this hierarchy of creatures, in God creating them first from the less perfect, and then to the more perfect.

> *"'To whom can you compare me, or who is my equal?' says the Holy One. Lift your eyes and look: he who created these things leads out his army in order, summoning each of them by name"* (Is 40:25-26).

FRUIT > Good order is the foundation of all things, but order means priority. It is best to do things systematically, for disorder is our worst enemy. We must have our priorities right, especially, the values by which we live, must have their priorities, for our values are guides by which we navigate ourselves through life. Spiritual goods must come before material goods; God's will before our own will; Divine law before human law; self-discipline before self-indulgence; and so on. Our happiness does not consist in flying high, but in walking orderly. The main thing is to make sure that the main remains the main.

THE PURPOSE OF CREATION

ROOT > God created the world to show forth and communicate his glory. But his glory consists in sharing with his creatures his own truth, goodness and beauty. He created the world to provide a place where his purpose and goal for humankind might be fulfilled. The culmination of God's purpose in creation is that he may dwell with human beings, that they shall be his people and that he might become 'all in all,' thus simultaneously assuring his own glory and our beatitude.

> *"This one, true God, of his own goodness created the world, not for increasing his own beatitude nor for attaining his perfection, but in order to manifest his perfection through the benefits he bestows on creatures both the spiritual and corporal" (Dei Filius 1: DS 3002).*

FRUIT > It is said that in Africa there is a fruit called the 'taste berry', because it changes a person's taste, so that everything eaten tastes sweet and pleasant. Sour fruit, even if eaten several hours after the 'taste berry', becomes sweet and delicious. Gratitude for all the creatures God has provided for our benefit, is the Christian 'taste berry'. When our hearts are filled with gratitude, nothing that God sends us seems unpleasant to us. Gratitude sweetens a sorrowful heart. Singing God's praises, lightens your life's burdens.

CHALLENGE OF CREATION

ROOT > Science that can stir the embers of fires that went out even millions of years ago, has transformed the world. Technology, through its electronic inter-dependency, is recreating the world in the image of a global village. Both science and technology have taken the human race from caveman to the present jet-aircraft age. All this is a significant expression of human beings' dominion over creation. But we are challenged by creation, to use these precious resources of science and technology, to promote our integral development and for the benefit of all.

> *"A person who believes in the essential goodness of all creation is capable of discovering all the secrets of creation in order to perfect continually the work assigned to him by God. There is a great challenge to perfect creation, be it oneself, be it the world" (John Paul II – CTH p. 21).*

FRUIT > A particular challenge, that we as human beings face, is to acknowledge that our dominion over created things is not absolute, for it is limited by some of our concerns for the good of the whole human race. For example, we are to place all the advancements at the service of the human persons, of their inalienable rights in conformity to God's will. We are to use the fruits of advancement not selfishly, and to improve the quality of life for our neighbours. With a kind of religious respect for creation, we are to protect the environment, at least for the sake of future generations to come; Otherwise, the means of unlimited progress would end in unlimited disaster.

SUMMIT OF CREATION

ROOT > God loves all his creatures and takes care of each one, even the sparrow. However, Jesus said, "You are of more value than sparrows," or again, "Of how much more value is a man than a sheep!" Human being is the summit of the Creator's work, as the Bible expresses clearly, distinguishing the creation of human being from that of other creatures. God destined all material creatures for the good of the human race. Human beings and through them all creation, are destined for the glory of God.

> *"What are human beings that you spare a thought for them or the child of Adam that you care for him? Yet, you have made him a little less than a god, you have crowned him with glory and beauty, made him lord of the works of your hands, put all things under his feet" (Ps 8:3-6).*

FRUIT > Because human being is the summit of creation, all progress achieved by science and technology must be ordered to human beings, from whom all progress takes its origin. In fact, it is in the personal and in the moral values of human beings, science and technology find both evidence of their purpose and awareness of their limits. Human person being the summit of creation also means that animals, plants and all inanimate things are by nature destined for the common good of past, present and future humanity.

IN THE IMAGE OF GOD

ROOT > Of all the visible creatures, only human person is able to know and love the Creator. We are the only creatures on earth that God has willed for our own sake, and we alone are called to share, by knowledge and love, in God's own life, and this is the fundamental reason for human dignity. Created in the image of God, human persons can enter into a dialogue with him. Human person is not God, but lives dependent on God, in relation analogous to that of a son to his father.

> *"What made you establish man in so great a dignity? Certainly, the incalculable love by which you have looked on your creature in yourself! You are taken with love for her; for by love in deed you created her, by love you have given her a being capable of tasting your eternal good"* (Catharine of Siena, Dialogue iv, 13).

FRUIT > Some people, whenever they look inside themselves, are afraid. Some others have always disliked themselves at any given moment. There are still others for whom the total of such moments is their life! Such persons lack self-esteem for they are not aware, that they are in the image of God. It is difficult to make a person miserable while he or she feels self-worthy, and claims kindred to God. If you love yourself meanly, childishly or timidly, even so, shall you love your neighbour.

HUMAN FINALE

ROOT > Human persons are created to know, love and serve our Creator here on earth in order to reach heaven in a blessed eternity. God gained nothing by bringing us into existence and gains nothing by our obedience to his will. All the benefits of being created are on our side. God wants us to be at peace in this life and perfectly happy in the life to come. On both counts, peace of soul here on earth and beatitude in eternity, depends on our faithful submission to the will of God.

> *"Human being is more precious in the eyes of God than all other creatures. God attached so much importance to our salvation that he did not spare his own Son for the sake of us. Nor does he ever cease to work, trying every possible means, until he has raised us up to himself and made us sit at his right hand" (John Chrisostom, I Gen Sermo 2).*

FRUIT > During most of the year, the trees are either bare or green. But for a short while, autumn showcases them with vivid golds and reds, dark browns and yellows. Leaves are the most beautiful at their finale, for they have fulfilled the reason for their existence. The reason for human existence is peaceful joy in this life and beatitude in the next, by loving God althrough and pleasing him doing his will. Without love, our lives would be only like sounding brass and tinkling symbols. When we reach our final season, love is what will make us more beautiful than autumn leaves.

AT OUR SERVICE

ROOT > We cannot reach our end which is peace in this world and beatitude in the next, without using needed means. That is why, the rest of the creatures exist as our means. They are everything that in any way enters or touches our lives. Every person, place or thing; every pleasure and pain; every circumstance in which we find ourselves; every thought and every desire; every sight we see and sound we hear. All are intended by God as means to be used by us to reach our glorious end.

> *"Creation was given and entrusted to humankind as a duty, representing not a source of suffering but the foundation of creative existence in the world. A person who believes in the essential goodness of all creation is capable of discovering all the secrets of creation, in order to perfect continually the work assigned to him by God" (John Paul II – CTH p. 20).*

FRUIT > For the creatures to serve us as a source of creative existence, we must use them discriminately. That is, we must discriminate or separate, and classify them according to their importance. We can distinguish four kinds of creatures in our lives; there are those that God wants us to enjoy; others, he wants us to endure; still others, he wants us to remove. And finally, there are creatures, he wants us to sacrifice. We must also take care to use the creatures dispassionately, that is, use them to fulfil our real needs, not necessarily to enjoy what we want.

GENUINE PIETY

ROOT > Through creation we discover our Creator and are led to profound feeling of wonder and gratitude. When we contemplate beauty in creation, we are led to enthusiastic praise, and are overwhelmed by his Divine Majesty appearing in his marvellous works. With these reminders, we are submerged in profound humility. God has kneaded, moulded and formed us like clay. At every instant we are in our Creator's hands, and nothing created escapes God. This is the basic attitude of genuine piety.

> *"I know that you are all powerful: You have told me about great works that I cannot understand, about marvels which are beyond me. Before, I knew you only by hearsay, but now, having seen you with my own eyes, I retract what I have said and repent in dust and ashes" (Job 42:1-4).*

FRUIT > Whatever our possessions, we shall all be happier if we steadily grow in a spirit of humility which can thank God for his mercies. Have you ever thought of it, that only smaller birds sing? You never heard a note from the eagle nor from the turkey, nor from the ostrich. But you have heard from the canary, the wren and the lark. The sweetest music of thanksgiving comes from those who are small in their own estimation and humble before God.

REDEEMED

ROOT > Our first parents, tempted by the evil one, let their trust in the Creator die in their hearts, and abusing their freedom, they disobeyed God's command. The result was that harmony in which they had found themselves was destroyed; The control of the soul's spiritual faculties over the body was shattered; harmony with creation was broken; and decay entered into human history. However, God did not abandon humankind. He announced the coming of the Messiah and Redeemer and with him victory over evil.

> *"The essential joy of creation is, in turn, completed by the joy of salvation, by the joy of redemption. The Creator of man is also his Redeemer. Salvation not only confronts evil in each of its existing forms in this world, but proclaims victory over evil" (John Paul II – CTH p. 21).*

FRUIT > Evil has become almost a necessary part of the order of the universe; to ignore it is childish; to bewail it is senseless. It enters like a needle but spreads like an oak. Who can deliver us from evil? Only God can. To liberate a single human being from evil, is beyond the combined legislation of the world's parliaments, the combined power of the world's armies, the combined wealth of the world's banks. Only God who created us out of nothing, can prevent us from going back to nothing through evil. That is why, he sent his own Son Jesus Christ to save us.

RE-CREATED

ROOT > Sacred history does not stop with the present but moves on into the future, until God would have achieved fully his plan for humankind. His plan was the ultimate salvation of human beings, for which he would go on re-creating them. The conversion of Israel was already a step towards re-creation. Likewise, God intended a future re-creation for all people which would be accompanied by the marvels of a new exodus from sin and death, to life and grace. According to God's plan, this re-creation would be made in Jesus Christ.

> *"The work of Redemption is to elevate the work of creation to a new level. It comes as if drawn to the sphere of divinity and of intimate life of God. In this realm, destructive power of sin is defeated and indestructible life is revealed in the Resurrection of Christ" (John Paul II – CTH p. 22).*

FRUIT > We are born incomplete. Hence, God will go on re-creating us or converting us. Conversion is both a moment and a process of transformation that deepens and extends through the whole of one's life. Yesterday I was over-indulgent and short-tempered, but I repented. That was conversion. But does this mean that I will never more get short tempered or over-indulgent? No. Probably I will fall into it as early as tomorrow. But if I am open to God's grace, he will convert me deeper and re-create me into still a newer person.

NEW IN CHRIST

ROOT > In the beginning God made Adam the head of the human race, and entrusted the world to his dominion. In the end, the incarnate Son of God entered history as the new Adam. God made Christ the head of the redeemed humanity so that all beings, heavenly as well as earthly, are to be unified in him. Because Christ has in himself the fullness of the Spirit, he communicates the Spirit to other human beings for their spiritual renovation, and to make of them new creatures.

> *"All who are guided by the Spirit of God are sons of God; for what you received was not the spirit of slavery; you received the Spirit of adoption, enabling us to cry out 'Abba, father!' And if we are children then we are heirs, heirs of God and joint-heirs with Christ provided we share his sufferings, so as to share his glory" (Rom 8:14-17).*

FRUIT > We become renewed by sharing in the Spirit of Christ; but that is possible only if we are ready to share in his pains. Nobody wants pain in one's life. But we realise that our times of greatest growth were somehow deeply connected to our times of greatest pain. God is relentless in bringing us to maturity in Christ; he will not stop until every area of our life is healthy, until every relationship is healed, until everything about us is scrutinised and empowered for love; but that means incredible pain.

NEW HUMANITY

ROOT > As the consequence of human rebellion against God at the beginning of human history, the present world was destined to dissolve and disappear. But in Christ, a new creation has already begun, as the prophets had foretold. This new creation is to be found, primarily in human beings who are renewed interiorly by Baptism according to the image of our Creator. The renewed persons become in Christ new creatures, new beings, after the cleansing of the fallen nature.

> *"So for any one who is in Christ, there is a new creation: the old order is gone and a new being is there to see. It is all God's work; he reconciled us to himself through Christ and he gave us the ministry of reconciliation, I mean, God was in Christ reconciling the world to himself" (2 Cor 5:17-18).*

FRUIT > By Baptism we are re-created, transformed, born again, set free and spiritually disposed to obey God and follow the leading of the Spirit, for in baptism we die with Christ to our brokenness and rise with him to new life, which we celebrate at Easter.

Easter is an extra-ordinary adventure, reminiscent of the dual between death and life, of the free decision of fateful destiny between our perdition and our salvation. It would have been useless for us to have been born, if we had not been granted the good fortune of being born again.

NEW BIRTH

ROOT > Our new birth in Christ cannot be equated with physical birth, for the relationship of God with the believer is a matter of the Spirit, rather than of the flesh. Hence, while the physical tie of a natural father and son can never be annulled, the father and son relationship which God desires with us, is voluntary and not indissoluble during our probationary time on earth. Hence, our membership in God's family remains conditional on our faith in Christ throughout our earthly existence, a faith ever growing into spiritual maturity.

> *"In all truth I tell you no one can enter the Kingdom of God without being born through water and the Spirit; what is born of human nature is human, what is born of the Spirit is spirit. Do not be surprised when I say: you must be born from above" (Jn 3: 5-7).*

FRUIT > The spiritually grown become more and more free from egocentric concerns of childhood. To them, their religious belief is dynamic, affecting and directing their whole life, motives and behaviour. They are open, allowing their religious convictions to intensify and grow more valid through deeper study, reflection and prayer. Many find spiritual maturity boring, for it seems to have no apparent practical or financial purpose. But, in fact, spiritual maturity does have a great practical impact, for with it, we can deal effectively with crucial issues of life.

UNIVERSAL NEW CREATION

ROOT > The new creation which is primarily in human beings, extends also to the universe, because the plan of God is to bring all things under Christ as one head, to reconcile all things in and through him. Thus, there is a subtle movement from God's action in the original creation to his action in the final re-creation of the whole universe in Christ. Creation of the universe and redemption in Christ thus merge.

> *"Christ exists before all things and in him all things hold together. God wanted all fullness to be found in him and through him to reconcile all things to him, by making peace through his death on the cross" (Col 1:17-20).*

FRUIT > Once, many people thought that we can solve every human problem with a rational response and make a better world. But it has not worked to perfection. Management and control are breaking down everywhere. The new world order looks very likely to end in disorder. We can't make things happen the way we want them to, at home, at work or in government, certainly not in the world as a whole. We seem to have reached the edge of chaos. But God's promise is that out of turbulence a new order will jell. For Christ is holding the reign.

NOT YET COMPLETE

ROOT > The new creation which formally began at the Pentecost has not yet reached its completion. We who are interiorly renewed by the Spirit still long for the redemption of our body on the day of the general resurrection. The surrounding world, in the meanwhile, is now subjected to frustrations, but seeking complete liberation from its servitude, marching towards its inevitable completion, when it will enjoy the glorious liberty of the children of God.

> *"It was not for its own purposes that creation had frustration imposed on it, but that the whole creation itself might be freed from its slavery to corruption. The whole creation, until this time, has been groaning in labour pains" (Rom 8:20-22).*

FRUIT > Winter is always a difficult season to pass through. I detest the cold weather and the gloom of winter months. I prefer to live where it is warm, but that is not possible. There is a season for everything. So too, we cannot escape the winter pains of our hearts. But the pains of life is a reminder that we are not yet fully recreated beings in Christ. The universe too, has not yet been fully transformed by the Spirit. But, as our hope lies in the magnificent flowers that will bloom next spring after a long winter, so we hope for God to end the groanings of humanity in his own time.

ONGOING RENEWAL

ROOT > There are different ways in which God invades the interior of a human being in order to transform the person into a new creation. One can be this: As you are walking in a dark thick grove, your heart is suddenly opened to the unspeakable glory of God with an inward apprehension of all that God is, such as you never had before, widely different from all the ideas that you ever had of God or things divine. As a result, you inwardly long that God be everything to you. This is the moment of conversion; but from now on, yourself must do something, so that conversion goes on all your life until you become fully renewed.

> *"In the plan for the salvation of the human race, everything depends on the living relationship which we can establish between Christ and ourselves. But this saving relationship with Christ demands some personal initiative on our part, it requires response from our liberty, from our faith, from our love" (Pope Paul VI).*

FRUIT > The on-going renewal of a person until one becomes fully transformed in Christ, involves a constant exercise of one's freedom, faith and love. True freedom is liberty to do what God wants. But we cannot freely choose what is pleasing to God unless our faith in him is deep. Faith is the capacity to trust God while not being able to make sense out of everything. Finally, love must always accompany faith, for faith without love is no living grace, as love without faith is no saving faith.

DESTINY IN SIGHT

ROOT > History is tending to its destiny of universal perfection in Christ, to the new heaven and to the new earth. The Apocalypse anticipates this: "The first heaven and the first earth have disappeared... Then, he who sits on throne declared, 'See, I am making all things new'" (Apoc 21:1-5). This will be the final creation of a transformed universe, when the definitive victory of the Lamb is achieved.

> *"What we are waiting for, relying on his promises, is the new heavens and new earth where uprightness will be at home. So, then, my dear friends, while you are waiting, do your best to live blameless and unsullied lives so that he will find you at peace" (2 Pet 3:13-14).*

FRUIT > True Christians live by hope. Hope means expectancy for oneself, and for the world, when things are otherwise hopeless. Our hope is, that one day, the entire human race and the universe will be fully transformed into new creation; that one day, races will be free from injustices to one another; that war will be banished; that family life everywhere will be secure, and all people be brought into one fellowship with God in Christ. But, Christians can hardly separate these hopes from their faith in Jesus as the Lord of both heaven and earth.

FEAR NOT!

ROOT > There are no *ifs* in God's heart. As his love for us is unconditional, so is his plan, to take us to our destiny of universal perfection in Christ. Independently of what we do or do not, God, by the power of the presence of his pervasive Spirit, is guiding us towards the new heaven and the new earth. God is saddened, indeed, when we do things that might frustrate his plan. But, God can draw good out of evil because, while the power of doing evil is ours, the effects of our evil deeds are outside our control, and therefore, in the hands of God, who can turn even the evils we do, into stepping stones to our destiny.

> *"There is no need to be afraid little flock, for it has pleased your Father to give you the Kingdom" (Lk 12:32).*

FRUIT > We fear the future more than the present. Just think of the number of insurance companies in every country? What are they for? The viability of so many companies is directly attributable to our basic fear of tomorrow, a fear that causes us to spend billions of pounds each year, trying to insure ourselves against minor setbacks or major catastrophes, while millions suffer and die for want of basic needs. There is only one way to tackle this fear of the future, that is, by trusting in God who is the Lord, not only of the present, but also of the future.

March:

THE FATHER

Week 1
The Father's Face

Week 2
The Father's Children

Week 3
Divine Providence

Week 4
Abba, Father

REVEALED IN CHRIST

ROOT > The revelation of God to the people of Israel reached its final, unsurpassable fullness in Jesus of Nazareth. In Jesus Christ, God gave himself and made his revelation complete. In Christ, God communicated to the world whatever he had to say and give. This revelation did not come from a distance. Rather, the infinite distance that separates human beings from God was bridged to the point that God allowed himself to be touched by human hands. Allowing oneself to be touched implies unreserved intimacy with God in Christ Jesus.

> *"What was from the beginning, what we have heard, what we have seen with our own eyes; what we have looked upon and touched with our own hands; the Word, who is life. We testify and proclaim to you the everlasting life which was with the Father and has been made visible to us" (1 Jn 1:1-4).*

FRUIT > When the disciples of Jesus touched Jesus, they were touching God. Their experience of God became so intimate through Christ. In the Eucharist, we can have a similar intimacy with God through faith, for it is the most sacred body and blood of Jesus, God made visible. The great mystery of the Eucharist is that God's love is offered to us, not in the abstract, but in a concrete way; not as a theory, but as food for our daily life. It is the love of God for all people, of all times and places.

MORE THAN AN IMAGE

ROOT > The revelation of the Father is accomplished not simply by virtue of a resemblance between the Father and the Son. Jesus is more than a visible image of the Father. In him, the Father is really present, in his words and actions. To look at Jesus is to discover the Father in him. There is perfect unity of thought and action between the Father and the Son. It is an identical reality that belongs to both to the Son and to the Father. We can see the Saviour only by recognising in him the invisible features of the Father.

> *"Have I been with you all this time, Philip, and still you do not know me? Anyone who has seen me has seen the Father; I am in the Father and the Father is in me. What I say to you I do not speak of my own accord: It is the father, living in me, who is doing his works" (Jn 14:9-11).*

FRUIT > Jesus Christ is *more* than the image of God but human beings are created *only* in the image of God. Because we are in his image, we are not hopelessly confined to the world of our own fantasies and illusions; we are not prisoners of our own human categories of thoughts. God can communicate essential things to us in human language and through human experiences. Hence, we are not ever condemned to doubt about Truth. Besides, because we are in the image of God, we can respond to God and have fellowship with him, and uniquely reflect his love, glory and holiness.

FATHER'S LOVE

Root > In Christ's parable of the prodigal son (Lk 15), the father's compassion evokes a mother's tenderness. At the sight of his son's distress, the father was filled with compassion, ran, fell upon his neck and kissed him repeatedly. We cannot disregard this maternal aspect which is one of the marks of the Father's love. The parable discloses the Father's heart to us in the most telling way, and at the most poignant moment, it shows us a merciful tenderness, that is the mark of a mother's heart.

> *"Jerusalem, Jerusalem! You kill the prophets and stone the messengers. God has sent you! How many times have I wanted to put my arms round all your people, just as a hen gathers her chicks under her wings, but you would not let me" (Mt 24: 37).*

Fruit > Revealing God's maternal affection, Jesus lovingly touched sick people, including lepers, while curing them. How much of affection we express to one another by touching them? We all hunger to touch and to be touched, not necessarily in a sexual embrace of love, but in genuine human affection, to touch our face, look into our eyes, lay their hands gently on ours, kiss us on the cheek, embrace us tenderly. Most of us suffer from a deadly disease of skin hunger. But the fear of rejection seems to be greater than the fear of the disease. So we continue to repress our deep need for affection. Perhaps, that is why, we have become such a violent people!

FATHER'S FORGIVENESS

ROOT > To justify his benevolent approach to sinners, Jesus invoked the attitude of the Father. He answers his critics through parables of mercy, especially the parable of the prodigal son, in which the Father's eagerness to forgive and reinstate the repentant son in his friendship, is the decisive argument. In establishing friendly relations with those whom others would have wanted to place in the catalogue of sinners, Jesus simply follows the course laid out by the Father.

> *"If you kept a record of our sins, Lord, who could stand their ground? But with you is forgiveness, that you may be revered. My whole being relies on your promise. For with the Lord is faithful love, with him generous ransom" (Ps 130:3-8).*

FRUIT > One way for us to return God's generous forgiveness of our debts, is that we show generosity in forgiving our neighbour's debts to us. Debt can be of many kinds. It could be also money. While almost all of us take a firm line on sexual sins, many of us never or rarely forgive debts. People mostly lend money at interest. Many don't forgive even the failure to pay interests, knowing well that interest works night and day, in fair weather and in foul, gnawing at the debtor's substance with invisible teeth. Therefore, a creditor seems to be worse than a tyrant, for a tyrant owns only your person, but a creditor owns your dignity as well.

FATHER'S AUTHORITY

ROOT > Jesus did not for an instant cease acting as the Son who receives everything from the Father, including the Father's authority. When he taught, he did so with an inborn authority. The Scribes invoked the authority of the Law, whereas Jesus had no need of recourse to an external authority. Moreover, he did not hesitate to correct the law. By that, he implied that he was endowed with an authority superior to the law, which can only be a divine authority. He even attributed to his words an eternal value that belongs only to the words spoken by God himself.

> *"For I have not spoken of my own accord; but the Father who sent me commanded me what to say and what to speak, and I know that his commands mean eternal life. And therefore what the Father has told me is what I speak" (Jn 12:49-50).*

FRUIT > God is our Author, for he has created us. Hence his authority over us, is sovereign. We drive our lives, but it is God who holds the reins. God is in all the events of history, as surely as he is in the march of the seasons. Nothing that is attempted in opposition to God can ever be successful. Events of all sorts creep and fly exactly as God pleases. Things do not happen in this world; they are brought about. To know that nothing happens in God's world apart from God's will, may frighten the Godless, but it stabilises the believers.

FATHER'S POWER

ROOT > Jesus performed miracles in his own name, thus demonstrating a power belonging to him personally. And yet, instead of drawing the faith of the witnesses to himself alone, he always directed it ultimately to the Father, saying that he was accomplishing only the Father's works. As he walked on the sea, he said to the frightened apostles, "It is I. Don't be afraid" (Mt 12:27). These are words God himself said to his people, "Do not fear, for I am the Lord your God" (Is 43:1-3). Thus we see that the power which Jesus demonstrated was the Father's own power.

> *"If I am not doing my Father's work, there is no need to believe in me; but if I am doing it, then even if you refuse to believe in me, at least believe in the work I do" (Jn 10: 37-38).*

FRUIT > Referring to God's almighty power, John Knox said that a person with God on his side is always in the majority. The arm of God never tires when human strength gives way. If God be God, then no insoluble problem should exist. And if God be our God, then none of our problems should be without its appropriate solution. Yes, God has in himself all power to support us and save us, as he has all the wisdom to direct us, all mercy to pardon us, all grace to enrich us, and all happiness to crown us.

FATHER'S WILL

ROOT > Far from showing himself to be a man who acts exclusively on his own, according to his own ideas and desires, with complete independence, Jesus considered himself as one who had a mission to carry out. He had been sent by the Father, and hence all of his activities were deployed in order to attain the goal that had been assigned to him. He once said that his food was to do God's will, thus implying that what sustained his life was doing Father's will.

> *"The basic attitude of hope, on the one hand encourages the Christian not to lose the sight of the final goal which gives meaning and value to life, and on the other, offers solid and profound reasons for a daily commitment to transform reality in order to make it correspond to God's plan" (John Paul II – TMA 46).*

FRUIT > There are peculiar storms in the Indian Ocean, called typhoons and monsoons. They are peculiar in that they do not move practically at all from east to west or north to south; instead, they play around a circle. Therefore, the navigators when they run into a monsoon, would first locate its centre and go round it. By and by, they narrow the circle. When they get into the centre, they are in a dead calm. A monsoon is like God's will. Try to get out of it, and you will find it a destructive force. Get into it, and you are in a calm; and you find it is good, acceptable and perfect.

FATHER OF THE HUMAN RACE

ROOT > In creating the world, God's first intention was not only to create the universe, but to give himself adopted children in Christ. He deployed his power in the work of creation, precisely because he wanted to be the Father of the human race. When he brought forth the physical universe, he was destining it to be the dwelling place of those who were to be his children. Moses refused to attribute to himself the fatherhood of his people, because true fatherhood belongs only to God, and he described the obligations of fatherhood in concrete terms.

> *"Was it I who conceived all these people, was I their father, for you say to me, 'carry them in your arms, like a foster-father, carrying an unweaned child, to the country which I swore to their fathers'?" (Num 11:12).*

FRUIT > God the Father loves all human beings without exception, for all are his children and destined to be with him through Christ Jesus. Hence Jesus repeatedly called every one to trust in the Fatherly love of God. When we fail to love God as our Father, we turn our love on ourselves, and in our self-centredness, we forget and reject other humans and even begin to hate them. Why there is so much suspicion, bitterness, vindictiveness, hatred, violence and discord in our world? The evil in the world simply originates from our lack of trust in God's love for ourselves and for the whole human race.

FATHER OF EACH ONE

ROOT > Though God revealed himself as the Father of the Chosen People as a whole, in his dealings with them, this collective Fatherhood often found its expression in God's personal love and care for individuals. Hence, God at times called individuals within the community as 'his sons and daughters' (Dt 32:19); Individuals invoked God by the name of 'Father' in their supplications for protection. In the Book of Wisdom, the just man is described as a son of God as the one enjoying the paternal love of God, not merely by the reason of his membership in the Chosen People, but by reason of his or her behaviour.

> *"He claims to have knowledge of God and calls himself as the child of the Lord. He proclaims the final end of the upright as blessed and boasts of having God for his father. Let us see if what he says is true, for if the upright man is God's son, God will help him and rescue him" (Wis 2:13, 16-18).*

FRUIT > When the small daughter of a woman was asked which child was her mother's favourite, the little girl replied: "She loves Jimmy best, because he is the oldest; and she loves Johnny best, because he is the youngest; and she loves me best, because I am the only girl." No matter to what height you have risen or to what depth you have fallen, God like a mother loves each of us best. This is not only because each of us is his creation and each of us has been redeemed by his Son, but also because of some characteristic personal quality, may be unknown to others, but well known to the Father.

THE BEGOTTEN SON

Root > Jesus is the begotten Son of the Father and so he could call him 'Abba', thus revealing the priority of the Father to whom he owes his whole being as the Son, and the unreserved intimacy he enjoys in his dialogue with the Father. As the Father's begotten Word, Jesus is the very imprint of God's being, his living expression. While speaking of the Eucharist, Jesus affirmed that the food he gives endures eternally, because he bears within himself the seal of the Father.

> *"In all truth I tell you, you are looking for me not because you have seen the signs but because you had all the bread you wanted to eat. Do not work for food that goes bad but work for food that endures for eternal life which the Son of Man will give you, for on him, the Father, God himself has set his seal" (Jn 6:27).*

Fruit > The lofty sealing of some Anglican Cathedrals in England, is adorned with magnificent frescoes. As you stand on the pavement and look up at it, your neck stiffens, your head grows dizzy and the figures become hazy and indistinct. Hence, the authorities of some such Cathedrals, have placed a broad mirror near the floor. In it the picture is reflected and you can sit down in front of it and study the wonderful work in comfort. When we try to get some idea of the heavenly Father, Jesus Christ does for us something like what the mirror does in these Cathedrals. Since he is the express image of God, he interprets God to our dull hearts.

THE ADOPTED CHILDREN

ROOT > Jesus reveals a Father who is first and above all his own Father, and he affirms that he is the Father's only begotten Son. But his relationship with his Father became the source of adoption for his disciples. The Father's paternity, concentrated in his relationship with Jesus, is destined to extend to all human beings. This means, that when we call God 'Father', we first mean it to be the Father of Jesus. However, it is from this initial Fatherhood, that all believers in his Son become his adopted sons and daughters.

> *"He chose us in Christ before the world was made to be holy and faultless before him in love, marking us out for himself beforehand, to be adopted sons, through Jesus Christ. Such was his purpose and good pleasure to the praise and glory of his grace, his free gift to us in the Beloved"* (Eph 1:3-5).

FRUIT > Christians are pilgrims and strangers on this earth, but we are not orphans, for we have been adopted by God as his children by faith in Christ. When we become Christians, we gain all the privileges of children in God's family. One of these outstanding privileges is that of being led by the Spirit. We are no longer cringing and fearful slaves; instead, we are the Master's children. What a privilege! Because we are God's children, he has already given us wonderful gifts: his Son, forgiveness, and eternal life; and he encourages us to ask him for whatever we need.

HIS EXTRAVAGANT LOVE

Root > In the Father's plan, freedom is given to human beings so that they may freely respond with most spontaneous and deepest filial love towards him. In other words, the Father wanted to find, in his adopted sons and daughters, the reflection of the love rendered to him by his only begotten Son. However, by endowing us with freedom, the Father assumed the risk of subjecting himself to rejection and hostility by his own children. As free creatures, we now have power to confront our Creator and reject his authority. In this risk-taking, we clearly see the extravagant love of the Father for us.

> *"Look, today, I am offering you life and prosperity, death and disaster. If you love your God and follow his ways, you will live; but if your hearts turn away, if you refuse to listen, I tell you today, you will most certainly perish" (Deut 30: 15-18).*

Fruit > Freedom is such a precious gift from God that the history of the world is none other than the progress of the consciousness of freedom, but abuse of it, can draw blood even from God's heart! What strikes us most poignantly is how completely God the Father has chosen to depend on his children for his paternal sorrows and joys! We are not denying that God, in his divine nature, remains immutable and impassable. Yet, in the love-relations he has freely entered into with us, he too experiences suffering or joy, according to the right or wrong use of our individual freedom.

CHILDREN'S GRATITUDE

ROOT > How we enjoy watching our infant granddaughter coo and babble with the joy of being alive. Everything delights her. She flashes her ready smile to every one. She trusts that all her needs will be met and she concentrates on the delights of her ever expanding world. That is her way of praising God for her gift of life! It is strange, that as we grow up we lose the child-like spirit of gratitude to the Father, who has given us all that we are as human beings and all that we have become and are becoming, because he has adopted us as his children.

> *"It is good to give thanks to God, to make music for your name, to proclaim your faithful love at daybreak and your constancy all through the night. You have brought me joy, by your deeds at the works of your hands I cry out, 'How great are your work, O God'" (Ps 92:1-4)!*

FRUIT > One morning, there was a little puddle by the roadside. I saw some small brown birds gathered round it, taking turns to hop in for a great time of splashing. Then they flew up in the bushes nearby and sang gaily. Birds and animals seem to enjoy and appreciate every little blessing that comes their way. Yet, human beings seem to take so many blessings from God for granted. When I sit down to the table to eat without thanking God for it, I am like the hog under a chestnut tree eating chestnuts, and does not so much as look up to see where the chestnuts come from.

CHILDREN'S INTIMACY

ROOT > The revelation of God, as realised in Jesus, totally entrusted the very Being of God to human beings, so that the disciples of Jesus could not only see and hear but touch that Being. Intimacy was thus established with a person who was God. This intimacy was meant to endure in its effects, beyond the moment when it was initially established. In other words, the intimacy which God established between him and human beings through Christ can never be taken back. The humanity which received the Word of life can never again lose it. What has been seen and heard has become the inheritance of the human community.

> *"The Word became flesh, he lived among us, and we saw his glory, the glory that he has from the Father as only Son of the Father, full of grace and truth. To those who did accept him he gave power to become children of God" (Jn 1: 14, 12).*

FRUIT > God is transcendent, but he is also immanent in all that exists, especially in human beings. He is in our minds, in our thinking and imagining. We can experience him in every material thing for he is in them sustaining them. As long as we live in this material world we have no other way of meeting God. What is still more delightful is that the Spirit of God indwells within the believer, so that we can experience a special intimacy with him, in quiet moments of prayer. God normally is a quiet giver, and you will rarely notice the gift at the time. God's gifts are like little seeds which fall noiselessly.

FILIAL LOVE

ROOT > God is truly our Father since he has created us and because he gives us life. In undertaking the work of salvation Jesus made all of us the adopted children of the Father and thereby elevated us to the highest possible status, establishing us in a relationship of filial intimacy with the Father. He wanted to communicate his divine sonship to us, so that we might be children of the Father in his likeness. He is prompting us to respond to our Father with filial love, so that we might come to share more and more in his love.

> *"Jesus said to him, 'You must love the Lord your God with all your heart, with all your soul, and with all your mind'"* (Mt 22:37).

FRUIT > What is filial love? Filial love for God our Father will arouse in us the desire to collaborate with him, to consecrate our every task to God's cause. Filial love will lead us to filial trust in the fatherhood of God, with a boundless reliance on his goodness and omnipotence, in the conviction that he intervenes to enrich even our human life on earth, let alone the life to come. Filial love will urge us to entrust our life to the Father's initiatives, which procure for us that supreme freedom that makes us masters of ourselves and our feelings. Finally, filial love will lead us to brotherly love, that springs from an awareness of God's universal fatherhood.

PATERNAL BENEVOLENCE

ROOT > Divine Providence is the solicitude with which the Father governs the course of events in the universe and in each human life. Even more, Providence can be seen as the vigilance with which he protects each individual and provides for the most mundane needs. Above all, it is proof of the Father's paternal benevolence that is concerned with every aspect of our lives. Providence is not occasional sympathy on the Father's part for human needs; but it is part of God's much vaster benevolence which guides humankind to its final destiny

> *"In the Church's history, every Jubilee is prepared for by divine Providence. This is true also of the Great Jubilee of the year 2000. With this conviction we look today with a sense of gratitude and yet with a sense of responsibility at all that has happened in human history since the birth of Christ" (John Paul II – TMA 17).*

FRUIT > The gratuitous solicitude of the Father who wants to deliver us from our anxieties, cannot be seen as an invitation to passivity on our part. The intervention of Providence in the smallest details, should not lead to a slackening of human efforts. Not only every one must work to obtain food and clothing, but we must strive to make our faculties and personal resources to bear fruit. We can never claim, on the excuse that our capacities are very limited, to be dispensed from the effort to make best use of whatever we have.

SCIENCE OBJECTS!

Root > Some scientists object to the idea of divine Providence because they see it as the Creator's intervention into the functioning of the laws of nature which he himself has established, and conclude that God is a dictatorial ruler; To them, divine Providence tends towards magic and superstition. They assert that the majesty of God is incompatible with Providence, for it determines the smallest details of human existence, and they add that Providence does not explain why God who governs with his omnipotence and wisdom, should allow turmoil and disaster.

> *"Agreed, the ship is the product of a craving for gain, its building embodies the wisdom of the shipwright; but your Providence, Father, is what steers it, you having opened a pathway even through the sea, and a safe way over the waves, showing that you can save, whatever happens"* (Wis 14:2-3).

Fruit > Providence will not be credible to those who limit themselves to an exclusively scientific conception of the universe. Scientific research into the energies of nature cannot discern the supernatural energy, which belongs to a different order, beyond physico, chemical and biological elements. In accordance with the teachings of revelation, it is necessary to understand that the Father manifests his paternal love in his Providence; Providence cannot be grasped scientifically. It can be perceived only through the eyes of faith.

EXTENDS TO MATERIAL THINGS

ROOT > The Divine Providence relates essentially to the work of salvation and helps assure the supernatural destiny of humankind. However, we have signs of God's Providence extending to all aspects of human life. Since the Father's dominion over the earth is complete, his gracious will must extend to all the material conditions of life as well, and to its spiritual goals. Jesus emphasises this point when he counsels his disciples to avoid worry about food and clothing.

> *"Now if that is how God clothes a flower which is growing wild today and is thrown into furnace tomorrow, how much more he will look after you! But you must not set your hearts on things to eat and things to drink; nor must you worry. Your Father well knows that you need them"* (Lk 12:28-32).

FRUIT > There are at least two things about which we should never worry. First, the things we cannot help. If we cannot help them, worrying is certainly the most foolish and useless. Secondly, the things we can help. If we can help them, let us set about it and not weaken our powers by worry. We must weed our garden and pluck up the smallest roots of worry. If we let them get a start, they will crowd out all the beautiful things that ought to grow in our hearts. Before sleep, gently lay every troubled thought away; drop your burden and care in the quiet arms of prayer.

IN EVERY DETAIL

ROOT > Those who object to the idea of divine Providence because God is intervening in trivial matters, forget that this divine intervention is justified by the greatness of the Father's love. He has willed to be our Father in the most perfect way possible. His Providence neglects no detail because, by virtue of his immense love, he attaches value to everything that concerns us. He never sacrifices the benefits of a superior order for the satisfaction of material needs. Rather, he provides material needs for the sake of the spiritual needs.

> *"Can you not buy two sparrows for a penny? And yet, not one falls to the ground without your Father knowing. Why, every hair on your head has been counted. So there is no need to be afraid; you are worth more than many sparrows"* (Mt 10:28-31).

FRUIT > The convergence of various accidental causes is called 'chance'. Can 'chance' explain events in our life? No, if it did, it has made a football of human life, a play thing of irrational influences. Events are not governed solely by accidental causes, but by a benevolent intention of Providence which organises the entire framework of human life, for the sake of a superior destiny. Human life is guided in all its detail by a power that measures and disposes everything in accordance with a benevolent goal. Thus, chance is caught up in the solicitude of Providence. There are no chances against God.

EMBRACES ALL

ROOT > Divine Providence reveals a solicitude that seeks to assure the essential destiny of all human beings. It emphasises the personal intervention of God who wants to act as the shepherd of all his people. By involving himself in the fate of humanity, God shows how he carefully watches over all whom he loves. He takes care of every one. His vigilance does not overlook any one, including those who are well and strong, to protect them and keep them healthy

> *"But I say this to you, love your enemies and pray for those who persecute you; so that you may be children of your Father in heaven, for he causes his sun to rise on the bad as well as the good, and sends down rain to fall on the upright and the wicked alike" (Mt 5:44-45).*

FRUIT > Though the divine Providence embraces all creation and all human beings, the Father is especially gracious to those who seek his Kingdom above everything else. To give God first place in my life means, to fill my heart with his desires, to take his character for my pattern, and to obey him in everything. People, objects, goals and other desires, all compete for priority. Any of these can quickly pump God out of first place, if I don't actively choose to give him first place, in every area of my life.

EMBRACES SINNERS

ROOT > The benevolent plan that governs the work of salvation is inspired by God's special love for sinners. From the beginning, the Father reacted to human offence with a very great love and concern, for he wants to save us all. So, we can see that Providence shows a generous love for those living in sin. Far from excluding sinners from his solicitude, the Father turns to them with gracious kindness. This attention continues throughout their earthly life for the sake of their conversion which is always possible until the very last moment.

> *"I tell you, there will be more rejoicing in heaven over one sinner repenting than over ninety-nine upright people who have no need of repentance" (Lk 15:7).*

FRUIT > The basic fact of Christianity is that God pardons and accepts believing sinners. The almighty is working on a great scale and will not be hustled by our peevish impetuosity. There is no divine attribute more wonderful than the patience of God. Sin's misery and God's mercy are beyond measure. What a world this would be, if God sat on a throne of justice only! Those who had fallen into great sins but repented, have realised that God has been a God of great mercies and now, through his mercies, they have a conscience as sound and quiet, as if they had never sinned.

IN HUMAN SUFFERING

ROOT > The purpose of Providence is not to provide the most pleasant and convenient life. Since it is ordered to the fulfilment of the benevolent plan that included the work of redemption by Christ on behalf human race, it is inevitably committed to the path of suffering and sacrifice. As such, the sufferings, far from being obstacles to the action of Providence, becomes part of its unfolding. The reason why God's paternal love does not spare the believers suffering, is so that we can share in Christ's passion and make of this suffering an offering, that ennobles our lives and makes us more fruitful for diffusing goodness in the world.

> *"You will be betrayed even by parents and brothers, relations and friends; and some of you will be put to death. You will be hated universally on account of my name, but not a hair of your head will be lost. Your perseverance will win you your lives" (Lk 21:16-19).*

FRUIT > In this world, even good people are not spared suffering. Far from being protected from suffering, they are often subjected to it in a more vigorous way. Why? By putting us to test, God toughens us and moulds us back to his own image. In God's plan, trials are beneficial to us, for they bring out the best in us. Our Father who seeks to perfect us in holiness, knows the value of the refiner's fire. When a goldsmith puts gold into the crucible and the fire begins to work on the dross, it begins to wriggle and wriggle and as the dross is burned out, it gets quieter, until at last the surface is so calm that the refiner sees his own face reflected and puts out the fire.

THE ULTIMATE GOAL

ROOT > The Father's Providence is not merely the extension of his work of creation. Providence proceeds from the gracious will that sends the Saviour into the world. In other words, it belongs to the supernatural level of the diffusion of salvation and grace to all people through Christ. He takes an interest in our material and spiritual life, so that he can give us all his Son the Saviour, in the hope that we may participate in the filial dignity of Jesus to the Father. Thus, the ultimate goal of the Father's Providence is the summing up of all things in Christ.

> *"And it is in him that we have received our inheritance, marked out beforehand as we were, under the plan of the One who guides all things as he decides, by his own will, chosen to be, for the praise of his glory, the people who would put their hopes in Christ before he came" (Eph 1:11).*

FRUIT > The solicitude that the Father shows for the most mundane needs of our daily life is closely linked to his decision to save humankind as children in Christ. This does not mean that God has subjected all human beings to his paternalistic control, stifling the autonomy of free human behaviour. On the contrary, he seeks to promote it. Freed from anxiety for material needs, we are better able to act with the fullest personal spontaneity to respond to God's love, to collaborate with him in all things, and seek after the most radical liberation wrought by the work of Christ's redemption.

CALL GOD 'ABBA'

ROOT > Jewish prayer avoided naming Yahweh. The divine name was pronounced only once a year during the solemn liturgy of the feast of Atonement. Respect for God's transcendence nurtured a climate of fear that forbade all familiarity. Jesus on the contrary wanted the Father to be called by his name in prayer. Not only we are invited to use the name 'Father', but we are encouraged to say, 'Abba' which literally means 'Daddy', in a spirit of tender familiarity.

> *"All who are guided by the Spirit of God are sons of God; for what you received was not the spirit of slavery to bring you back into fear; you received the Spirit of adoption, enabling to cry out, 'Abba, Father!' (Rom 8:14-16).*

FRUIT > A king sits with his council deliberating on high affairs of state involving the destiny of nations, when he suddenly hears the sorrowful cry of his little child who has fallen down or been frightened by a bee. He rises and runs to his relief, assuages his sorrow and relieves his fears. Is there any thing unkingly here? Does it not even elevate the monarch in your esteem? And yet, we some times think it dishonourable for our heavenly Father, the King of kings, to consider the small matters of his children, when we cry to him, 'Abba, Father' in our needs!

PRAY TO THE FATHER

Root > We can pray to Jesus Christ and to the Holy Spirit directly. But Jesus taught us to pray to the Father. Why? It is to the Father, all prayer is ultimately addressed. Prayer addressed to Christ or to the Holy Spirit reaches the Father even if the Father is not named. Once a prayer has penetrated the mystery of the Holy Trinity, it can never stop midway. All prayer is brought to the Father by Jesus Christ in the Spirit. So too, answer to prayer springs from the Father, who lavishes his gifts through Christ and the Spirit.

> *"When you pray, go to your private room, shut yourself in, and so pray to your Father who is in the secret place, and your Father who sees all that is done in secret will reward you" (Mt 6:6).*

Fruit > A fine fresh wind is blowing in at the window but my wind chime is not sounding. Why don't I hear its soft music strains? Perhaps I have put it away in the storage room, because some of its strings were broken. There is a gracious revival in the Church and believers are greatly refreshed by the visitations of the Holy Spirit, but I am personally in sadly unbelieving condition, why? May it not be, I have neglected private prayer to our heavenly Father, due to the fact that family concerns and business have kept my heart in the storage room and my soul has lost its spiritual strings?

WHY, PRAYER?

ROOT > Father himself has the supreme responsibility for his Kingdom. Then why to pray for the coming for his Kingdom? The Father wants his children to collaborate with him. And we do that first by prayer. Our petitions are means through which a co-responsibility is exercised, which has a guarantee of authentic efficacy. The Father knows all our material needs. Then, why pray for them? Again, the purpose is to highlight human collaboration in the Father's work. Father is the first to show solicitude, but he wants our co-operation, by asking him for our needs.

> *"Christian prayer is co-operation with God's Providence, his plan of love for men" (CCC 2738).*

FRUIT > When a petition is granted, it signifies that the human entreaty has influenced the Father's will to the point of new act on his part. Some deny that such a thing is possible with God, for he is immutable; Yes, but in his relation with his children, the Father has freely decided to be receptive to our requests with a promise to grant them. Because of his love, he continually accedes to the influence our requests exercise on his way of acting. The co-operation to which he invites us, is not merely a facade. The Father wants our supplication to have the fullest possible efficacy.

HOW TO PRAY?

Root > The 'Our Father' is a prayer of petition. Prayers of petition incur the danger of being filled with self-concern. Contrary to the purpose of prayer, which is to acknowledge God's sovereignty and absolute control over our lives, petitions that are too self-centred, would place human desires in the forefront, subordinating God to human plan. In order to preserve us from this danger, Jesus asks us to give, in our prayers, priority to the Father's interests. That is the meaning of the first three petitions in the 'Our Father'.

> *"Our Father in heaven, may your name be held holy, your Kingdom come, your will be done on earth as in heaven"* (Mt 6:9-10).

Fruit > Our prayer must be first addressed to the three concerns of the Father himself: the proclamation of his name, the spreading of his Kingdom, and the fulfilment of his will. The veneration of the name implies a certain inward attitude of adoration and praise. However, this worship could remain rather superficial, if it were not accompanied by the coming of a Kingdom, in which the Father exercises greater control over human destiny. Then, too, the expansion of the Kingdom assumes its full dimension only if it implies the accomplishment of the father's will within human heart.

FILIAL TRUST

ROOT > The trust that inspires the prayers of Christians must be filial trust. This is not merely a creature's trust in its Creator. It is the trust that impels a child to open his or her soul to the father without reservation. The supreme example of trust is given us in Jesus' final cry from the cross: "Father, into your hands, I commend my spirit" (Lk 23:46). Jesus wants to lead us along the same path. When he tells us that the Father gives good things to those who pray to him, he wants to arouse in us a specifically filial trust, rooted in the Father's paternal love.

> *"Our fearlessness towards him consists in this, that if we ask anything in accordance with his will, he hears us. And if we know that he listens to whatever we ask him, we know that we already possess whatever we have asked of him"* (1 Jn 5:14-15).

FRUIT > A neighbour's dog was very fond of visiting my garden, and as he never improved my flowers, I never gave him a cordial welcome. Walking along quietly one evening, I saw him doing mischief. I threw a stick at him and advised him to go home. But how did the good creature reply to me? He turned round and waggled his tail, and in the merriest manner, picked up my stick, brought it to me and laid it at my feet. Since then we are friends. As the dog mastered the man by confiding in him, we children of God can even master our heavenly Father, by our filial trust in him.

PERSEVERANCE

ROOT > When Jesus recommends perseverance in prayer he does not name the Father, at least according to the texts of the two parables about the importunate friend and the nagging widow (Lk 11:5-8; 18:1-8). Yet, he has the Father in mind since he has exhorted his disciples to pray to the Father. We can even say, that the full meaning of the parables shines through, if we look at the Father, who is much more obliging than the friend and much more compassionate and just than the judge. Perseverance is all the more certain of attaining the goal, because it touches any father's heart.

> *"The battle of prayer is that of humble, trusting and persevering love. This love opens our hearts to three life-giving facts of faith about prayer: It is always possible to pray; Prayer is a vital necessity and prayer and Christian life are inseparable" (CCC 2742).*

FRUIT > Some mercies are not given to us except in answer to importunate prayer. There are blessings which, like fruit, drop into your hand the moment you touch the bough. But there are others which require you to shake the tree again and again, until you make it rock with vehemence of your exercise, for only then will the fruit fall down. By making us repeat our petitions, the Father wants us to achieve a more dearly won victory. To persevere, trusting in what hopes we have in the Father, is courage in a Christian; only the coward despairs.

WITH AND FOR OTHERS

ROOT > The Father desires harmony among his children. He is therefore particularly moved by prayers said in union with others. The filial relationship with the Father that prayer demands always requires charity, love of neighbour. The Father loves all his children with the same love, and it is in the unity of this love that he desires to receive the petitions addressed to him. He does not take sides for one of his children against the other, and he rejects all the divisions that drive human hearts apart.

> *"If we pray the 'Our Father' sincerely, we leave individualism behind, because the love that we receive frees us from it. The 'our' at the beginning of the Lord's prayer, like the 'us' of the last four petitions, excludes no-one. If we are to say it truthfully, our divisions and oppositions have to be overcome"* (CCC 2792).

FRUIT > Prayer pleases the Father in the measure that it is accompanied by an attitude of profound goodwill and fellowship. It is not enough to proclaim a personal affection for the Father. A truly filial attitude must reflect the fellowship that the Father has established in his Son Jesus. Brotherly or sisterly love is in itself a guarantee that prayer will be heard, since it offers the Father a filial heart that more closely resembles the Saviour's, and conforms more closely to the Father's great plan for gathering the human race into one family united in love.

UNANSWERED PRAYERS?

ROOT > No one is assured of receiving exactly what he or she asked for, for we do not know to what extent we are asking for good things. In any case, we will receive either precisely what was asked for, or the good things implicit in the intention of our prayer. Jesus proclaims the efficacy of all prayer in vigorous terms. The underlying reason for the efficacy of the petition is the Father's love. We are not speaking only of God's kindness towards his creatures. The specific reason why prayer is answered is Father's gracious love for his children.

> *"Ask, and it will be given to you; search, and you will find; knock, and the door will be opened to you. Every one who asks, receives; every one who searches, finds; every one who knocks, will have the door opened" (Mt 7:7-8).*

FRUIT > Why some prayers are not answered? Perhaps we are asking for things that are not good. If you were to tell your child that you would grant him anything he asks for, you would not intend by that, to give him a poisonous drug if he were to ask for it. When God appears to refuse what has been asked for, it is because he wants to give something better. If you ask for silver, will you be angry if he gives you gold? If you seek bodily health, should you complain, if instead, he makes your sickness turn to the healing of spiritual maladies?

April:

JESUS CHRIST

Week 1
The Incarnation

Week 2
The Good News

Week 3
The Universal Saviour

Week 4
The Sole Mediator

WORD MADE FLESH

Root > Jesus, the Word of God, was existing from the beginning in God, and he was God. He was the creative Word by whom all things have been made, enlightening the darkness of the world, in order to bring the revelation of God to human beings. In the Incarnation, he entered openly into the history, by being made flesh. He then became the object of a concrete experience of human beings. By this means, he perfected his twofold activity as revealer and author of salvation. As the only Son of God, he has brought truth and grace to save the world

> *"Christianity has its starting point in the Incarnation of the Word. Here, it is not simply the case of man seeking God, but of God who comes in Person to speak to man of himself and to show him the path by which he may be reached"* (John Paul II – TMA 5).

Fruit > Those who believe in the Word, who acknowledge and accept the Word, enter through him into the life of the children of God. Those who reject the Word, remain in the darkness of the world and are judged thereby. Every one must face this formidable prospect: If he or she is brought into contact with the Gospel of Christ directly, or if the divine Word is attained indirectly through other ways. To every person the Word speaks; and God awaits an answer from every person, and a person's eternal destiny depends upon this answer.

MORE THAN A WORD

ROOT > Jesus is more than the Word of God. He is the Light, the Truth, the Life; he is the Good Shepherd; he is the Son of God; he is the Son of Man. Jesus does not see his mission as simply the diffusion of the Word. He accomplishes the mission of a Saviour. He liberates the humankind from evil. Jesus did not present himself solely as the Divine Word. More fundamentally, he appears as the Son who lives by the life of the Father, and wants to communicate his life to human beings. He is the vine that nourishes the branches.

> *"God created the world through the Word. The Word is the eternal Wisdom; the Thought and the substantial image of God; eternally begotten and eternally loved by the Father, as God from God, light from light, he is the principle and the archetype of everything created by God in time" (John Paul II – TMA 3).*

FRUIT > Since the Incarnation of God, human beings are called to take position, when confronted by Christ who puts us in contact with God himself. The attitude we take towards God's Word and his person, determines our attitude also towards God. After taking a position, we see ourselves introduced to a life of faith, hope and charity, or the opposite; either we are bathed in the light, or cast into the darkness of evil. Those who accept the Word and put them into practice, are like those who build their house on rock. Those who accept it but do not put it into practice, are like those who build their house on sand.

THE CENTRAL TRUTH

Root > Through the Incarnation, the whole fullness of deity dwells bodily in Christ. Incarnation is the process of God's abasement and humiliation to the point of annihilation through death on the cross. Faith in the incarnation of God is not the result of human speculation. It does not have any true parallels in other religions. It is a truth revealed by God, and the Holy Scriptures bear unanimous witness to it. The first Christian communities considered and experienced the Incarnation to be the central truth of their faith.

> *"The becoming one of us on the part of the Son of God took place in the greatest humility. Everything returns to its origin. Jesus Christ is the recapitulation of everything; at the same time, the fulfilment of all things in God; a fulfilment which is the glory of God" (John Paul II – TMA 5,6).*

Fruit > God came as a man among human beings, and because he was wholly man and infinitely loving, he came to enter into every human being, into all of humanity and the world, through the presence of his love. That is the event which dominates history, working to bring together everything in heaven and on earth in Jesus Christ. Christ being the visible expression of a unique and eternal act of God's love, calls for a response of love from every one of us, so that he could gradually achieve the incorporation of all humankind into himself.

NOT A MYTH

ROOT > From the beginning to this day, the Incarnation has been continually opposed. Some have called it a myth. They say that in Jesus the man, God manifested his saving presence only in a particularly powerful way. But to us, the Incarnation is the central point of biblical witness. The Church has always defended the Incarnation giving at the same time reasons for its credibility. The martyrs, past and present, have given their very lives as a witness to this truth.

> *"For us men and for our salvation, he came down from heaven and became man. He suffered, died, rose on the third day, and ascended into heaven. He will come again to judge the living and the dead" (Nicene Creed).*

FRUIT > The doctrine of the Incarnation has been baptised in blood; sword have been drawn to slay the confessors of it; it has been sealed by martyrs at the stake or the block where they have been slained by hundreds. But for most of us believers, our witness would be in fulfilling our secular vocation in a way that one's life would not make sense if the Incarnation is a myth. The messenger's personal life is at least half of her or his message. As a Christian, I must witness to God made flesh, if necessary, using words. But, what use walking anywhere to preach, unless we preach as we walk?

GOD AND MAN

ROOT > Jesus was truly a man. He spoke and did everything
as any other human being. He was a noble character, strong
and fearless, kind and loving. He suffered crucifixion and
died on the cross. But he was also truly God. He spoke and
acted as only God could. He worked miracles and forgave
sins, showed power over life and death as only God could. If
Jesus is not both true God and true man, we are not saved.
Salvation means overcoming the gulf between God and us,
and we are saved only if God comes in person as one of us.

> *"The unique and altogether singular event of the Incarnation
> of the Son of God does not mean that Jesus Christ is part
> God and part man; nor does it imply that he is the result of
> a confused mixture of the divine and the human. He became
> truly man while remaining truly God"* (CCC 464).

FRUIT > If I can read the New Testament and still not see
that Christ is both divine and human, I can look all over the
sky at high noon on a cloudless day, and will not see the sun.
Because Jesus is wholly God and wholly man, he revealed
to us who God is and who man is. Because he is both God
and man, he can make of human beings that which they
should be. As a result, all who are incorporated into Christ,
are in the process of being humanised and divinised. In other
words, by uniting us with himself, Christ allows us to achieve
our fullest potential.

SOMETHING NEW

Root > In ancient times, God had spoken to the human race in many and various ways. But in order to introduce into human history his definitive salvation, opening it to all humankind, God intervened in history with absolute newness, only in the birth of his Son Jesus Christ. If there were, before Christ, many religions such as Hinduism, Buddhism and other Greco-Roman pagan religions, they were essentially ordered to prepare for the coming of Christ. The Incarnation is what makes Christianity new, for Jesus is not a prophet speaking in the name of God, but is God himself.

> *"Christ is God who comes in Person to speak of himself to man and to show him the way by which to reach him. The religion founded upon Jesus Christ is a religion of glory; it is a newness of life for the praise of the glory of God" (John Paul II – TMA 6,5).*

Fruit > Christianity can no more be compared with other religions, than Jesus Christ can be compared with other human beings. Some try to water down Christianity, by squeezing the supernatural out of it. Because its founder is the Son of God, the transcendence cannot be separated from it. There are great difficulties, no doubt, in Christianity, but they are nothing compared to the difficulties that will follow, if its divine origin is denied. Christianity is neither a creed nor a ceremonial, but life connected with the divine Saviour from above.

THE CENTRALITY OF CHRIST

ROOT > Human history started from the creation of humankind, and arrived at Christ through the Chosen people, but now continues to expand from the time of Christ via the Church, to the whole of humanity. Because the coming of Christ is temporal centre of everything that happens in history, it gives meaning to history and its saving efficacy. Because of the Incarnation, the cosmic events are no more profane, but are sacred. That is, whatever happens in the world, has become a means for God to become incarnate, to reveal himself and give his grace.

> *"Thanks to the Word, the world of creatures appears as a 'cosmos', an ordered universe. And it is the same Word who, by taking flesh, renews the cosmic order of creation"* (John Paul II – TMA 3,4).

FRUIT > Are there Christians among us who have long been absent from the world? Have they emigrated to a 'spiritual' universe that they have created for themselves, as if they have nothing to do with this life? Such Christians should return to their mother earth. For God is present now, as yeast in dough, precisely in the mundane realities of our earthly life, and hence we can now encounter him only in and through the daily details of our human life, and be divinised by Christ. There is no real 'spiritual life' unless life itself is lived fully. A Christian who is absent from life is a person who has separated himself or herself from the incarnate God.

THE EVANGELIZER

ROOT > Jesus was a comprehensive evangeliser. He communicated the Good News using a variety of literary forms such as short discourses, parables, and similes. He evangelised by certain unconventional attitudes towards the poor and the needy. He communicated by means of a great number of miracles; He communicated with his actions, his silences and gazes. He communicated extra-ordinary religious experience whenever he called someone to follow him. Finally, he sealed his total communication by his death and resurrection.

> *"Jesus made a tour through all the towns and villages, teaching in their synagogues, proclaiming the Good News of the Kingdom and curing all kinds of illness. When he saw the crowd he felt sorry for them for they were like sheep without a shepherd" (Mt 9:35-36).*

FRUIT > God is a communicating Being and hence he made his only Son an evangeliser. The Gospel Jesus preached is the power of God operating towards the total transformation of the humankind. And it works! Thousands will testify that it does. No one who wants to climb out of his or her sad past should overlook the Gospel. It is the God's way out and there is no other. But we must note this: The medicine of the Gospel has been prescribed by the Good Physician. We may neither dilute it nor add ingredients to make it more palatable; we must serve it neat.

THE HEALER

ROOT > Jesus' activity as a healer is one of the first and best attested episodes of the New Testament. In his time, the scientific knowledge that we have today about the diseases, was absent. There were no surgery of any note. Rules of hygiene were rudimentary and the same is true of cures and medicines. It is in this context, Jesus went about healing the sick and curing all sort of maladies. He not only healed the body but also the souls of the sick, by prompting forgiveness for the sins and eliciting faith in their hearts.

> *"'Heal the sick!' The Church has received this charge from the Lord and strives to carry it out. She believes in the life-giving presence of Christ, the Physician of souls and bodies. This presence is particularly active through the sacraments and in altogether special way through the Eucharist" (CCC 1509).*

FRUIT > Once I was so ill that literally I was near the gate of death. The convent sisters who were around me, holding me down, because I was in convulsion, were praying for me too. My God! I rose up, not gradually, but suddenly again. Was it the power of their prayer? I firmly believe it was. When I rose up, I enjoyed the kind of rehearsal of that grand rising, when from beds of dust and silent clay, I shall rise at the trumpet of the angels and the voice of God. In every healing there is a pledge of resurrection, and Christ is the Life and the Resurrection.

A FRIEND OF THE NEEDY

Root > The poor and the needy can be always found in great number in every epoch and every society. In our Lord's time too, there were lots of people discriminated against and excluded from society because of illness, low income, social status, religion or moral behaviour. But Jesus became friend of all these. Acceptance, compassion, understanding and forgiveness were his habitual attitudes towards them. Thus he revealed that the nearness of the Kingdom was the saving nearness of God to all the needy.

> *"For John came, neither eating nor drinking, and they say, 'He is possessed.' The Son of man came, eating and drinking, and they say, 'look, a glutton and a drunkard, a friend of tax collectors and sinners.' Yet, Wisdom is justified by her deeds" (Mt 11:18-19).*

Fruit > As children of the same heavenly Father, how concerned are we, and what do we do for the victims of rejection, segregation, inequality, injustice, sin and evil in our times? When a member of a family suffers and dies, do not the other members grieve? How can we, then, see in the faces of millions the lines that rejection has cut, the mouths that segregation has twisted, the eyes that inequality has darkened, and those whose light that injustice has extinguished, and still remain quiet with a peaceful conscience?

JESUS FORGIVES

ROOT > Jesus is the incarnate mercy of God and hence he forgave all sinners including his own executioners. A generous man because he is aware of his own sinfulness, can take a tolerant attitude towards those who sin. Jesus' forgiveness of sinners is not such a tolerant attitude. He being the sinless one, his forgiveness is a gesture of absolute goodness. Jesus wanted to educate us to imitate him in mercy and forgiveness. He has called us to pardon always. He completed his hard lesson of forgiving others, when he asked us to love our enemies.

> *"You have heard how it was said, 'You will love your neighbour and hate your enemies.' But I say this to you, love your enemies and pray for those who persecute you; so that you may be children of your Father in heaven, for he causes his sun to rise on the bad as well as the good" (Mt 5:44-45).*

FRUIT > Our human nature demands justice. So, anyone who does good should receive good, and any one who does evil merits evil. Thus, when evil has been done to us, we see only two possible attitudes: that of vengeance and that of justice. But Jesus wants us to oppose revenge and surpass human justice, with the attitude of pardon and love for our enemies. The power to forgive sins is a precious legacy that Jesus has left the Church. When we approach the sacraments, not only we are forgiven, but receive a share in the divine power to forgive and love our enemies.

JESUS CONVERTS

ROOT > Among the converts Jesus made, Zacchaeus was one. He was a tax-collector, rich, but considered by every one a sinner. However, like all human beings he was also searching for true and lasting happiness. He met Jesus not out of curiosity but attracted by the irresistible force of the good, and by an intense desire to receive the gift of inner sight. When Jesus was dining with him, he told the Master that he would give half of his goods to the poor. Thus, he began a new life, a life of reconciliation, not only with God but also with the brothers and sisters, defrauded by his greed.

> *"Jesus said to him: 'Today salvation has come to this house, because this man too is a son of Abraham; for the Son of man has come to seek out and save what was lost' " (Lk 19:9-10).*

FRUIT > Zacchaeus' restitution of his ill-gotten gains is a true act of conversion to a life he had neglected. It is a recovery of authentic happiness. Like Zacchaeus, from what to what I need conversion 'today'? Note, Jesus' emphasis on 'today'. In our lives, 'today' is more important than 'yesterday and tomorrow', for the past is made up of so many 'todays' and the future will be made up of many 'todays'. It is today, we need conversion. It is today, Jesus is calling each of us to meet him. He awaits our willingness to receive him.

JESUS REVEALS

FRUIT > The heart of Christian religion is that Jesus Christ has revealed God, in his person, and has communicated him as the Father, just as he has revealed himself as the Father's Son and the Holy Spirit as the Divine Love. In Jesus Christ, the ineffable God becomes seeable, touchable and speakable. The God Jesus has revealed is a kind, merciful and provident Father, not the one who oppresses and punishes, but a Father who considers all human beings as his children, a Father who wants to share his supreme goodness with his children.

> *"To see Jesus is to see the Father. For this reason, Jesus perfected revelation by fulfilling it through this whole work of making himself present and manifesting himself: through his words and deeds, his signs and wonders, but especially through his death and resurrection and the final sending of the Spirit of truth" (DV 4).*

FRUIT > We cannot, by any amount of searching, fully find out God. The more we try, the more we are bewildered. Then Jesus Christ appears. He is God stooping down to our level, and he enables our feeble thought to get some real hold on God as he is. Science must always be prepared to alter course, when new facts demand such action. Revelation of Christ, on the other hand, is final. Hence, instead of complaining that God has hidden himself, we must give him thanks for having revealed so much of himself in Christ.

JESUS DIES

ROOT > Jesus healed many people and relieved their sufferings. But he did not come to eliminate sufferings and death from human existence. So, suffering and death still remain in the world, keeping us always on the alert towards our everlasting destiny. But Jesus gave suffering a profound and redemptive meaning. He himself did not avoid suffering and death. On the contrary, he shared fully our human nature except in sin, and with full knowledge and freedom, he made himself vulnerable to the most painful form of human suffering and death.

> *"If anyone wants to be a follower of mine, let him renounce himself and take up his cross and follow me. Anyone who wants to save his life will lose it; but anyone who loses his life for my sake, will save it" (Lk 9:23-24).*

FRUIT > God not only descended to us human beings to become a human being, but descended to the total dereliction of one condemned to death. Jesus calls us to take up the same descending way. It is the way of suffering, but is also the way to healing. It is the way of humiliation, but is also the way to resurrection. It is the way of tears, but of tears that turn into tears of joy. It is the way of hiddenness, but is the way that leads to light for all to see. It is the way of oppression, persecution and death, but also the way to full revelation of God's love.

JESUS RISES

Root > Jesus rose from the dead. His resurrection is a transcendent event, because in the resurrection, Jesus' humanity instantaneously passed from death to the divine life of God. However, the risen Jesus remains solidly linked to our physical world which he confirmed through his appearances. By his resurrection, our broken friendship with God was repaired. Since then, the divine life of God is streaming through the risen humanity of Christ into all of humanity. As a result, human beings can be set free from slavery of sin and its consequences.

> *"Christ, like a divine leaven always and ever more fully penetrates the life of humanity, spreading the work of salvation accomplished in the Paschal Mystery" (John Paul II – TMA 56).*

Fruit > The risen Jesus is actively present in our world, and it is possible for anyone who believes to get totally incorporated into Christ. The risen Lord is present with us in a relationship more intimate than that we can find between two human persons. People today believe in existence, and some times, only in existence! Hence most people are absent to God who is present in their human existence. God is waiting for us, and that, in the midst of our mundane life. To meet God we have no need to look further.

SAVIOUR OF ALL

ROOT > God has manifested and accomplished his will to save all human beings, in a unique and definitive way, in the mystery of Jesus and his Church, which is the sacrament of salvation on earth. Any faith, grace and salvation that there may be outside of Christianity, draw their saving power substantially from death and resurrection of Christ. The grace of Christ is the cause and the substance of salvation for every one, whether they are inside or outside the Church. Jesus is the sole and universal Saviour of all.

> *"The Son of God became man, taking a body and soul in the womb of the Virgin, precisely for this reason: to become the perfect redeeming sacrifice. The religion of the Incarnation is the religion of the world's redemption through the sacrifice of Christ, wherein lies victory over evil, over sin and over death itself" (John Paul II – TMA 7).*

FRUIT > Saved! What a sweet sound it is to the one who sees the vessel going down; but discovers that the lifeboat is near and will rescue him from the sinking ship! But to be rescued from sin and death is greater salvation still, and demands a louder joy. We will sing it in life and whisper it in death and chant it throughout eternity: saved by the Lord! I heard some one saying, "Oh, I would give my eyes for salvation!" But I said to him, "You shall have it, without giving your eyes. Give your heart to Jesus Christ and take his salvation free!"

JESUS' CLAIM

ROOT > Jesus was consistent in claiming to be the sole and definitive Saviour of humanity. What are the core bases of his claim? He was fully aware during his earthly life that he was the Son of the heavenly Father, and the Messiah whom the Father had sent to save the humankind. He proclaimed that his death and resurrection is the reality that saves all people. He revealed God as the Father whose love is the origin of man's redemption in Christ. Jesus' message shows that adoption by God as his sons and daughters in his Son, is a Christian privilege, but open to all to receive.

> *"Jesus Christ is one Saviour of the world, yesterday, today and for ever. Christ entered the world to give witness to the truth, to rescue, and not to sit in judgement, to serve and not to be served"* (John Paul II – TMA 40,56).

FRUIT > Christ is the A and the Z of the salvation alphabet. He is not only the helper of our salvation, but the God of it, the maker of it, the all-in-all of it. As human beings, we cannot manufacture salvation for ourselves. Eternal salvation must come from an eternal God. Therefore, human beings should row away from their fantasy of self-sufficiency, before it turns into a torpedo to work their ruin. Salvation that makes us new creatures must be the work of him who sits on the throne and makes all things new.

MYSTERIOUS WAYS

ROOT > In God's plan, no one is deprived of the chance to be saved. Those who do not know Christ and live in other religious traditions, are also offered salvation by mysterious paths known only to God. Obedience to one's own upright conscience, the doing of good and the avoidance of evil, adherence to the truth and consistency between faith and life, are these mysterious ways. In such cases, people receive salvation, because they practise good on the basis of Christ's teachings.

> *"Though God, in ways known to himself, can lead those inculpably ignorant of the Gospel to that faith without which it is impossible to please him, yet a necessity lies upon the Church and at the same time a sacred duty to preach the Gospel. Hence missionary activity today as always retains its power and necessity" (AG 7).*

FRUIT > Missions are a 'must', not a 'may be'. The special person called to do missionary work is every person who knows Christ as the Saviour. A missionary in North India told the Christmas story to a group of Hindu villagers and then read it from the Scriptures. One asked, "How long has it been since God's Son was born in the world?" "About two thousand years', came the answer. "Then," asked the villager, "who has been hiding this Book all this time?" That is it – hiding the Book. For, after all, is not our keeping the Book from those who need it, the same as hiding it?

THE CHALLENGE!

ROOT > There are challenges today which the saving universality of Jesus is facing. One challenge is 'pluralism', which is a form of society embracing many minority groups and cultural traditions, due to a large-scale migration of people to the North and the West. Another challenge is the slackening of Church's missionary outreach towards non-Christians and the re-awakening of the non-Christian religions to their role as a source and guarantee of human values. Still another challenge is the fascination of a new religiosity, which offers a culture and life-style, as an alternative to the empty and superficial life prevailing in many developed countries.

> *"Mission renews the Church, imparts fresh vigour to Christian faith and identity, and gives new enthusiasm and new reasons to go forward. Faith strengthens when it is given away! All peoples, open your door to Christ"* (John Paul II – RM 3).

FRUIT > The way we have to face the modern challenges to the saving universality of Jesus is not to dilute the incomparable necessity of Christ to human salvation, but to reaffirm that Jesus is the sole, universal Saviour of the world, and assert again that everything good and true that may be found in other religious traditions and movements, are a preparation for the Gospel. Hence, we have a need to increase our efforts to preach the Gospel, especially by personal witness to our faith in Christ, for any person touched by Jesus Christ, is already a good publicity for the Gospel.

PERSONAL EXPERIENCE

ROOT > Christians have a personal experience of the saving power of Christ, when they are incorporated into Christ through Baptism. In the words of St Paul, we become 'God's field', 'God's building', 'God's temple'. The image of the 'mystical body' is the best expression of the believer's living participation in the saving mystery of Christ, a participation by which we become one with Christ. Incorporation into Christ brings the believer into relation with the Trinity, and at the same time, establishes a relationship with fellow Christians.

> *"Rediscover baptism as the foundation of Christian existence according to the words of the Apostle: 'As many of you as were baptised into Christ have put on Christ'" (John Paul II – TMA 41).*

FRUIT > To be a Christian is not merely to understand the mystery of Christ. I am a Christian when I have recognised Jesus as a faithful friend, a model of my human fulfilment and a teacher of fraternal life. I am a Christian when I experience Jesus as the Messiah and Saviour of my own personal existence. Because of union with Christ, the baptised do not form a shapeless jumble of closed individual existences, but a living organism, full of inter-connections with one another, each exercising one's own function in the mystical body of Christ.

ECCLESIAL EXPERIENCE

ROOT > Our encounter with the Saviour at baptism is actually an encounter with the community of faith, for Baptism takes place in the context of the ecclesial community. We express and celebrate this communion, in a special way, in the liturgy of the Eucharist for it is in the Eucharist, we live together our experience of being saved by Christ's paschal mystery. The experience of Christ by the baptised in the context of the community, has its vibrant expression in the 'consecrated life', which is by its nature a personal and communal experience of Christ, a life in Christ and in the Church, with a particular apostolic mission in the world.

> *"We were baptised into one body in a single Spirit and we were all given the same Spirit to drink. And indeed the body consists not of one member but of many" (1 Cor 12:13-14).*

FRUIT > We can bring to maturity our ecclesial experience of the salvation in Christ, through active participation in liturgy and common life of prayer, through a positive attitude to obedience and collaboration, with a readiness to serve at all the levels that exist in the body of Christ. We can take part in ecclesial movements which promote maturation of faith and human solidarity. Our experience of the saving grace of Christ can become more intense, if we form a genuine communion with every human person, discriminating none because of religion, race, sex or social standing.

CONVERSION EXPERIENCE

ROOT > Among the many spiritual experiences which reveal the saving power of Christ, conversion-experience is one. This experience gives us not only enlightenment, but also strength to overcome the spiritual, moral and even physical disabilities. Conversion is an experience of lived salvation and can be, in some cases, a radical change of one's fundamental option in favour of Christ, or a partial correction and improvement of one's life of faith. The sacrament of Penance or Reconciliation, is a definite means for a believer to experience conversion.

> *"Christ instituted the sacrament of Penance for all sinful members of his Church: above all for those who, since Baptism, have fallen into grave sin and have thus lost their baptismal grace and wounded ecclesial communion. It is to them the sacrament of Penance offers a new possibility to convert and to recover the grace of justification" (CCC 1446).*

FRUIT > Being converted at the Sacrament of Reconciliation is not a finished event. Conversion can continue all one's life. Conversion can be accomplished as an on-going event in daily life, by gestures of reconciliation, concern for the poor, defence of justice, by the admission of faults to one's brothers, fraternal correction, regular examination of conscience, spiritual direction, acceptance of suffering, endurance of persecution for the sake of righteousness. Taking up one's cross each day and following Jesus is the surest way for on-going conversion.

CULTURAL EXPERIENCE

Root > The religious life of Christians becomes the Christian culture, which is a new culture of leavening and transforming any other human cultures, into a civilisation of love. This culture does not reject any thing that is authentically human or religious in other cultures. But, this culture is not static but dynamic, for it spurs the world to transcend continuously its own limits and dark sides, until it reaches its fulfilment in the universal Saviour. This calls for Christian missionary endeavour, along the lines of practical inculturation of faith in today's world.

> *"Missionary endeavour begins with the proclamation of the Gospel to peoples and groups who do not yet believe in Christ, continues with the establishment of Christian communities that are a sign of God's presence in the world. It must involve a process of inculturation if the Gospel has to flesh in each people's culture" (CCC 854).*

Fruit > Practical inculturation of faith calls for focusing our missionary efforts on areas particularly relevant for today, such as human dignity, equality of human beings, universal brotherhood, the inviolability of life, respect for nature, world peace, through just distribution of the world's goods. Our inculturation efforts must touch also the celebration of liturgy. It must correspond to the genius and culture of the different peoples. The mystery of the Saviour must be celebrated in all cultures in such a way that they themselves are not stifled by it, but saved and fulfilled.

UNIQUE MEDIATION

ROOT > Jesus Christ is the unique Mediator between God and humankind. Jesus, as the second person of the Holy Trinity, had played his role as Mediator already in God's work of creation, and of his covenant with Israel. But, when God willed to save all people concretely by means of the unique efficacy of the mystery of Jesus' death and resurrection, Jesus became the unique and unsurpassing Mediator. "There is only one God and there is only one Mediator between God and humanity, himself a human being, Christ Jesus, who offered himself as a ransom for all" (1 Tim 2:5-6). Hence, humankind's only way to salvation is through Christ Jesus.

> *"Christ the Redeemer of the world, is the one Mediator between God and man, and there is no other name under heaven by which we can be saved" (John Paul II – TMA 4).*

FRUIT > The fact that Christ is the sole Mediator does not, however, put an end to the role of human persons in God's work of salvation. Mediation of Jesus takes on sensible signs, in the persons to whom he confides a function in his Church. From the time of his earthly life, Jesus called men and women to work with him, to proclaim the Gospel, to bring about the signs of the presence of his Kingdom. They are responsible for his Word, for his Church, for Baptism, for the Eucharist and forgiveness of sins. Thus, his envoys prolong his mediation.

ABSOLUTE DISTINCTION

ROOT > There is a qualitative difference between Christ and other non-Christian mediations of salvation. We accept that all religious traditions, since the beginning of creation, are human search for God, a search which itself is a divine gift from above. However, there is a radical difference between Christian and other religions, which consists in the mystery of Jesus Christ, in his historical self-revelation and in his special presence in the Church which makes the Church sacrament of salvation to humanity. Christianity is not opposed to other religions, but in it, there is a qualitative leap due solely to the mystery of Jesus.

> *"Christ is the one Mediator between God and man and the sole Redeemer of the world, to be clearly distinguished from the founders of other great religions" (John Paul II – TMA 38).*

FRUIT > Those who believe in Jesus Christ as the only Mediator will vigorously reject all divinations, fortune-telling, prophecies in groves, amulets, incantations, and sorcery, for they are means opposed to God's own means offered to us in Christ. They will also keep away from occult-cults, which are cultural responses to personal and social crises. On the surface, these cults seem to offer some kind of answer, but in reality, they cause havoc: young people are brain-washed, families split, idols and pictures of ordinary human beings are worshipped, sometimes leading to large scale mass suicide.

THE WAY TO THE FATHER

ROOT > Our supreme goal is life in the Father's house. And the way to that house is Jesus Christ. As the Son of God, he is oriented to the Father, and by following him we share in his orientation. We do not, any longer, attain the supreme goal of human existence by following a rule of conduct. We have to follow the person of Jesus Christ. In order to enter into communion with the Father, we have first to enter into communion with the Son. He is the way, for it contains within itself everything that is present in the Father.

> *"Thomas said, 'Lord, we do not know where you are going, so how can we know the way?' Jesus said, 'I am the Way, I am the Truth and Life. No one can come to the Father, except through me'"* (Jn 14:6).

FRUIT > Christ is the way, but if we will not tread it, we shall not reach the Father's house. A minister was going up the aisle of his church during a revival, when a young man earnestly cried to him, "Sir, can you tell me the way to Christ?" "No. I cannot", was the deliberate answer. The young man answered, "I beg your pardon; I thought you were a minister of the Gospel." "So I am", was the reply. "Then how is it that you cannot tell me the way to Christ?" "My friend," said the minister, "there is no way to Christ; he himself is the Way. Christ is here."

RELIGIOUS DIALOGUE

Root > God is present in every human being. He wants every one to find fullness of life in him. This is the mystery of unity already existing among all peoples, in spite of the differences of creed. The Church wishes to see the mystery of this unity be fully realised so that perfect harmony may come about. For this reason, the Catholic Church is in favour of dialogue with other Churches, with non-Christians and with those who profess no religion. The purpose of this dialogue is to establish positive and constructive relations with individuals and groups of differing creed, and to be mutually enriched.

> *"All this has to be done freely. The Church regards religious freedom as an inalienable right, a right that goes with the duty of seeking the truth: only in a climate of respect for the freedom of the individual can inter-religious dialogue develop and bear fruit" (John Paul II – AHM 2).*

Fruit > We are not to force our own creed on others. That is, we are not to recruit members actively. We are not to use persuasive or evocative advertising methods that will visibly force people to join the Catholic Church. We are not sent into the world as sales representatives urging people to buy goods with miraculous properties or as insurance agents selling all risk policies. Our task is not to persuade workers to join multi-national commercial enterprise. We are the disciples of a living person whom we want our brothers and sisters come to know, and freely choose to follow him.

PRAYER TO CHRIST

ROOT > When Jesus taught his disciples to pray to the Father, he did not mean that the Father alone should be addressed in prayer. We know he granted many petitions for miraculous cures addressed to himself. He counselled his disciples: "You believe in God; believe also in me" (Jn 14:1). He declared, "If you ask me for any thing in my name, I will do it" (Jn 14:14). When we make a request 'in his name', it is inspired by faith in his name, by faith in him as the Son, which implies his omnipotence.

> *"To pray 'Jesus', is to invoke him and to call him within us. His name is the only one that contains the presence it signifies. Jesus is the Risen One, and who ever invokes the name of Jesus, is welcoming the Son of God who loved him and who gave himself up for him" (CCC 435).*

FRUIT > Pray to Jesus, he is a place of refuge in the day of strife. Pray to him, when the problems oppress you, and when your strength fails, he will teach you wisdom and banish your distress. If we forget the name of Jesus in our prayers, we have lost the muscle and sinew from the arm of prayer. 'In the name of Christ', is the one unbuttressed pillar on which all prayer must lean. Take this away, and it comes down with a crash. Let this stand, and prayer stands like a heaven-reaching minaret, holding communion with the skies.

MEDIATION OF THE CHURCH

ROOT > The unique God, alone in the absolute transcendence of his being, has raised up many mediators between himself and his people. He prepared and announced the mediation which his Chosen People would exercise between him and humanity. This mediation of Israel was fulfilled in the mediation of Jesus Christ, the sole Mediator with unfathomable grandeur which comes to him as the Son of God. Nevertheless, Christ as the head of the new Israel, exercises his mediation through the Church, his body which he has raised up.

> *"The Church is both the means and the goal of God's plan: prefigured in creation, prepared for in the Old Covenant, founded by the words and actions of Jesus Christ, fulfilled by his redeeming cross and resurrection, the Church has been manifested as the mystery of salvation by the outpouring of the Holy Spirit" (CCC 778).*

FRUIT > We are living at a time when the Church is frequently seen more as an obstacle in the way, rather than as the way to Jesus. Nevertheless, the Church is the body of the Lord. Without Jesus there can be no Church, and without the Church we cannot stay united with Jesus. Have you ever met any one who has come closer to Jesus, by forsaking the Church? To listen to the Church, is to listen to the Lord of the Church. Specifically, this means taking active part in all the aspects of the Church's life, especially the liturgical life.

THE MEDIATION OF MARY

ROOT > It is certain that all the grace that came upon Mary flowed exclusively from the mediation of her Son. But the Mediator, when he died, entrusted her with a mission with regard to his followers, who were represented by the well-beloved disciple (Jn 19:25). This is the mission which she continues to fulfil invisibly, associated with all the elect, but in an eminent manner, praying with all the elect for the Church, but in a prayer, the efficacy of which was already seen at the marriage in Cana (Jn 2:3). By virtue of being the mother of the head, she is in a certain way mother of the whole body.

> *"Mary, taken up to heaven, continues to win for us gifts of eternal salvation by her manifold acts of intercession. Therefore, the Blessed Virgin is invoked by the Church under the titles of Advocate and Mediatrix. These, however, are to be so understood that they neither take away nor add any thing to the dignity and efficacy of Christ the one Mediator"* (LG 62).

FRUIT > It is well known that the heart has two movements: distole and diastole. Mary is always performing those two movements: absorbing grace from her Son Jesus and pouring it forth on us. Salvation is occasionally more obtained by calling on the name of Mary than by invoking that of Jesus. This is not because he is not the source and the Lord of all graces, but because, when we have recourse to the Mother, her intercession is more irresistible than our own. When she prays to her Son, it seems as if she rather commands.

May:

CROSS AND RESURRECTION

Week 1
Suffering

Week 2
Dying

Week 3
Rising

Week 4
Living

SUFFERING SERVANT IN LOVE

ROOT > The sufferings of Jesus throughout his human life, especially his passion and death, is the most convincing sign that God loves us. Christ came to redeem us from sin, but sin basically being non-love or conditional love or love with self-love, Jesus suffered all the frightful sufferings, out of unselfish and unconditional love for us. Suffering in itself is evil, hence it is not Christ's suffering that redeems; only his love redeems. Suffering in itself is worth nothing; only love gives life.

> *"We had all gone astray like sheep, each taking his own way, and God brought the acts of rebellion of all of us to bear on him. Ill-treated and afflicted like a lamb led to the slaughter-house, he never opened his mouth" (Is 53:6-7).*

FRUIT > Non-love is the root cause of our individual and collective sufferings, found in the hurt feelings of a neighbour because of a thoughtless word, as well as in the mass slaughter of a race. Non-love or love with self-love ends in broken homes, in disrupted communities, in reducing labourers into virtual slaves and the like. Every form of non-love, however obscure, produces suffering, generates disorder where there should be harmony, hatred where there should be love. There are infinitely more people who die from hunger and war caused by global self-love, than from earth quakes or natural disasters.

SUFFERING SERVANT IN SOLIDARITY

ROOT > Jesus made us see God's love for us by being in solidarity with us in our suffering. His Son became our partner and companion in suffering, thus enabling us to turn it into a way to liberation. If we are poor, we know that Jesus was poor too. If we are afraid, we know that Jesus too was afraid. If we are beaten, we know Jesus too was beaten; and if we are tortured to death, we know Jesus too suffered the same fate. Jesus as a faithful friend walks with us the lonely road of suffering, but bringing us divine consolation and true liberation.

> *"Ours were the sufferings he was bearing, ours were the sorrows he was carrying. He was crushed because of our guilt, the punishment reconciling us fell on him, and we have been healed by his bruises" (Is 53:4-5).*

FRUIT > Being deeply aware that Jesus is in solidarity with us in our suffering can, not only take away a lot of sting from our suffering, but also release new life within us through suffering. This is the reason why the victims of poverty and oppression are often more deeply convinced of God's love, than others are. That is why, the question, "How can God really love the world when he permits all that frightful suffering?" is raised, less by these people who have themselves tasted sufferings, than by those who have merely heard and read about it.

THE CENTRALITY OF THE CROSS

Root > God who wanted to reverse the effects of human rebellion against him, carried out his plan in a way we could never expect. He set in motion a process that led to his Son coming into the human society as a man. His Son lived truly a human life and chose to experience the very effects of our sin, namely the whole range of human suffering from the womb to the tomb, as the path to his glory and our reunion with God. Hence, leave out the cross and you have killed the religion of Christ. We do not understand Christ until we understand his cross.

> *"Then he said to them, 'You foolish men! So slow to believe all that the prophets have said! Was it not necessary that the Christ should suffer before entering into his glory'?" (Lk 24:25-26).*

Fruit > The response most people spontaneously give to suffering is: preventing, avoiding, denying, shunning, keeping clear of and ignoring. All this indicate that suffering does not fit into our programme of living. When we react to them as uninvited, undesirable and show the door as soon as we can, what happens? We are again rebelling against God's plan and thus invite more suffering which has been already the result of human original rebellion against God. God's way revealed in Jesus is the way of the cross, the only way to our glory.

THE MEANING OF THE CROSS

ROOT > The meaning of the cross is that it is the symbol of victory over evil. All those who have come to know Christ must confess that the turning point of the human race is the cross of Christ. For, from the moment he was crucified on the cross, the power of evil received its mortal wound. Evil dies hard, but from that moment it was doomed. The cross is also the supreme symbol of God's love for humankind. What brought Jesus to the cross was not the Jewish and Roman authorities, but God's love which desired the restoration of humankind to himself.

> *"By suffering for us, Jesus not only provided us with an example for our imitation, but blazed a trail, and if we follow it, life and death are made holy and take a new meaning" (GS 22).*

FRUIT > Therefore, God does not witness to his love for us by taking us out of suffering, but rather by demonstrating his grace and love through them and in the midst of them. As true Christians, we cannot live without joy and we can have that joy even in suffering for the grace of Christ is present in it. To us, suffering and death are means to victory over evil and points of encounter with God's love. Thus the greatest suffering and the greatest joy can co-exist in the same life of a Christian, and every moment of his or her life can resound with Easter joy.

THE QUESTION OF SUFFERING

ROOT > God certainly cannot create suffering, for it is evil. Faith affirms that the first human beings fell from grace by rebelling against God and thus sufferings and death entered into the human race. The pity is that we their descendants still remain fallen. There is a voice inside our moral conscience that tells us that our immoral and unmoral acts are abnormal. There is something wrong in us, something dislocated, with the result we continue to suffer, because we freely make wrong choices. We make ourselves suffer by virtue of our freedom. God wrote the drama, but we keep changing the plot.

> *"It was through one man that sin came into the world, and through sin death, and thus death has spread through the whole human race because every one has sinned" (Rom 5:12).*

FRUIT > What can console a believer in the midst of sufferings is that the very God who has allowed us to suffer stands by, forming us into fuller human beings in Christ Jesus. 'Why?' and 'Why me?' are the most commonly asked questions by the sufferers. We will never have the complete answers in this life, because we are dealing sometimes with irrational chaos, at other times with mystery, and always with Mysterious One who is forming us into the likeness of his Son Jesus Christ. It is only later that we will see how it all adds up to some grand and glorious purpose.

IT CAN BE REDEMPTIVE

Root > As all the rivers run into the sea and all the clouds empty themselves upon the earth, so did all the acts of human frailty gathered together to the crucifixion of Christ. But Jesus bore them all in love and obedience to the Father for the salvation of humankind, thereby transforming all our sufferings into means of salvation. Jesus, the new Adam, through his obedient acceptance of suffering and death, restored to the Father a renewed humanity, thus giving us new hope of happiness in a life without suffering and death.

> *"Son though he was, he learnt obedience through what he suffered; when he had been perfected, he became for all who obey him the source of eternal salvation" (Heb 5:8-9).*

Fruit > There is an extra-ordinary force concealed within suffering, which is capable of raising up the world, because the redemption Jesus achieved on his cross was not only victory over sin, but also over suffering and death. This force is the strength of Jesus' redemptive love, strength for a world perpetually harassed by a destructive selfishness. So, let us go to our Redeemer who waits for us in the midst of suffering. Before human beings ever suffered, suffering belonged to him, who entered into it, transformed it, with all the power of divine love, thus reclaiming it as a free gift to the Father.

ACCEPTANCE OF SUFFERING

ROOT > Illness cannot drive Christians into listlessness or sterility, but impels them to participate and share in the redemption; for they know that, although Christ's redemption is complete, it still remains open to the participation of the believers who can appropriate its saving effectiveness. Because we know that through suffering we participate by faith in Jesus' passion, death and resurrection, we do not face suffering of any kind with an attitude of avoidance or refusal or unwilling resignation, rather we welcome it when it comes.

> *"It makes me happy to be suffering for you now, in my own body to make up all the hardships that still have to be undergone by Christ for the sake of his body, the Church"* (Col 1:24).

FRUIT > Even at the purely human level, we can grow to maturity if we can integrate sufferings into our upward climb. We are such sour fruits that nothing will ripen us but heavy blows, and suffering can be such a blow. But for believers, suffering can be also an occasion to meet the triumphant Christ and receive his salvation. The sufferings we mention here are those that come to us in the ordinary course of life; To bypass these sufferings and invent new ones of our own manufacture, such as sacrifices we choose to make in Lent, is like deliberately choosing to sit on sharp rocks in order to suffer.

PATIENCE IN SUFFERING

ROOT > A Christian without patience is like a soldier without arms, but one who is patient is invincible. Strengthened by the infinite patience of God towards us, we are patient in suffering. Hope is the foundation of patience, and hence, we believers who hope to come through suffering more matured in Christ reaping redemptive fruits hidden in suffering, are patient in suffering. As the farmer waits for the crop to grow and patiently hopes for early or late rains, so we wait in patience to inherit the promises hidden in suffering.

> *"If mercy has been shown to me, it is because Jesus Christ meant to make me the leading example of his inexhaustible patience for all other people who were later to trust in him for eternal life" (1 Tim 1:16).*

FRUIT > Christian patience is not passive resignation to suffering. That would be contrary to our essential human dignity, for suffering is evil. We must do all we can to control and reduce this evil as Jesus did during his ministry on earth. This calls for our participation in political, social and economic restructuring that work towards removal of all pain, all tears from every human eye. If we are to become more human, and if Christians are to become more like the children of God, we cannot remain passive in the face of suffering, but keep fighting against it.

CHRIST'S DEATH: VITAL

ROOT > The rebellion of the first human beings against God deprived them and their descendants, of friendship with God. Since then, all the evidence, drawn from every succeeding age and from every environment and circumstance of human history, have proved conclusively that human beings by themselves were absolutely helpless to restore their lost friendship with God, for no finite creature could ever satisfy the claims of God's justice; Only the infinite God could restore it and hence the necessity for the death of the Son of God.

> *"Christ himself died once and for all for sins, the upright for the sake of the guilty, to lead us to God. In the body he was put to death, in the spirit, he was raised to life" (1 Pet 3:18).*

FRUIT > No scene in sacred history ever gladdens the soul like the scene on Calvary. Nowhere a Christian finds such a consolation as on that very spot where misery reigned, where agony reached its climax. Calvary preaching, Calvary theology, Calvary books, Calvary meditations: these are the things we need today, but woefully missing. Without the death and resurrection of Jesus, the Gospel is a beautiful tale about an exceptionally saintly person, a tale that might inspire good thoughts and great deeds; but there are other stories of the sort.

CHRIST'S DEATH: VOLUNTARY

ROOT > If an innocent man was forced to suffer for the guilty, then that would be flagrantly unjust; but if he became a willing substitute, it would be legitimate, and justice would in no way be violated. Jesus willingly and freely came into the world to accomplish the work of our salvation. The Father wanted to save the world and his Son was willing to carry out his Father's plan. He deliberately emptied himself, came into the world as man, took upon himself the form of a bondservant, and was obedient unto the death on the cross.

> *"Who, being in the form of God, did not count equality with God something to be grasped. But he emptied himself, taking the form of a slave, becoming as human beings are, he was humbler yet, even to accepting death, death on a cross" (Phil 2:18-19).*

FRUIT > Lovers say 'yes' to one another on a particular day, and they do so in joy and in full liberty. After marriage, they must work out their 'yes' in daily life and live out their commitment. In the same way, Jesus freely said 'yes' to the Father to become man and die for us. It is our turn now to say freely 'yes' to God's love. The 'yes' of Jesus to love us, was perfect and complete; whereas our 'yes' to love God and our neighbour and to surrender our life to that love, can only take place step by step, day by day.

CHRIST'S DEATH: VALUABLE

ROOT > The value of the work of Jesus is seen in the fact that God has been satisfied. His justice could only be satisfied with an infinite sacrifice. God in his infinite love has provided such a sacrifice. The resurrection of Christ fully demonstrates that the divine righteousness has been satisfied and because of the infinite value of the work of Christ, it will never be necessary for atonement to be repeated. The value of this atonement for the sins of humankind provides a universal, all-time righteous basis for forgiveness, cleansing and reconciliation.

> *"This is the Revelation of God's love, that God sent his only Son into the world that we might have life through him. Love consists in this: it is not we who loved God, but God loved us and sent his Son to expiate our sins" (1 Jn 4:9-10).*

FRUIT > The heart of Christ dying on the cross, became like a reservoir in the midst of mountains. All the tributary streams of human iniquity ran down and gathered into his heart, as into a vast lake shoreless as eternal, to redeem us all. To deny the value of Christ's sacrifice as the only means of forgiveness, is to hamstring the Gospel and to cut the throat of Christianity. If I do not believe in the reconciling power of Christ's death, I must never go to see believers die, for I will find that they trust in nothing else. A dying Christ is the last resort of the believer.

CHRIST'S DEATH: VICARIOUS

Root > God desires all to be saved and the work of Christ on Calvary is sufficient for all to be saved. Christ died for all manifesting the universal provision whereby all people might be brought to God. But when we speak of the vicarious nature of Christ's death, we are not so much thinking of the universal provision made in the death of Christ, rather of the substitutionary character of his death. That is, the Lord Jesus is substitute for all who believe. He bore our sins and died on our behalf.

> *"He was bearing our sins in his own body on the cross, so that we might die to our sins and live for uprightness; through his bruises, you have been healed" (1 Pet 2:24).*

Fruit > When Jesus hung upon the cross and died the death of a man in love for all humanity, he took upon himself all the deaths of all those who would believe in him. He was incapable of not opening his heart for all human beings, for he is Love of God made flesh. On Calvary, all of humanity was joined together in him. The whole of his Body was nailed to the cross. Take away the cleansing blood of Jesus from Christianity, and what is left to the guilty? Deny the vicarious death of Christ, you have denied all that is precious in the New Testament.

OUR DEATH: A CONSEQUENCE

ROOT > The Church has always taught that the overwhelming misery that oppresses human beings, their tendency to evil and death, cannot be understood apart from original sin. Adam has transmitted to us a sin with which we are all born, and as a consequence we all die. That is why the Church baptises for the remission of sin, even infants who have not committed any personal sin. Sin has caused not only death, but also it distorts and darkens our all other experiences in life.

> *"The Church's Magisterium teaches that death entered the world on account of man's sin. Even though man's nature is mortal, God had destined him not to die. Death was therefore contrary to the plan of God the Creator and entered the world as a consequence of sin" (CCC 1008).*

FRUIT > The fact that our death is certain, adds urgency to our lives. Remembering our mortality helps us to realise that we have only a limited time in which to bring our life to fulfilment. It matters not how long you live, but how well. Could we so live that when we die even the undertaker will be sorry? Instead of worrying about death, we must live every moment of our lives to the full, as if it is the final one. And the secret of fulfilment in life is love. In fact, death is not the greatest loss in life. The greatest loss in life is when love dies inside us, while we live.

OUR DEATH: FEARFUL!

ROOT > We are tormented not only by pain and advancing deterioration of our body, but even more so, by a fear of perpetual extinction. The intuition of our heart abhors and repudiates our absolute ruin and total extinction from the face of the earth. Why? Because we bear in ourselves an eternal seed, that cannot be reduced to mere dust. Therefore, even the modern advanced technology cannot calm our fear of death. There is in each of us a desire for a higher life, which cannot be satisfied by biological life for any length of time.

> *"Although the mystery of death utterly beggars the imagination, the Church has been taught by divine revelation, and herself firmly teaches that man has been created by God for a blissful purpose beyond the reach of earthly misery"* (GS 18).

FRUIT > Our fear of death argues for immortal life that waits for us in its fullness, after we pass through our biological death and this must reduce to a great extent our natural fear of death. To say the least, it is a poor thing for us to fear that which is inevitable. Besides, we must learn to look at death as a sharp corner near the beginning of life's procession down eternity. Those who do not believe in immortal life fear death as the greatest of evils, but those who believe in it, desire death as a rest after labours, and as the end of ills.

OUR DEATH: FINAL 'YES'

Root > Death for a human being is not something that happens to a person from the outside, but is distinctively a human act, related to the precious nature of human freedom. That is, as the final moment of our free human life, death is the decisive act of human freedom, in which I can either accept or reject the mystery of God and thereby put the final seal on my destiny. The free act by which we give ourselves in death, over into the hands of God's love and mercy, is the way in which believers enter fully into the dying of Christ.

> *"It was now about the sixth hour. The veil of the sanctuary was torn right down the middle. Jesus cried out in a loud voice saying, 'Father, into your hands I commit my spirit.' With these words, he breathed his last" (Lk 23:44-46).*

Fruit > When we accept death as an act of obedience to the Father, it becomes a trustful offering to the God of love and life. Death thus becomes our final free act of love, with the awareness of being on the cross together with Jesus. Believers who try to live all their lives in loving obedience to the Father, must have said innumerable times their 'yes' to the Father. And those who say the same 'yes' also at their death, reach their final stage of development, the final step in their climb towards transformation, the ultimate liberation from their limitations, so that they may emerge into perfect life.

OUR DEATH: THE GATEWAY

Root > When Christians unite their death to that of Jesus, it becomes a step towards him and an entrance into everlasting life. That is why, the Church for the last time speaks to dying Christians Christ's words of pardon and absolution, seals them for the last time with a strengthening anointing and gives Christ's viaticum as nourishment for the journey. To those who die in God's grace and friendship and are perfectly purified, death is the gateway to return to their Creator and to see Jesus their Redeemer face to face.

> *"For God has called man and still calls him so that with his entire being he might be joined to him in endless sharing of divine life beyond all corruption. Christ won this victory when he rose to life, since by his death he freed man from death" (GS 18).*

Fruit > Death is God's 'delightful' way of giving us life. Real pain is in life and death is the end of pain. Death is only putting out the lamp at the rise of a new dawn. Do prepare for your death, by doing every act as if it were the last. Happy is the Christian who falls asleep with the Lord's work in his or her hand. There is nothing morbid about getting ready to die. For a Christian, it is a preparation for life's greatest adventure. If we live to live for ever, we will never fear dying. No one would find it difficult to die, who died every day a little to self-love, and lived a life of love for God and neighbour.

HIS RISING: BASIS OF FAITH

Root > The golden thread that has bound together twenty centuries of Christianity is faith in the event of Jesus' resurrection. From the beginning, Jesus' resurrection has been the basis of faith and the essential content of Christian preaching. The first Christians spoke of it with involvement and never with detachment. His death and resurrection were the essential elements of apostolic kerygma. It was considered as the keystone of the mystery of Christ, the absolute criterion of the truth of the Gospel.

> *"The resurrection of Jesus is the crowning truth of our faith in Christ, a faith believed and lived as central truth by the first Christian community; handed on as fundamental by Tradition; established by the documents of the New Testament and preached as essential part of the Paschal Mystery along with the cross" (CCC 638).*

Fruit > The divinity of Christ finds its surest proof in his resurrection. His Lordship also depends on his resurrection. Our justification hangs on his resurrection. Most certainly, our ultimate resurrection rests here. The silver thread of resurrection runs through all the blessings, our rebirth onward to our eternal glory, and binds them together. The resurrection of Jesus is the cornerstone of Christian doctrine. It is the keystone of the arch of Christianity, for if that fact could be disproved, the whole fabric of the Gospel would fall to the ground.

HIS RISING: WHAT IS IT?

Root > The resurrection has to do with the entrance of Jesus' body and his entire humanity into unending life. It is a concrete event that, even before it concerns his disciples, essentially concerned Jesus Christ. The resurrection was not the consequence, but the cause of the disciples' faith. The resurrection indicates the fact that Jesus was restored, together with his humanity, to God's glorious, full and immortal life. Therefore, his risen body, while maintaining its identity and human reality, was rendered capable of living for ever in God.

> *"In his risen body, he passes from the state of death to another life beyond time and space. At Jesus' resurrection, his body is filled with the power of the Holy Spirit: he shares the divine life in his glorious state, so that Paul could say that 'Christ is the man of heaven'" (CCC 646).*

Fruit > The resurrection was not a simple re-entry into earthly life, to be followed by a second death. The resurrection is not simply the immortality of the soul. The resurrection is not re-incarnation, such as Hindus and Buddhists believe in. It was not the transmigration of the soul of Christ from one body into another. It concerns his body and humanity which entered into eternal life. And the resurrection was not something that the disciples made up because of fraud or hallucination; it was a historical fact.

HIS RISING: HISTORICAL

ROOT > The resurrection is a historical event, because the various writings of the New Testament provide ample and consistent evidence concerning it. Its historicity receives added proof from the fact that it is the high point of the four Gospels, and the thread linking together the Church's preaching from that of Peter on the Pentecost to our days. Resurrection, though a transcendent event, it is solidly linked to history, through the recognition of the empty tomb and of the reality of his appearances to his disciples.

> *"Mary Magdalene and the holy women who came to finish anointing the body of Jesus, were the first messengers of Christ's resurrection for the apostles themselves. They were the next to whom Jesus appears: first Peter, then the Twelve"* (CCC 641).

FRUIT > The resurrection is a fact better attested than any event recorded in any history, whether ancient or modern. The gospels do not explain the resurrection; the resurrection explains the gospels. Belief in the resurrection as historical, is not an appendage to Christian faith; it is the Christian faith. Christianity, in its very essence, a resurrection-religion. The belief in the resurrection lies at its very heart. If you remove it, Christianity is destroyed.

HIS RISING: REVEALS WHO HE IS

ROOT > Resurrection reveals Jesus as the Lord. It reveals him as God and the Son of God. It confirms the divinity of Jesus who along with his risen humanity returned to the loving communion of the Father. The resurrection completes the revelation of God as Trinity: the Father glorifies the Son by exalting him to his right hand; the Son, through his redeeming sacrifice, deserves this glorification; and the Holy Spirit proves himself as the Spirit of life and resurrection.

> *"The resurrection of the crucified one shows that he was truly, 'I AM', the Son of God and God himself. Christ's resurrection is closely linked to the Incarnation of God's Son, and its fulfilment in accordance with God's plan"* (CCC 653).

FRUIT > Christ was God, not because he was Virgin-born, but he was Virgin-born because he was God. So too, Christ is God not because he rose from the dead, but he rose from the dead because he is God. Christ demands more complete allegiance than any dictator who ever lived. The difference is that he has the right to, for he is divine. We marvel not that Christ performed miracles, but rather he performed so few. He who could have stormed the citadels of men with mighty battalions of angels, let men spit on him and crucify him.

OUR RISING: IS POSSIBLE

ROOT > The resurrection is the event that has repaired our friendship with God, in which the divine life streams abundantly into the humanity of Christ, and through him into all humanity. This influx of the risen Christ is real and efficacious. Because he is risen, he has the spiritual power to transform us absorbing us to himself, in order to make us children of the Father. In every human being we find a hope for immortal existence and the resurrection of Christ is the fulfilment of this hope.

> *"Now if Christ is proclaimed as raised from the dead, how can some of you be saying that there is no resurrection of the dead? If there is no resurrection of the dead, then Christ cannot have been raised, then our preaching is without substance and so is your faith" (1 Cor 15:12-14).*

FRUIT > The Lord asked us to renounce and die to ourselves. What does that mean? We are called to die to the lower part of ourselves, so that we may have new life of the risen Christ. It means, if we give our time to the Lord, he will give us his eternity; if we give him our death, he will give us his life; if we give him our nothingness, he will give us his all. When we give ourselves to the Lord, we don't put ourselves as it were in wet cement which only hardens, and you never get yourself back. On the contrary, to renounce all for the Lord, is to gain all, to descend is to ascend, and to die is to live.

HUMANITY IS RISEN

ROOT > The risen Jesus is a new man who involves the whole of humanity in the destiny of newness. This was evidenced by what Peter said to a needy man at the Temple, after the resurrection. He was a lame man who was begging. Peter did not have any money, so he gave him the most valuable thing he had, the gift of the risen Christ. In the name of the risen Jesus, he cured him. Thus, Jesus' resurrection is an event of liberation, for it radically transforms humanity, freeing them from snares of sin, suffering and death.

> *"Peter said, 'I have neither silver, nor gold, but I will give you what I have: in the name of Jesus Christ the Nazarene, walk!' Then he took him by the right hand and helped him to stand up" (Act 3:6-8).*

FRUIT > The rising of the human race that the resurrection of Jesus effects, comes through the spiritual freedom that he offers to any one who believes in him. This freedom touches the heart of our being in all its humanity, and takes effect in every sphere: physical, psychical and social. It is meant to be everywhere visible; but the core of this spiritual freedom does not depend on the manner in which it is made visible. For example, a sick or mentally handicapped or oppressed person can still be spiritually free, even if that freedom has not manifest itself in other visible areas of his life.

RISING EXPERIENCE: EUCHARIST

ROOT > We can experience the risen Christ in the eucharistic communion, in the breaking of bread, as did the disciples of Emmaeus (Lk 24:35). Eucharist is not only the memorial of the death and resurrection of Jesus, but also a participation in the real life of the risen Christ. Eucharist is the Sacrament of the continuous saving presence of the risen Lord. In it, our saving encounter with him is realised. The risen Christ is present in his Mystical Body which is his Church and in his Eucharistic Body.

> *"Eucharist is called the 'breaking of bread' because Jesus used this rite, part of Jewish meal, when as master of the table, he blessed and distributed the bread, above all at the Last Supper. It is by this action, the first Christians signified that all who eat the one broken bread, Christ, enter into communion with him and form but one body in him" (CCC 1329).*

FRUIT > In human beings we can see angels and devils, saints and brutes, benevolent souls and malevolent power-maniacs. However, when we have learnt from personal experience, how much Jesus cares for us and how much he desires to be our daily food in the Eucharist, we are able to see every human heart as a prospective dwelling place for Jesus. When your heart is touched by the presence of Jesus in the Eucharist, then you will receive new eyes capable of recognising the same presence in the hearts of others, good or bad.

RISING EXPERIENCE: CONVERSION

ROOT > We can have a rising experience with Jesus, when we truly return to him in faith and full abandonment to his power. We have the example of the apostles Peter and Thomas. Seeing the risen Jesus, they were converted. Conversion, then, does not belong only to Lent, the time before Easter; but it is an integral part of Easter. It is an on-going passage from unbelief to faith, from sadness to joy, from the paralysis of fear to the enthusiasm of the mission. For Christians, Jesus' resurrection is an experience of mercy, forgiveness, spiritual renewal and participation in Jesus' victory over evil.

> *"Baptism is the principle place for the first and fundamental conversion. It is by faith in the Gospel and by Baptism that one renounces evil and gains salvation, that is, forgiveness of all sins and the gift of new life" (CCC 1427).*

FRUIT > There is a risen joy in being converted. By 'joy' we do not mean the transient pleasure which comes from comfort, or false happiness of the simple mind that is unaware of the human degradation, or the 'virtuous' resignation of a pseudo-mystic, or the blind optimism of the one who figures that it is better to laugh than to cry. By 'joy' we mean the calm, the interior serenity, and the profound peace which permeates and emanates from a person, who believes with all strength in the victory of the Saviour over evil, despite all the sufferings in the world.

LIVING FOR EVER

ROOT > Science tells us that nature does not know extinction; all it knows is transformation. It must be so with human life. Primitive people did not philosophise, but had their own instinctive way of believing in the human being's immortality. It was a belief rooted in an obscure experience of the self, and in the natural aspiration of the spirit in us to overcome death. However, God from the beginning and finally in Christ has revealed that after our life on earth, we have eternal life, a life of ineffable bliss without corruption.

> *"And hence, the Creator of the world, who made every one and ordained the origin of all things, will in his mercy give you back the breath of life, since for the sake of his laws, you have no concern for yourselves" (2 Mac 7:23).*

FRUIT > Even before the end of a full life, we recognise that we are made for more than what is on the menu here. We hunger for greater love, deeper relationships, complete understanding and to have it all without end. And that is what going to be. Any of us who live a life of love, never really dies; rather, we become more like the God of love and discover that love is the key to life, that love is even stronger than death. For all who live and love and die, God shouts a resounding 'yes', that sustains us in ecstatic existence forever.

HEAVENLY LIVING

ROOT > Heaven is the state of happiness that comes from knowing God fully, loving him perfectly, and living with him in union with Jesus Christ. Even in this life, to know a truth is one of great human joys. But love is greater than knowledge. Love gives the greatest joy to the human heart. Hence, the full knowledge of God in heaven would be a thrilling ecstasy of love. So brilliant and ecstatic is the vision of God enjoyed by those in heaven, that they need to receive from God a special power, to enable them to see him and not be burned by the sight.

> *"And eternal life is this: to know you the only true God, and Jesus Christ whom you have sent" (Jn 17:3).*

FRUIT > When congratulated on his eighty-first birthday, Pope John XXIII said: "Any day is a good day on which to be born, and any day is a good day on which to die." About the same time he said: "God did not make this beautiful world to be a cemetery." Five days before his death he said to those at his bedside: "Do not worry about me. My bags are packed and I am ready, in fact, very ready to leave." When they told him that he had only a few hours to live, he said: "Well. This is not a time to cry. This is a moment of joy and glory."

LIVING IN THE RISEN BODY

ROOT > We believe in the resurrection of the body, that is, of the whole person. The discovery of the empty tomb and the appearances of the risen Christ to his amazed disciples, is a sign that in Jesus, the whole of nature, material and spiritual will be redeemed. It is not just a question of our rising individually from the dead but together as a human race in what is called 'General Resurrection'. Our final salvation will not only be individual, but together in perfect unity with Christ and of the whole human race united to him.

> *"What is sown is perishable, but what is raised is imperishable; what is sown in contemptible, but what is raised is glorious; what is sown is weak, but what is raised is powerful; what is sown is natural body, and what is raised is a spiritual body" (1 Cor 15:42-44).*

FRUIT > In order to be perfectly happy in heaven, we will have to have our body with us, because our body does a great deal for the salvation of our souls. It follows, that in heaven, we will meet all those who are our friends and relatives on earth, in a glorified state. Since the resurrection of the body also means the resurrection of the whole human race, here on earth, we have to learn not only to be related to God on a one to one basis, but we have to learn to relate to each other, because we will be related to each other in eternity also.

THE BEYOND IS HERE

Root > Christians pass over to the reality of risen life in baptism. "You have died," says St Paul, "and your life is hidden with Christ in God." Hence we have already begun the eternal life. We are not merely looking forward to it after death. The decisive transition has taken place in baptism. Hence, physical death has no longer the finality it once had and our true life in Christ is not extinguished by it. The only difference between 'Now' and 'After' is that now we live by faith and signs, but after death we will live by sight and in fullness.

> *"United with Christ by baptism, believers already truly participate in the heavenly life of the risen Christ, but this life remains hidden with Christ in God. The Father has already raised us up with him and made us sit with him in the heavenly places in Christ Jesus" (CCC 1003).*

Fruit > There is no such thing as dying and then going to heaven. We are in heaven already if we love God and neighbour unconditionally. Have we not seen people with heaven in them? To know how much love is related to heaven, just look at the bride and groom at the altar on the day of the nuptial Mass. Heaven is there, because love is there. You can also see heaven in a missionary nun, who is spending herself among the lepers. The beauty of such a person is a kind of imprisoned loveliness, that comes from within, breaking down the barriers of flesh.

THE RIGHT TO LIVE

ROOT > When God creates human beings, he creates them in his image, to live, and to live with him for ever. Hence, any type of direct killing of human life is morally wrong. It follows, that direct abortion, that is to say, abortion willed either as an end or a means, is gravely contrary to the moral law. Human life must be respected and protected absolutely from the moment of conception. From the first moment of existence, a human being has the rights of a person, among which is the inviolable right of every innocent being to life.

> *"Whatever is opposed to life itself, such as any type of murder, genocide, abortion, euthanasia, or will-full self-destruction, whatever violates the integrity of the human person, all these things and others of their like are infamies indeed. They poison the human society; they are a supreme dishonour to the Creator" (GS 27).*

FRUIT > The Catholic Church teaches that formal co-operation in an abortion constitutes a grave offence; that the inalienable right to life of every innocent human individual, ought to be a constitutive element of a civil society and its legislation; that pre-natal diagnosis is morally licit, but it is gravely opposed to the moral law, when this is done with the thought of possibly inducing abortion, depending upon the results; and that it is immoral to produce human embryos, intended for exploitation, as disposable biological material.

WE CHOOSE TO LIVE

ROOT > A person who truly wants to love God and to be with God for ever, will be given the grace and help to fulfil that desire. Hell is basically love-lost. The Church teaches that there is judgement of God after our death. The Last Judgement will reveal the good each person has done or failed to do during this earthly life. Heaven, hell, and judgement remind us that we are given desperately important choices to make on earth. Our choice for God is not once and for all. It is a daily decision. And it is not sufficient for us to say that we choose to follow Christ. We must choose to do his will.

> *"Today, I call heaven and earth to witness against you: I am offering you life or death, blessing or curse. Choose life, then, so that you and your descendants may live" (Dt 30:19).*

FRUIT > Although God knows how we would choose our eternal destiny, he leaves us free to do the choosing. God urges, strengthens, even nudges us throughout life to make wise choices, but it is we who actually decide. The crucial question is: what do I choose to do with the present moment and become by it, for eternity? By the way we choose in our present moment, we become richer or poorer for heaven, kinder or more cruel, loving or selfish. We gradually become what we choose as we pass through our present moments, and they turn into days, weeks, years and eternity.

THE LIVING CHRISTIANS

ROOT > Risen life is eternal life, but eternal life is a life of loving. Jesus said, "keep my word, you will never see death." And the sermon on the mount sums up all his words into twofold love: love of God and love of neighbour. Christians who keep the sermon on the mount as their rule of life, live a life of love, and if we love as Jesus has asked us to, we are already living eternal life. Eternal life is not the last stage of a rocket, projected into space and destined to orbit eternally. Eternal life is already with us, in our loving life.

> *"Blessed are the poor in spirit. Blessed are the gentle. Blessed are those who mourn. Blessed are those who hunger and thirst for uprightness. Blessed are the merciful. Blessed are the pure in heart. Blessed are the peace-makers. Blessed are those who are persecuted in the cause of uprightness"* *(Mt 5:3-10).*

FRUIT > Human beings were created out of love, and for love. Therefore, our vocation is love, not human love alone, but, beginning with human love and through it and in it, it is also a love divinised and transformed by the presence of the risen Christ. The final purpose is for the human being to be with all other human beings, loving with the love of the Trinity, which is heaven. As a product of love, a Christian chooses to love all the way and thus return to God's own love. It is our destiny to do so.

June:

HOLY SPIRIT

Week 1
The Spirit in the Trinity

Week 2
The Spirit in Creation

Week 3
The Spirit in the Church

Week 4
Life in the Spirit

GOD IS TRINITY

ROOT > God revealed by Jesus is a personal God, who is the communion of three persons. From all eternity the Father freely generates in love the Son, and with the Son, he breathes the Holy Spirit. The Christian Good News is the Gospel of the Trinity and the divinity of God cannot be thought of, except as the divinity of the Father, the Son and the Holy Spirit. God handed over his Son to death out of his infinite love for humankind. But the Son in his death entrusted himself to the Spirit in a faithful and filial abandonment.

> *"Inseparable in what they are, the divine persons are also inseparable in what they do. But within the single divine operation each shows forth what is proper to him in the Trinity, especially in the divine mission of the Son's Incarnation and the gift of the Holy Spirit" (CCC 267).*

FRUIT > Since the Trinity lives a community life bound by mutual love, we too are called to care for each other in love. That is the way to live a fulfilling human life. Today so many people claim to know the way to live, but unfortunately each claim conflicts with the other. The film and television industries have their gospel; the gambling strips of modern cities have theirs; the print industry and political heavy weights have their own version. In the midst of all these confusing claims, the Trinity call us to live as they do: in communion of love.

THREE IN ONE

ROOT > The intimate life of God is so rich that it is formed by three persons, but distinct among themselves. The being of the Father is beginning of everything; the essence of the second person is being the Son and the third person claims his very origin from the Father through the Son. Every divine person has his own activity in our salvation and has a specific relationship with humanity. Everything comes from the Father, everything is accomplished by the Son and everything is experienced by us through the Spirit.

> *"The whole Christian life is a communion with each of the divine persons, without in any way separating them. Every one who glorifies the Father does so through the Son in the Holy Spirit; everyone who follows Christ does so because the Father draws him and the Spirit moves him" (CCC 259).*

FRUIT > Each night before falling asleep, set aside three minutes. During the first minute, pick out the high point of your day, something good that happened to you like escaping a car accident. Speak to the Father about it and thank him for it. During the second minute, pick out the low point of the day like chastising your child, not to correct but to vent your anger. Speak to Jesus and ask him to forgive you. During the third minute, look ahead to tomorrow, to some critical point-like having to confront someone who has been spreading false rumour about you. Speak to the Holy Spirit, and ask him for wisdom and courage to deal with it properly.

SPIRIT IS GOD'S GIFT

Root > The Holy Spirit is Father's gift to human beings, because the ineffable mystery of God becomes an experience for the believer only by the power of the Spirit, and through the Spirit, the incommunicable God in his mercy, draws near to people and becomes God among us. Because the Spirit represents the eternal mutual love between the Father and the Son, God gives himself to his creatures and unites himself to them, in the Spirit.

> *"Through the Holy Spirit, God exists in the mode of gift. It is the Holy Spirit who is the personal expression of this self-giving; he is person-gift. Here we have an inexhaustible measure of the reality which only divine revelation makes known to us" (John Paul II – DeV 10).*

Fruit > The natural spirit, the purely human spirit, the spirit that is not holy cannot grasp the deep meaning of the mystery of God. It is almost like expecting a rabbit in a cage to learn Shakespeare. He cannot do so. You would have to put your own brain inside of the rabbit's brain. So too, the brain of a scientist cannot understand the mysteries of God's love if it lacks the Spirit. Therefore, we cannot teach people about who God is, unless we first prepare these people to receive the gift of the Spirit of God. It is the Holy Spirit who woos the soul, draws it into closer fellowship with God.

IN THE SPIRIT: GOD SPEAKS

ROOT > Sacred Scripture, being the Word of God spoken to human beings, offers the possibility of meeting God in open dialogue. But it is impossible for God's self-revelation in his Word, to become possible without the Holy Spirit, for it is he who renders what is invisible into visible. That is, the Holy Spirit is the mouth of God. As our interior thoughts go out through our mouth, and are revealed to others, so the very Son of God, the Word, is expressed by the Holy Spirit, as if by a mouth.

> *"Sacred Scripture, is the speech of God as it is put down in writing under the breath of the Holy Spirit" (DV 9).*

FRUIT > You will hear some people say, "Oh! Jesus was a great teacher! He, Gandhi, Churchill and Plato have done a great deal for the world!" Such people call Jesus simply as one of the great. This is because they have not read the Scriptures with Holy Spirit within them. It is the Spirit who can reveal Jesus as he truly is and unless God imparts his Spirit to hear his voice in the Scriptures, one hears nothing but meaningless words, because the Scriptures are inspired by the Spirit. One proof of the inspiration of the Bible, is that it has withstood so much poor preaching!

IN THE SPIRIT: WORD IS ALIVE

ROOT > The Bible would remain a dead letter if the Holy Spirit does not make it forceful to today's reader, because the Word is living through the Spirit who dwells in it. Holy Spirit acts so that the Word of God becomes now 'spirit and life'. The Spirit has the force to challenge us with the Word, calling us to create communion with God and with one another. Besides, it is the Spirit who prepares our heart for listening, and makes the heart capable of welcoming the Word.

> *"The Paraclete, the Holy Spirit, whom the Father will send in my name, will teach you everything and remind you of all I have said to you" (Jn 14:26).*

FRUIT > Commentators of the Scriptures are good in their own way, but ultimately it is the Holy Spirit who makes the passage clear. How often have we found our utter inability to understand some part of divine truth! We ask some of God's people and they help us a little. But we are never satisfied until we take the passage to throne of heavenly grace and implore the Spirit to enlighten us. Then how sweetly it is opened to us! We can eat of it spiritually. It is no longer husk and shell; it comes as bread.

IN THE SPIRIT: THROUGH THE CHURCH

ROOT > As Jesus had promised, the Father sent the Holy Spirit to the Church at Pentecost. Hence, the Spirit of Truth teaches us everything for salvation through the Church. The Spirit teaches not only from the Word, but also from the Traditions of the Church. The function of the Spirit in the Church is to introduce the believers to the fullness of truth and make it vital part of our spiritual life. The Spirit also ignites an increasingly more vital desire in our hearts, to love the things we already know, and wish to know what we do not know.

> *"What was accomplished by the power of the Holy Spirit at Incarnation, can only through the Spirit's power now emerge from the memory of Christ. The Spirit makes present in the Church of every time and place the unique Revelation brought by Christ to humanity making it alive and active in the soul of each individual" (John Paul II – TMA 44).*

FRUIT > Immediately after the resurrection, Jesus breathed upon his disciples saying: "Receive the Holy Spirit." Thus, he gave the Spirit first to his Church; this is the beginning of the outpouring of the Spirit. Then at Pentecost, there comes another. But see how the Church has grown by this time: Blessed Mother, the apostles and 120 others. Therefore it is the Spirit who gradually unfolds himself in the Church. When we detach the Spirit from the Church, we are apt to grow awry. We need to listen to the Church. It is the way to Jesus, for his Spirit dwells in the Church.

IN THE SPIRIT: WE KNOW GOD

ROOT > To know God is to communicate with him through Jesus in the power of the Holy Spirit. That is, to know God is to have a relationship with God, which the Spirit alone makes it possible in the life of the believer. We cannot love God without knowing him and we cannot know him without loving him. Because the Holy Spirit is the Spirit of Truth, it is he who enlightens us, purifies us, baptises us from above and puts us in such a relationship with God that we are made loving children of God.

> *"In all truth I tell you no one can see the Kingdom of God without being born from above. No one can enter the Kingdom of God without being born through water and the Spirit"* *(Jn 3:3-5).*

FRUIT > We thirst for truth, but we shall not reach it until we reach the source which is the Holy Spirit. One might as well try to catch sunbeams with a fish-hook, as to lay hold of God's revelation, unassisted by the Holy Spirit. The Holy Spirit has not promised to reveal new truths, but to enable us to understand the truth Christ has already revealed about God. The minds of those who are not born in the Spirit can easily hear and mentally comprehend the facts set forth by Christ, but only the Spirit of God can turn the power of those truths into an inward spiritual experience.

CREATION IN THE SPIRIT

Root > Creation is the start of God's self-communication with his creatures and the start of the history of salvation. It is the belief of the Church that everything that exists outside of the divinity, has been created by God from nothing, through the Word in the power of the Spirit. It is through the Holy Spirit God animates life, unites the creatures with himself, saves them from non-existence, sustains them, renews them and directs them to their fulfilment.

> *"It belongs to the Holy Spirit to rule, to sanctify, and animate creation for he is God co-substantial with the Father and the Son. Power over life pertains to the Spirit, for being God he preserves creation in the Father through the Son"* (CCC 703).

Fruit > One night I had a dream in which I was riding a tandem bicycle with Jesus. At first, I sat in front; Jesus in the rear. I could not see him but I knew he was there, to help me when need arose. After sometime, Jesus and I changed seats. Suddenly everything went topsy-turvy. When I was in control, the ride was predictable, even boring. But when Jesus took over, it got wild! I could hardly hold on. "This is madness", I cried. But Jesus just smiled and said, 'Pedal!' So I learnt to shut up and pedal. When we are co-operating with the Spirit to make this world a better place, we are pedalling with Jesus.

COSMIC SALVATION IN THE SPIRIT

Root > One salvific value of creation is that God wanted all his creatures to be glorified by sharing in his being, wisdom and goodness. And the Holy Spirit accompanies the people in this fundamental journey towards their glorification. The salvific value of creation consists also in the fact that cosmos as a whole also participates in the goodness of God, with the result, it is not mere the scenery for the revelation of God-man, but also it reveals God's will to communicate with creatures; and again it is through the Holy Spirit, that the created world becomes a place for God's communication.

> *"The Spirit searches the depths of the Father and of the Word-Son in the mystery of creation. Not only is he the direct witness of their mutual love from which creation derives, but he himself is this love. He himself, as love, is the eternal uncreated gift. In him is the source and the beginning of every giving of gifts to creatures" (DeV 34).*

Fruit > Since it is God's salvific plan that not only the human beings but the whole of Creation should share in his divine goodness through his Spirit, we have a responsibility for Creation. We are committed to give an accounting to our Creator of our relationship with nature. Yes, we love nature as the reflection of God's goodness; but our love cannot merely consist in our aesthetic admiration of it, or in our using it for our development, but also in doing everything to save it from extinction. If we fail in this, we are endangering the very existence of humanity, since nature is an integral part of human existence.

CREATION IS GOOD BY THE SPIRIT

ROOT > After creating everything, God said, "It is good" (Gen 1:10). Creation is good, not merely because it derives its existence from the wisdom of God, but also because the Holy Spirit who co-operated with the Father and the Son in creating the world, also put order in the world and rendered it beautiful. Even at the beginning of creation the Spirit swept over the face of water (Gen 1:2). This means, that at the time the Spirit was about to move, creation had no beauty. Only when it received the Spirit's work, it became an attractive beauty of resplendent world.

> *"I want to awaken in you a deep admiration for creation, until you in every place, contemplating plants and flowers, are overcome by a living remembrance of the Creator"* (St Basil).

FRUIT > When we look at plants and flowers, do we remember God? This requires a religious contemplation of creation by means of 'spiritual senses', those new senses given to Christians by the Spirit, to understand the divine traces hidden in every being. If we have the spiritual senses open, we would look out on a mountain and think of the power of God; on snow-flake, and dwell on the purity of God; on the sunset and think of the beauty of God. This is a sacramental outlook, a penetrating glance, that perceives the eternal through time and the divine through the human.

HUMANITY IS SPIRITUAL

ROOT > God breathing his Spirit into human beings, instilled life into them. After sin, it is again the Spirit who transmits new life ransomed by Christ. The Spirit always incarnates in human beings the image of God, with the result that each human being becomes a child of God in his Son. In this sense, humanity itself is called to become spiritual. But to be spiritual does not simply mean to have a life superior to corporal life; it means rather life in the Spirit oriented towards God who is our final destiny.

> *"He who no longer lives according to the flesh but is led by the Spirit of God, is called son of God, made in the image of the Son of God; he is called spiritual. As the capacity to see resides in a healthy eye, so does the operating force of the Spirit, exists in a purified soul" (St Basil).*

FRUIT > Only through human beings, all other creatures can achieve the destiny of their existence, because only human beings are spiritual. Being spiritual, they alone can be mediators between God and the rest of creation. In other words, human beings are priests of the cosmos, for only they can return to God for a personal encounter with him. But we can carry out this work of mediation and priesthood, only in the power of the Spirit. Without the Spirit of God, we can do nothing; without the Spirit, we are branches without sap and coals without fire.

THE IMPRINT OF THE SPIRIT

ROOT > Human being is made in the image and likeness of God (Gen 1:26). But we must immediately add that we are created *in Christ*, in the image of the invisible God. This is so because, although the image of each person came out of God's hands pure, it was disfigured by sin, but restored by Christ with his death and resurrection. Redemption, in fact, is the restoration of the divine image. However, we thus return to our original image of God thanks to the Holy Spirit, who once again fuses us to the image of Christ from whom everything comes to us through the Father.

> *"It is in Christ, the image of the invisible God, that man has been created in the image and likeness of the Creator. It is in Christ, the Redeemer and Saviour, that the divine image, disfigured in man by the first sin, has been restored to its original beauty and ennobled by the grace of God"* (CCC 1701).

FRUIT > I was once watching the distribution of used clothes to street people. Suddenly I found myself wondering, "What would be like to walk about in another's clothes or in another's shoes?" Then it occurred to me, that it is something like this, that I am called to do as a Christian, to walk about in the shoes of Jesus, to go where Jesus would go, to do what Jesus would do. Being Christian is to be the walking image of Jesus in today's world. Every character has an inward spring. Is Christ that spring for me? Every action has a key note. Is Christ that note to me?

JESUS ANOINTED WITH THE SPIRIT

ROOT > From his conception onwards, Jesus is being anointed by the Spirit, especially in his baptism. The Spirit which is the power of freedom from evil, leads Jesus into the desert to combat and overcome evil. The Spirit brought forth the sacrificial offering of Christ in his redeeming death. Though it is the Father who raises Jesus, the resurrection takes place through the Holy Spirit. Jesus does not experience the Spirit as a force which invades him from without, for he is in the Spirit and the Spirit is in him; it is his own Spirit.

> *"You know what happened all over Judea, how Jesus of Nazareth began in Galilee after John had been preaching baptism, God had anointed him with the Holy Spirit and with power and God was with him" (Acts 10:37-38).*

FRUIT > We sit by the fireplace in my house. I pick up some tongs, take a glowing coal from the fire place, and set it on the hearth. What happens? The coal slowly loses its glow and dies. So too, if we cut ourselves away from Jesus, the anointed one, we become useless as dead wood, for we are left without his Spirit. The signs of being anointed in the Spirit are seen in its fruits: faith, joy, patience, self-denial, fervour in prayer. These are the fruits on the fig tree, the rest is leafage!

JESUS BESTOWS THE SPIRIT

ROOT > When Jesus died he 'gave up his spirit' (Jn 19:30). In doing so, he gave the Spirit back to the Father from whom he had received, but it also meant that he gave to his believers the breath of his Spirit. After his resurrection, he breathed on his disciples saying 'receive the holy Spirit' (Jn 20:22) to make them new men capable of fulfilling the mission entrusted to them, that of bringing to each person the very life which he received from the Father. At Pentecost all this comes in a superabundant way.

> *"God raised this man Jesus to life, and of that we are all witnesses. Now raised to the heights by God's right hand, he has received from the Father the Holy Spirit, who was promised and what you see and hear is the outpouring of that Spirit" (Act 2:32-34).*

FRUIT > A boy would not comb his hair, wash behind his ears, clean his fingernails or come to the table with clean clothes. When he went out of the door he always slammed it. His parents begged, coaxed and pleaded to no avail. One day, he came down, hair combed, clean clothes, hands washed and clean behind his ears. When he went out, he closed the door gently. Any reason for this change? He had met Elizabeth, his sweet heart, his future wife. Encounter the Holy Spirit and you will change for the better, for he is the Spirit of love.

IN THE ONE CHURCH

Root > The Church is the mystery of communion, for it is the sacrament of the Trinity. The Holy Spirit is the one who accomplishes unity between the believers and to their head, thus enhancing the collegial character of the Church. The Spirit is also at work to accomplish unity between non-Catholic Churches and the Catholic Church. The Spirit achieves not only unity of the Church, but also its diversity, by granting a variety of charisms and gifts to individual faithful as well as to local churches, without harming the unity.

> *"Giving the Body of the Church unity through himself and through his power and through the internal cohesion of its members, this same Spirit produces and urges love among the believers" (John Paul II – TMA 45).*

Fruit > "Is it a strong Congregation?" "Yes," was the reply. "How many members are there?" "Thirty." "Thirty!" "Are they so wealthy?" "No, many of them are poor." "How then can you say it is a strong church?" "Because they are earnest, devoted, at peace, loving each other, following the Word of God in all things, together in prayer, striving together to do the Lord's work." Yes, such a congregation is strong, whether thirty or three hundred members. Not spires and crosses rearing to the sky, but it is such Churches that silently testify to the presence of the Spirit in them.

IN THE HOLY CHURCH

ROOT > The Spirit is holy for he is God's indwelling, and the Church is holy because the Spirit is her soul. It is not mere moral holiness, though the moral holiness of innumerable children of the Church is due to the direct action of the Holy Spirit. The holiness of the Church is the holiness that touches the essence of every believer and transforms them. The holy Spirit accomplishes this holiness of the Church, through the communion of the holy things: the sacraments, the Word and Charisms. Because the Church is holy, she is the temple of God, and her members living stones.

> *"If anybody should destroy the temple of God, God will destroy that person, because God's temple is holy; and you are that temple" (1 Cor 3:17).*

FRUIT > There are three kinds of Church-members: 'Old Faithful,' 'Once-in-a-Whilers', and the 'Almost Nevers'. They never come. Perhaps I should not say, 'never'. They do come on Easter or on Christmas. Some have a basic allergy to 'Church,' for they say it is not perfect. Well, if they can find a perfect Church, by all means they can join it. Then it will no longer be perfect! Because the Church is holy, she is not perfect, free of sinners. Jesus compared Church to a net. The net is open to all kinds of fish. So too, the Church is open to all kinds of people: good people, selfish people, thoughtless people. Jesus said it would be this way.

IN THE CATHOLIC CHURCH

ROOT > The Catholicity of the Church means primarily its qualitative fullness and secondarily its quantitative fullness, which in fact is derived from the first. The Holy Spirit is at the root of the Church's qualitative fullness, which extends to all the faithful and to every local church. By the action of this fullness, which is the fruit of Easter and Pentecost, every local church is truly in the universal Church, a family of God, a holy people, united in faith, love and peace.

> *"The Church was, in the fundamental sense of qualitative fullness, Catholic on the day of Pentecost and will always be until the day of Parousia" (CCC 830).*

FRUIT > The Church cannot be closed unto itself. It cannot separate itself from the world, for that would be imprisoning the Spirit within its limits. We cannot limit the action of the Spirit within the Catholic Church alone. On the contrary, the Spirit is constantly urging the Church to open towards the world. And yet, how often we get so wrapped up in our own organisation or Church, that it leads to the building of barriers, rather than bridges, between us and the people of other religious beliefs!

IN THE APOSTOLIC CHURCH

ROOT > The Church is apostolic through the perpetual sending of the Spirit. The Holy Spirit guarantees the apostolicity of the Church by being the counsellor of the apostles and the Church, always present in their midst, as the teacher of the same Good News that Christ proclaimed. Ensuring true apostolic succession, the Spirit keeps constantly reminding the Church of its original vocation, of the revelation of Christ as the source of truth, of the fact that the Church is the beginning of the Kingdom, always on the move to accomplish peace, freedom, and justice.

> *"The unity of the Body of Christ is founded on the activity of the Spirit, guaranteed by the Apostolic ministry and sustained by mutual love" (John Paul II – TMA 47).*

FRUIT > The entire Church is apostolic. This means, individual believers are also apostolic. Often, an apostolate started by an individual, becomes an institutionalised apostolate. Mother Teresa felt called by the Spirit to help the poor, especially the dying on the streets of Calcutta, in India. She began using all the money she had to buy a small dirt-floor shack. Today, that shack has multiplied itself into over 100 schools for children and over 150 homes for dying people. Mother Teresa gave her 'loaves and fishes' to Jesus, and his Spirit multiplied them beyond her wildest dreams.

IN THE EVANGELISING CHURCH

ROOT > It is in the Church that humanity can discover the true God and it is through the Church, that God's loving plan for all humankind can be known by every one. Therefore, the Church has a serious obligation to make the call of God for salvation echo in every human heart. This is the meaning of evangelisation. However, it is the Spirit who inspires the Scriptures, gives the Word to humanity and enables the Word to take flesh in the world, and he does this in many ways, but especially through our work of evangelisation.

> *"In our own day too, the Spirit is the principle agent of the new evangelisation. He is the one who builds the Kingdom of God within the course of history, striking people's hearts and quickening in our world the seeds of full salvation which will come at the end of time" (John Paul II – TMA 45).*

FRUIT > A woman had a strange dream. An angel took her to a church to worship. The organist played, but no music came from the organ. The choir sang, the singers' mouths opened and closed, but no sound came from their lips. The congregation prayed, their lips moved, but no sound could be heard. The woman said to the angel, "Why don't I hear any thing?" The angel said, "There is nothing to hear!" Obviously, the Spirit was not working in any of them. So too, if an evangeliser does not have the Spirit, he can make no spiritual effect on any one.

THE SPIRIT IN THE BELIEVER

ROOT > Through Baptism the Spirit performs such a radical renewal that it can be compared to true and proper rebirth. It regenerates us in the Spirit. We cannot enter into the Kingdom of God without the rebirth through Baptism. The new life which the Spirit pours into believers is life in Christ. Confirmation is the pre-eminent Sacrament of the Spirit. With Confirmation, we participate in Pentecost and are sealed in the Spirit in order to grow in it. Yet Confirmation can be understood and lived, only in relation to Baptism.

> *"Holy Baptism is basis of the whole Christian life, the gateway to life in the Spirit, and the door which gives access to other sacraments. The seal of the Holy Spirit in confirmation marks our total belonging to Christ, our enrolment in his service for ever" (CCC 1213,1296).*

FRUIT > As baptised persons we listen to the Church, we listen to the Word of God in the Scriptures. We must also listen to the Spirit in our hearts. Praying is first and foremost listening to Jesus indwelling in us through his Spirit. He does not shout. He does not thrust himself upon us. His voice is an unassuming voice, very nearly a whisper, a voice of a gentle love. This listening must be a very active and attentive listening, for in our restless and noisy world, God's so loving a voice, is easily drowned.

IN THE SACRAMENTS

ROOT > The sacraments derive their effectiveness solely from the Spirit, because he always transforms that which he touches. The Holy Spirit, through the Church's sacraments, puts us in a lively and efficacious contact with the Saviour and his salvific work. Christ who fulfilled salvation in the Spirit, applies same salvation to every believer in his Spirit. Holy Spirit lives in the sacraments and secretly works their effects. The Holy Spirit, not only makes the sacraments possible, but permits every one of us to accept the mysteries of Christ.

> *"The sacraments are powers that come forth from the body of Christ, which is ever-giving and life-giving. They are actions of the Holy Spirit at work in his body, the Church"* (CCC 1116).

FRUIT > By the mere fact that we turn on the faucet, water comes out. The water does not come because we subjectively believe that water will come forth. Likewise, the divine life of Christ is poured into our souls by the mere fact that we receive the sacraments. But it is Christ who baptises; it is Christ who forgives sins. There are ministers, of course, administering the sacraments, but they only loan to Christ their eyes, hands and limbs. It is he who gives the grace. That is why, even though we receive the sacrament from an unworthy priest, it would still be a sacrament.

IN THE EUCHARIST

ROOT > The Eucharist is not only the source and the summit of Christian life, but also is the synthesis of life in faith. The Eucharist contains the whole spiritual good of the Church, namely, Christ himself. Hence the action of the Spirit is nowhere else in the liturgy as evident as it is in the Eucharist. It is the Spirit which makes Christ present in the Eucharist; It actualises the paschal mystery and makes the eucharistic celebration an efficacious descent of the Spirit.

> *"In the most blessed Eucharist is contained the whole spiritual good of the Church, namely, Christ himself, our Pasch and living bread which gives life through his flesh – that flesh which is given life and gives life through the Holy Sprit" (PO 5).*

FRUIT > We become what we eat. We have received Christ in Holy Communion. Have we become Christ to others? Christ was a home missionary in the house of Lazarus. He was Sunday school missionary when he opened up the Scriptures and set men to studying the Word of God. He was missionary to the poor and the suffering, when he opened the spiritual eyes of a beggar. He was missionary to the rich when he opened the spiritual eyes of Zacchaeus. Even on the cross, Christ was a missionary to the good thief. In what way am I a missionary?

IN THE DIVINE LIFE

ROOT > As human beings, created in the image of God, we do possess a part of God's holiness. It is by participation in the Holy Spirit that we share in the holiness of God. The Spirit's presence in human beings is sometimes called 'sanctifying grace'. The sanctifying work of the Spirit is divinisation, namely, participation in God's divine nature. Moreover, as believers, we receive the 'seed of life', through Baptism, which gives birth to 'life in Christ' and the process of Christification in Christ.

> *"A special role is attributed to the Holy Spirit in divinisation: through the power of the Spirit who dwells in man deification already begins on earth; the creature is transfigured and God's Kingdom inaugurated" (John Paul II – OL 6).*

FRUIT > To live in sanctifying grace is to live spiritually. Living spiritually is more than living physically, intellectually or emotionally. It embraces all these but it is larger, deeper and wider. It concerns the core of our humanity. It is possible to lead a wholesome, emotionally rich and sensible life, without being a spiritual person; that is, without knowledge or personal experience of the terrain where the meaning and goal of my human existence are hidden. The spiritual life has to do with the heart of human existence. In this sense, spiritual life is life of the heart.

BECOMING CHILDREN OF GOD

ROOT > Christians who welcome the seed of life implanted in them by the Spirit and allow it to grow through faith and sacraments, are incorporated into Christ and become adopted children of God. Becoming adopted children is not a juridical affiliation. It is a true new birth and a true communion with the God's only Son, not only in name but in reality. It is a communion of blood, flesh and life. Again, it is the Spirit who makes us vividly aware of our status as children of God.

> *"All who are guided by the Spirit of God are sons of God; for what you received was not the Spirit of slavery, to bring you back into fear; you received the Spirit of adoption, enabling us to cry out: 'Abba, father!'" (Rom 8:14-15).*

FRUIT > Engineers understand engineers and brokers understand brokers and students at college understand the students at the same college. Why? Because they all have the same spirit. They are human to begin with, and then, they have the spirit of engineers, brokers and students. Similarly, if we have the Spirit of God, we will know and understand the will of God, and to do God's will in all things is the true mark of God's children. The filial love of Christians guided by the Spirit constantly urges them to conform to the Father's will, not from fear but from love.

PRAYING IN THE SPIRIT

ROOT > True prayer is the union of the soul with God. To pray always is to be continually in the presence of God and to be in communion with him. If prayer is understood in this sense, human beings on their own cannot really pray, they can utter only 'words' of prayer. They have to receive from God himself the gift of prayer. But, any gift of God comes to us through his Son as the gift of the Holy Spirit. Hence any form of prayer is the action of the Spirit, which continually moves the praying person into ever closer and filial relationship with the Father.

> *"The Holy Spirit whose anointing permeates our whole being, is the interior Master of Christian prayer. To be sure, there are as many paths of prayer as there are persons who pray, but it is the same Spirit acting in all and with all"* (CCC 2672).

FRUIT > God not only answers our prayer, but through his Spirit makes our prayer for us. He is more than a king who says to the petitioner, "Bring your case before me, and I will grant your desire." Rather, he is like the king who says: "I will be your secretary; I will write out your petition for you; I will put it in proper words so that your petition will be framed acceptably." This is goodness at its utmost stretch. In fact, if I could pray the best prayer in the world unaided by the Holy Spirit, God would have nothing to do with it. But if the Spirit made it, even though my prayer be broken and limping, God would look at it and say, "It is very good."

WITNESSING IN THE SPIRIT

Root > The Spirit's work is also to transform the believers into witnesses to Christ. We give witness to Christ in the power of the Spirit. When we become so involved in the Word of the Gospel, that it transforms and ferments our very existence, we are ready to witness to Christ before every one and at whatever cost. The action of the Spirit in such a witness, is found to the highest degree in the dying of men and women of yesterday and today as martyrs for Christ. Those who consecrate themselves in religious life also do so, inspired by the Spirit and can be called successors to martyrs.

> *"At the end of the second millennium, the Church has once again become a Church of the martyrs. In our own century, the martyrs have returned, many of them nameless, 'unknown solders' as it were of God's great cause" (John Paul II – TMA 37).*

Fruit > Witnessing does not always require the shedding of blood, but it does require the accepting of life's difficulties for Christ's sake: loneliness, sickness, old age, poverty, being misunderstood, failure in life and such other pains. However, even in trials and tribulations, the Spirit makes us experience true joy, the joy of the blessed. And there is something more in suffering for Christ's sake: As a storm puts a man on guard, and obliges him to exert his utmost efforts to avoid shipwreck, so the Spirit helps those who suffer, to have a guarded and persistent journey to the Father's house.

GIFTS OF THE SPIRIT

ROOT > Confirmation is the pre-eminent Sacrament of the Spirit, through which the Spirit confers his gifts. The gift of the Spirit can be something equivalent to a 'charism', the manifestation of the Spirit in a person for building up the Church. It can also be a spiritual 'gift' superior even to infused virtue. The Church has traditionally held that there are seven gifts of the Spirit: wisdom, understanding, counsel, fortitude, knowledge, piety and fear of the Lord. In the strength of these gifts, their recipients are called to be witnesses to their faith and to serve the human community.

> *"Preparing for the year 2000 is certainly not a matter of indulging in a new millennium, rather it is aimed at an increased sensitivity to all that the Spirit is saying to the Church and to the Churches, as well as to individuals through charisms meant to serve the whole community" (John Paul II – TMA 23).*

FRUIT > A sparrow was lying on its back, holding its legs towards the sky. A woman who saw it, asked the sparrow: "Why are you lying like this?" The sparrow replied: "We are told that the sky is going to fall today." The woman laughed uproariously and said to the sparrow: "Do you think that your toothpick legs can hold up the sky?" "No," said the sparrow, "but I must do what I can." Each of us have been given by the Spirit some gifts. When it comes to working for the building up of God's Kingdom, to what extent do I put to use the gift I have received, however small?

STRUGGLE IN THE SPIRIT

ROOT > For the Spirit to help us to reconstruct in us the disfigured image of God, we must collaborate with the Spirit, which will involve a struggle, a struggle to purify our souls from dregs of sin and to eliminate everything that can impede the work of the Spirit in us. It is true that human beings have been already redeemed and the Spirit is already given to the believers, but there still remains inherent in each of us the sad possibility of again becoming 'flesh', that is, of returning to the former condition of slavery, which can suffocate the beautiful work of the Spirit.

> *"Be guided by the Spirit and you will no longer yield to self-indulgence. The desires of self-indulgence are always in opposition to the Spirit, and the desires of the Spirit, are in opposition to self-indulgence; they are opposites, one against the other" (Gal 5:16-18).*

FRUIT > We all have to struggle against sin, if we want to live in the Spirit. There are seven major sins. Pride: it is a tendency to make ourselves our own law, our own god. Envy: it is sadness at the good of others, as if it is an affront to us. Anger: an unreasonable hostility towards those who harm us. Lust: the unreasonable focus on sexuality and the misuse of others for our gratification. Greed: a consuming focus on material possessions. Gluttony: the excessive love of eating and drinking. Sloth: the excessive avoidance of our responsibilities, duties and personal development.

REPENTANCE IN THE SPIRIT

ROOT > Because of our fallen human nature, there always exists the monstrous possibility of substituting ourselves for God, building up our own image and denying our nature as created in the image of God; and this possibility often becomes a reality. Therefore, Christians often experience spiritual defeat. But at the very instant of defeat, the Spirit comes to help. He intervenes with sweetness, to lift us up and place us back on track. We only have to repent and he grants forgiveness, and integrates us into the Body of Christ again.

> *"You must repent", Peter answered, "and every one of you must be baptised in the name of Jesus Christ for the forgiveness of your sins and you will receive the gift of the Holy Spirit" (Acts 2:37-38).*

FRUIT > It costs much to repent. It costs self-surrender and humiliation and the yielding up of the precious things to God. It costs the perseverance of long waiting and the faith of strong trust. But when we have really repented, we will find this difference: Whereas before it was hard for us to do the easiest things, now it is easy for us to do the hardest things, because the repentant person receives the joy of the holy Spirit. And this joy is unspeakable, for the Holy Spirit is the Comforter and Christ is the Comfort.

RENEWAL IN THE SPIRIT

ROOT > The Spirit not only moves us to repentance, but also renews in us the divine life. This renewal especially takes place in the Sacrament of Penance. A truly repentant Christian confessing to a sprit-filled priest, can truly experience the miracle of renewal. Through the newness thus produced, the Spirit forms the people of God, enables them to discover the charismatic dimension of the Church, offers them a multiplicity of spiritual gifts, with a view to their use for the community in forms both personal and communitarian.

> *"Alongside the traditional forming of associations, movements and new sodalities have sprouted, with a specific feature and purpose, so great that the Holy Spirit nourishes in the ecclesial community, and so great the capacity of initiative and the generosity of our lay people"* (John Paul II – ChL 29).

FRUIT > With diversity of its spiritual gifts, the Spirit opens up diversity of ministries in the Church, all aimed at the growth of the community, giving birth to many kinds of spiritual movements. These ecclesial movements emphasise in their character the primacy of every Christian vocation to holiness; the responsibility to profess the Catholic faith; the witness of a steadfast and committed communion; conformity with and participation in the apostolic goal of the Church and a commitment to a social presence in human society in order to permeate it with Gospel values.

July:

VIRGIN MARY

Week 1
Mary our Model

Week 2
Highly Favoured

Week 3
Marian Devotions

Week 4
Guiding Star

MODEL OF FAITH

Root > Faith is a firm belief in God, and in all the divine truths he has revealed. It is an implicit trust in his loving Providence overshadowing us at all times. Mary was a paragon of faith throughout her life. When her faith was tested at the Annunciation, by the arduous journey to Bethlehem for Jesus' birth, by having to flee to Egypt to protect her child, by losing her Son in the Temple, when she stood at the foot of the cross, and even after resurrection, when she prays with the apostles for the outpouring of the holy Spirit, Mary shines as perfect model of faith.

> *"Mary in fact constantly points to her divine Son and she is proposed to all believers as the model of faith put into practice"* (John Paul II – TMA 43).

Fruit > Our society today is experiencing a major crisis of faith. In this computer age, we have made such a vast strides in technology that we have become a self-sufficient, sophisticated people. God has become irrelevant in the lives of many people who put their faith instead in their own ingenuity. Assisted by Mary our model of faith, each of us has tremendous potential to counteract the decline of faith; Each one of us can bring hope into situations that are marked by discouragement and despair.

MODEL OF HOPE

ROOT > By hope we desire, and with steadfast trust, we await from God eternal life and the graces to merit it. Hope strengthens our trust and confidence, in the midst of all trials and tribulations, as well as all the joys and blessings of life. Mary's strong hope in the face of many trials and difficulties she had to endure, sets a course for us to follow. There were many occasions, such as when she kept standing at the cross, hoping to witness the outpouring of Jesus' redemptive love, casting all her anxieties on the Lord.

> *"Hope is the theological virtue by which we desire the Kingdom of heaven and eternal life as our happiness, placing our trust in Christ's promises and relying not on our own strength, but on the help of the grace of the Holy Spirit"* (CCC 1817).

FRUIT > If we live with a strong and vibrant hope, our whole lifestyle will reflect our deep trust and confidence in God. Without our even being aware of it, we will radiate our positive attitudes. People around us will begin to put their faith in God and to believe that God has a future and a hope for them. If you influence just one person each month, and if that person in turn influences one another person each month, do you know how many persons you will touch actually? Four thousand! Yes, you can make a difference.

MODEL OF CHARITY

ROOT > Mary shared the Good News with her cousin Elizabeth (Lk 1:39-56). She offers to her cousin, also pregnant, compassionate support. In moments of great joy and overwhelming grief, we need someone with whom to share, and that is what Mary did. She not only shares her own concerns, but she cares about Elizabeth and wants to be of assistance. The scene is a model for us as we share our own concerns, extend ourselves and reach out to others. When we forget ourselves and think more of others, we simply are following Mary.

> *"Mary Most Holy, the highly favoured daughter of the Father, will appear before the eyes of believers as the perfect model of love towards God and neighbour (John Paul II – TMA 54).*

FRUIT > If we are in danger, Mary will hasten to free us. If we are troubled, she will console us; if we are sick, she will bring relief. If we are in need, she will help. She does not look to see what kind of a person I have been. She simply comes to one who comes to her. John Bosco said: "People may well say that Don Bosco sees everything clearly, and that the Blessed Virgin leads him step by step. Yes, at every moment, in every circumstance, she has been protecting me from every danger, she shows me the task to be accomplished and helps me to carry it out."

MODEL OF PRAYER

ROOT > Prayer is primarily giving God our loving presence, by offering him our undivided attention and willingness to accept and respond to whatever he may ask of us. Mary is our model of prayer. Her prayer was grounded in the Scriptures, as we see it when she bursts forth in her memorable *Magnificat*. She was contemplative in her prayers. Contemplative prayer is a powerful in-depth prayer that leads us beyond words and beyond reflections about God, to the very reality of God dwelling within us. As Mary pondered God's workings and sought to give herself exclusively to him, her prayer for the most part became a silent attentiveness.

> *"As for Mary, she treasured all these things and pondered them in her heart" (Lk 2:19).*

FRUIT > Pondering before the Lord is sometimes called 'Meditation'. Some ask, "How can an average person, with a real life to live, mortgage or rent payments to make, a job to hold down, children to raise, a spouse to be married to, and a car that needs an oil change, take meditation seriously?" But, don't we meditate every time we turn around? Without thinking, we meditate upon the values, ideals, and goals cherished by the world! We reflect upon how much money we can pile up, if we buy a lottery ticket. After buying a new car, we ponder on the satisfaction it gives. Therefore, pondering before the Lord should not frighten us.

MODEL OF DISCERNMENT

ROOT > Discernment is a process by which we try to determine precisely what God wishes us to do in a given situation. Discernment means, not only making a prudent judgement, but doing so in light of God's purpose. The interior promptings and the dynamic presence of the Holy Spirit within Mary, empowered her to discern God's will in all the events of her earthly journey. The Annunciation is perhaps the event in Mary's life which most closely reveals the perfect discernment and the obedience, that the Holy Spirit worked in her.

> *"Mary who conceived the Incarnate Word through the power of the Holy Spirit and then in the whole of her life allowed herself to be guided by his interior activity, will be contemplated and imitated this year above all as the woman who was docile to the voice of the Spirit" (John Paul II – TMA 48).*

FRUIT > The procedure for discerning God's will consists of several steps: taking our concern to the Lord in listening prayer, striving to develop an objective and receptive frame of mind, sharing our problem with a competent person, and finally, reaching a conclusion. As we pray for guidance in discerning God's will, he may not give us specific directions, nor a step-by-step procedure to follow; but he does enlighten us, giving us the grace to comprehend his will more clearly. If our decision is in tune with God's will, we will enjoy genuine peace.

MODEL OF OBEDIENCE

FRUIT > Mary loved the Lord with all her heart and hence sought God's will in everything, especially his will of preference, that is, what will please him most. Being invited to become the Mother of the Messiah was a great privilege, but also a challenge. She was to become a mother in the most unheard of way, without a human father. But she said, 'yes', for she believed in the assurance of the angel that, by the Holy Spirit she would conceive the child. She is a model of single-hearted attentiveness to God's desires and total abandonment to his plans.

> *"Embracing God's salvific will with a full heart and impeded by no sin, she devoted herself totally as a handmaid of the Lord to the person and the work of her Son, under him and with him by the grace of almighty God, serving the mystery of redemption" (LG 56).*

FRUIT > Even in civil life, obedience is looked upon as of primary importance to the success of any undertaking. When a battle is in progress, the general is given supreme command to direct the manoeuvres of all the soldiers under him. But in spiritual life, obedience is more praiseworthy than any other virtue, for by it we yield up to God the stronghold of our very individuality. But it is a source of peace, of security, and of ever increasing merit. Actually, obedience simplifies life marvellously. It reduces the whole of our conduct to the observance of a single duty, that of doing God's will.

MODEL OF DISCIPLESHIP

Root > Mary is the first and perfect disciple of Jesus. God's personal, direct and immediate call came to Mary at the Annunciation. As it happens with anyone who is called to fulfil a special role in his plan, Mary too went through a life-long period of preparation, a life filled with difficulties and trials. Mary paid a high price to become and remain a faithful disciple, personally committing herself to the Lord with the words: "Behold, the handmaid of the Lord; let it be done to me according to your word" (Lk 1:38). From the beginning of her life, she strived to respond graciously and generously to God's call.

> *"Mary gave full expression to the longing of the poor of Yahweh and is a radiant model for those who entrust themselves with all their heart to the promises of God" (John Paul II – TMA 48).*

Fruit > A disciple is more than a follower. A follower is somewhat like a student, who learns by listening to the teaching of a professor, or under the instruction of a teacher. A disciple, on the other hand, observes the lifestyle of the master and follows him so closely that eventually he will be identified with his master. He strives to capture the mentality, the attitudes, the feelings, the heart of the master, in order to become like him. Unworthy or not, we too are being invited to become disciples of Jesus: to listen to his teaching, to observe his actions, to be imbued with his mind and heart.

MODEL OF SUFFERING

ROOT > Mary, though sinless, was not exempt from the hardships and heartaches which are the normal lot of humanity: problems in pregnancy, journey to Bethlehem, finding no room in the inn, flight into Egypt, losing the Son in the temple, letting her adult Son to leave the home for good, witnessing to the ridicule and hatred of her Son's enemies, walking with him in the way of cross and finally seeing him die on the cross like a criminal. Yes, Mary knows what it is to suffer; but her deep sufferings united with that of her Son, fulfilled an important role in the redemption of the human race.

> *"Her motherhood which began at Nazareth and was lived most intently in Jerusalem at the foot of the cross, is a loving and urgent invitation to all the children of God so that they will return to the house of the Father" (John Paul II – TMA 54).*

FRUIT > Affliction of any kind can be a powerful means of conditioning us to enter into a closer union with the Lord. To comfort us in our suffering, to aid and encourage us in our plight of suffering, Jesus gave us his Mother as our very own. But a mother cannot comfort her hurting child, if the child does not come to her. If we take our pain to Mary in prayer, she will soothe our suffering and bring it to Jesus, that he may sanctify it, and thus assuage our distress by giving it meaning and purpose.

FULL OF GRACE

Root > Grace is an unmerited gift bestowed on the human race by the benevolence of God, and includes all the supernatural charisms of the Holy Spirit. God made Mary 'full of grace,' by filling her with the Holy Spirit, so that she could become God's Mother. From the first moment of her conception, by a singular grace and privilege of God and by virtue of the merits of Jesus Christ, the Saviour of the human race, Mary was preserved from all stain of original sin.

> *"To become the Mother of the Saviour, Mary was enriched by God with gifts appropriate to such a role. In fact, in order for Mary to be able to give the free assent of her faith to the angel's announcement of her vocation, it was necessary that she be wholly borne by God's grace" (CCC 490).*

Fruit > I heard someone murmur, "God will not give grace to those who do not repent." The truth is, that God gives us grace to repent, and none of us can ever repent until grace is first given to us to lead us to repentance. I heard another saying, "But God will not give his grace to those who won't believe." The truth is, that God gives grace to people by which they are moved to believe. It is through the grace of God that we are brought to faith in Christ. Grace is omnipotence acting redemptively.

THE IMMACULATE

ROOT > The Catholic Church teaches that Mary was preserved from the effects of original sin from the very first moment of her existence. This unique privilege is called Immaculate Conception. It means that the new life of sanctifying grace, which was lost by original sin and is restored to Christians through Baptism, was given direct to Mary, from the first moment that she began to exist in the womb of her mother.

> *"The splendour of an entirely unique holiness by which Mary is enriched from the first moment of her conception comes wholly from Christ. The Father chose her in Christ before the foundation of the world, to be holy and blameless before him in love" (CCC 492).*

FRUIT > Does not the artist love the painting over which he has laboured and into which he has breathed his creative power? Does not the composer love the music in which the flame of his genius burns? Yes, they do. Similarly, God loves his masterpiece, the human soul, into which he has breathed his creative power and in which the flame of his genius burns. That is why, Mary who hates sin, still loves the sinners. She loves them because her maternal eye can penetrate the muck and mire of sin, which covers the splendour of the human soul.

VIRGIN MOTHER

Root > When the angel told Mary she was to become a mother, she questioned it: "How can this be?" (Lk 1:34). From this, the Church has always believed that in agreement with Joseph, Mary had pledged her virginity to God, so that she might be able to dedicate herself fully to the will of God. The Church also teaches that Mary always remained a virgin. Tradition has never known of another child of Mary except Jesus. There are some references in the Gospels to the 'brethren of the Lord', but 'brethren' among the Jews did not necessarily mean children of the same parents. It included cousins and relatives.

> *"Jesus was conceived solely by the power of the Holy Spirit in the womb of the Virgin Mary. The Church confesses Mary's real and perpetual virginity even in the act of giving birth to the Son of God made man. Mary remained as the Ever Virgin" (CCC 496,499).*

Fruit > When the Church proclaims Mary as 'Ever-Virgin,' she is speaking of her physical virginity, but more so of her spiritual virginity. It means that Mary is committed and belongs to God, more than to any earthly relationship or bond. Each Christian is called to be a 'virgin', in the sense, a part of her or him must belong totally and exclusively to God. At the same time, each Christian must be 'married', in the sense, that he or she must live out his or her love of God by loving real flesh and blood people, loving particular persons, not just all people in general.

THE MOTHER OF GOD

ROOT > Mary is the mother of Jesus Christ, God made-man. A mother brings forth a person not just a human body or a human nature. It was Jesus, a person, in Mary's womb. Since that person was God made-man, she is truly the Mother of God. All her gifts and privileges were given precisely because she was to be God's Mother. It does not mean that she existed before the Creator of heaven and earth. Yet, the Second Person of the Trinity, God the Son, became a member of the human family through Mary.

> *"Mary is acknowledged and honoured as being truly the Mother of God and the Mother of the Redeemer. Redeemed in especially sublime manner by means of the merits of her Son, and united to him by a close and indissoluble link, she is endowed with supreme office and dignity of being the Mother of the Son of God" (LG 53).*

FRUIT > Napoleon once uttered these remarkable words: "If Socrates would enter the room, we should rise and do him honour. But, if Jesus Christ came into the room, we should fall down on our knees and worship him." He was right, for Jesus is God. Mary was not mother of Jesus just because she brought him forth into the world. To think that simply bearing children makes one a mother, is as absurd as believing that a piano makes one a musician. Mary as mother, not only brought forth her child but also did what all mothers do: to see him growing into manhood, pleasing to God and to fellow human beings; Mary was truly the mother of Jesus as she is Mother of God.

OUR MOTHER

Root > Mary gave birth to Jesus not as a private person, but as Saviour of humankind. Even within Mary's virginal womb, Christ our Saviour bore the exalted title of the head of the Church. Through Baptism, we have been united with Christ to share with him his life and glory. We have become brothers and sisters of Christ, adopted children of the same Father. Hence Mary is our spiritual mother by grace. Since Mary is our mother, she has all of a mother's intense love and interest for us.

> *"The Virgin Mary is clearly the mother of the members of Christ, since she has by her charity joined in bringing about the birth of believers in the Church, who are members of its head. Mary Mother of Christ, is the Mother of the Church"* (CCC 963).

Fruit > A great treasure in any house is a good mother. Mary, our Mother, does for us what the best mother does in a house, indeed, more than what the best of mothers can do. As flies are driven away by a great fire, so the evils that come to torment us are driven away by Mary's ardent love for us. She brings a human smile even when sorrow has gained entrance into our hearts, heavenly light even when darkness has invaded our minds. She softens our hearts, makes things turn out well, sanctifies our actions and induces the spread of benevolence around us.

ASSUMED INTO HEAVEN

ROOT > It is the belief of the Church that at the end of her life on earth, Mary was taken up to heaven. The early Christians who treasured the bodies and tombs of the apostles and martyrs, never claimed to have the body of Mary or able to point to the place of her burial, for they believed that her body was taken up to heaven. Mary shared in an unique way with her Son in the work of redemption. That is why, the Church has always believed, that as he rose from the dead and ascended into heaven, so also she was lifted up both body and soul into heaven.

> *"The Most Blessed Virgin Mary, when the course of her earthly life was completed, was taken up body and soul into the glory of heaven, where she already shares in the glory of her Son's resurrection, anticipating the resurrection of all the members of his Body" (CCC 974).*

FRUIT > We are like tulip plant. In spring, this flower has a beautiful body but by the time fall comes, the tulip's body loses all its beauty, and at winter, only a bare bulb remains. So too, at the fall of our lives, our body would lose all its beauty and strength, but when the time of our resurrection comes, we will emerge with a beautiful new body. As a good salesman carries with him the best sample of his products, so Jesus attracts all of us to our destiny, by setting before us Mary, as the most sublime expression of his redemptive work.

OUR MEDIATRIX

ROOT > The motherhood of Mary for the Church in the order of grace, began with her consent at the Annunciation, and since then, it has been continuing to function uninterruptedly, and will do so until the entire humanity is redeemed. Taken up to heaven, she did not lay down this saving office. She intercedes with God to bring us the gifts of eternal salvation. Thus, she is our mediator-mother with God, but her mediation in no way obscures or diminishes Christ's unique mediation, as the universal and only Saviour of the world.

> *"Mary the unassuming woman of Nazareth, who two thousand years ago offered the world the Incarnate Word, leads the men and women of the new millennium towards the One who is the true light that enlightens everyone"* (John Paul II – TMA 59).

FRUIT > Mary prays that Jesus will change our weak hearts and make them strong and loving, just as at Cana he changed the water into wine. Our hearts are so often as weak as water, and they must be changed into the wine of unselfish love. But we cannot do this alone. Mary knows this best of all, and so she begs her Son to assist us. Comfortable Christians, of course, do not want to change. They have been lulled into complacency. They spend too much time in their overstuffed chairs watching TV. Mary's prayers are our hope.

MARY IN THE LITURGY

ROOT > The primary expression of Catholic faith lies in the liturgy as our worship of the Lord. Because of Mary's singular status among the saints, we honour her through liturgical celebrations and feasts. Mary is included in the many prayers of the Mass: the Canon, called the Eucharistic Prayer; Mary is mentioned in each of the four general Eucharistic prayers. In Masses that honour Mary, there are two Prefaces. Throughout the Church Year, feasts in honour of Mary occur with regularity. The Solemnities of Mary commemorate Marian doctrinal beliefs and supersede Sunday liturgies.

> *"The Church's devotion to the Blessed Virgin is intrinsic to Christian worship. The liturgical feasts dedicated to the Mother of God and Marian prayers such as rosary, an epitome of the whole Gospel, express this devotion to the Virgin Mary" (CCC 971).*

FRUIT > We know that a stone dropped from an aeroplane will fall to earth with an ever increasing velocity. The earth attracts the stone like a magnet. That attraction becomes stronger as the stone approaches the earth. That is why, the speed of falling stone increases with each second that it falls. There is also a natural attraction which God exerts on every human soul. The closer a person is to God the greater will be the attraction. The devotion we express to Mary at Masses celebrated in her honour will be pleasing to her, if every celebration brings us closer to God.

MARY IN SACRAMENTALS

ROOT > Sacramentals make ordinary things special by bringing us into contact with the 'sacred'. Sacramentals are objects, gestures and blessings that remind us of the sacred, and bring us close to God. There are many Marian sacramentals: Medals, Scapulars, Icons, votive Candles, Processions, Associations and Confraternities of the laity like the Sodality. We all reach out to God on our own wave-length. We all have our most comfortable and our most intimate forms of prayer. Mary fits into our personal prayer-life, in any form we choose.

> *"The Holy Mother Church has instituted sacramentals. These are sacred signs which bear a resemblance to the sacraments. They signify effects particularly of a spiritual nature. By them, men are disposed to receive the chief effect of the sacraments, and various occasions in life are rendered holy" (CCC 1667).*

FRUIT > Medals, an ancient sacramental from earliest times, are small coin-like objects, used as religious reminders. The catechumens were often given a medal with a cross inscribed on it. Martyrs were commemorated on medals, and when pilgrims visited cathedrals or holy sites in the Middle Ages, they received medals as reminders of the sacred locations. Medals in themselves are not amulets and, even if they are blessed, do not carry magical powers. Medals usually worn around the neck, serve as reminders, and excite one to deeper devotion and faith.

MARY IN SHRINES

ROOT > Throughout the Catholic world, thousands of churches, institutions, schools, colleges, hospitals, even entire town bear the name of Mary. Among the monuments outstanding in some countries are Basilicas or National shrines of Mary. Many shrines symbolise the significant roles Mary plays in human history. In particular, crowds of faithful make pilgrimages in their thousands to the revered shrines, where the Church has confirmed that an apparition of Mary has taken place.

> *"Marian shrines are scattered throughout the world. They are like so many milestones, set up to mark the stages of our itinerary on earth: they enable us to pause for a rest, to restore ourselves from the journey, to regain joy and security on the way, together with strength to go on. They are like oases in the desert, formed to provide water and shade"* (*John Paul II – Insegnamenti 19 March 1982*).

FRUIT > The experience one gets in the holy shrine at Lourdes is unique. Daily, many thousands do converge into that shrine. Whether you are a pilgrim or a tourist, whether you are a believer or not, when the Blessed Sacrament night procession starts, a heavenly and awesome silence descends upon them all, revealing the inescapable presence of the ultimate reality of God, behind the appearances. If you listened to that silence of the night, you would feel, as I did, that all of a sudden you had penetrated the very heart of the universe, an immense happiness sweeping over you with a flow of fulfilment.

MARY IN PRAYERS

Root > Mary has been honoured throughout history with many prayers. *Memorare:* It is generally attributed to Bernard of Clairvaux. *Salve Regina:* It has been sung in Latin at the Divine Office in the monasteries, since the Middle Ages. *Stabat Mater:* This ancient anthem of many stanzas is used during Lenten devotions. *The magnificat:* This canticle, spoken by Mary when she visits her cousin Elizabeth is recorded in Luke's Gospel. The *Hail Mary:* This is the most common Marian prayer among Catholics. It capsulises most perfectly the role of Mary in the Church.

> *"Hail Mary, full of grace, the Lord is with thee, blessed art thou among women and blessed is the fruit of thy womb Jesus. Holy Mary, Mother of God, pray for us sinners now and at the hour of our death. Amen." (Angelic Salutation)*

Fruit > In her many appearances around the world, Mary has always been pleading for us to 'pray, pray, pray.' As we concentrate on Mary's request, we discover that she is not necessarily asking for more and more prayers, or for longer time in prayer; rather, she is encouraging us to enter into the deeper, more contemplative life of prayer, manifested in Mary's own lifestyle. But when we can't enter into deep contemplative prayer, vocal prayers such as 'Hail Mary' always come in hand. They do help us to enter into deeper communion with God.

ROSARY

ROOT > The Rosary is a meditation–vocal prayer form of devotion, focusing on the main mysteries of salvation, using a set of beads. The rosary as we know it today, evolved gradually in the prayer of the Church. It combines vocal prayer with meditation on the scenes from Christ's life, called mysteries. Although there are various ways to pray the rosary, it traditionally is divided into fifteen decades: five Joyful mysteries, five Sorrowful Mysteries and five Glorious Mysteries. Each decade consists of an Our Father, ten Hail Mary's and a prayer of praise.

> *"Christian prayer tries above all to meditate on the Mysteries of Christ, as in the rosary. This form of prayerful reflection is of great value, but Christian prayer should go further: to the knowledge of the love of the Lord Jesus, to union with him"* (CCC 2708).

FRUIT > In our progress towards God, there are three stages, as in the rosary. The first one, that of knowledge, is represented in the joyful mysteries, which contain the goodness of incarnation and open us to the way of salvation. The second stage is one of effort and labour, which is often painful but which is shaped after our Lord's own example. The final stage, is glorious for it is rest in the possession of eternal life. The rosary is a true introduction to even the highest forms of prayer, one of intimate converse with Jesus and Mary.

TITLES OF MARY

ROOT > Titles of Mary arise from various grounds of our beliefs about her, from the places of her apparitions, from her outstanding virtues and in general, from her status as the Mother of God. Some Marian titles have become popular because of extra-ordinary religious experiences or insights in relation to Mary. Our Lady of Perpetual Help is one of the most familiar and famous icons of Mary; Our Lady of the Sacred Heart is of specific interest to those who honour Jesus' compassionate love. And there are titles such as Our Lady of Fatima and Our Lady of Lourdes referring to her apparitions.

> *"My soul proclaims the greatness of the Lord, because he has looked upon the humiliation of his servant. Yes, from now onwards all generations will call me blessed"* (Lk 1: 46-48).

FRUIT > One of the titles which I like very much is 'Mary, Queen of Apostles'. Between a queen and her subjects, there is usually a common bond, something which unites them, something which creates a natural relationship. Among earthly queens that common bond may be the land itself, the language, and the love for their native country. The common bond that exists between Mary the Queen and the apostles is their personal and intense love for Jesus. Apostles loved Jesus not in the same degree as Mary, but nevertheless in a very high degree.

VENERATION TO MARY

ROOT > While dogmas and teachings have come from Church officials, devotions and pious practices have originated from the laity, including our affections and devotions for Mary. But true devotion to Mary is always secondary, to devotion to the Lord. We do not adore Mary, which is given only to God and Jesus. Rather, we honour Mary with reverence accorded to the saints. Because Mary is the most revered of the saints, the tribute we give to Mary is pre-eminent. But our Marian spirituality must be rooted in Mary's close connection with Jesus.

> *"The affirmation of the central place of Christ cannot be separated from the recognition of the role played by his Holy Mother. But veneration of her, when properly understood, can in no way take away from the dignity and efficacy of Christ, the one Mediator" (John Paul II – TMA 43).*

FRUIT > The story is told of an inebriated gent who staggers into Saint Patrick's Cathedral and prays aloud in front of Mary's statue. He begs mother Mary to get him a good job. A sexton working behind the main altar thinks he can have some fun and so in booming voice chides, "Yes, Joe, but first you better give up drinking." The man curtly replies, "Jesus, you be quiet. I'm talking to your mother." As humorous as this anecdote may be, it portrays the attitude of many Catholics concerning devotion to Mary. In itself, this simply is not a true portrayal of Mary's role in the Church.

SAINTS AND MARY

ROOT > The saints are all real people, whose lives are held to be a witness and example to the Christian faithful. Sanctity does not consist in being odd, but it does consist in being rare. Mary has a unique position among all the saints, because she is the Mother of God, immaculate and full of grace. The history of the Church teaches us, that the greatest saints are those who professed the greatest devotion to Mary. All the saints, the earliest ones down to the medieval and modern ones, have been ready to see Mary as the Queen of heaven and the heart of the Church.

> *"The Blessed Virgin, by becoming the Mother of God, received a kind of infinite dignity because God is infinite; this dignity therefore is such a reality that a better is not possible, just as nothing can be better than God" (St Thomas Aquinas).*

FRUIT > We all have a calling to become saints. We can't be content with placing a statue of Mary in the middle of a bird-bath and let the whole business of saints go at that. We may be ordinary people and may not be full of grace as Mary was, but we can still become saints by loving God and neighbour in our own way. In the words of the poet John Oxenham: "To every one there opens a way – a high way and a low way. The high soul takes the high way; the low soul takes the low way. And in between on the misty flats, the rest drift to and fro. But to every one there opens a way. And every one decides the way his soul shall go."

THE WORLD NEEDS MARY

ROOT > The Lord has set before us a certain way of life. But our human nature is broken and so we can easily drift from the way of the Lord. There is so much noise, speed and confusion in the world, and so we are apt to be deaf to hear the voice of God and take a wrong off-ramp, as we journey through life. Being influenced by crisis of faith around, we can easily become fearful of the future, losing peace, serenity and genuine joy in the Lord. Therefore, we need help from above and there is no better person than Virgin Mary to offer us this help, for God has from eternity destined her to be our guiding star.

> *"She, the Mother of Fairest Love, will be for Christians on the way to the Great Jubilee of the Third Millennium, the Star which safely guides their steps to the Lord" (John Paul II – TMA 59).*

FRUIT > The virtue of hope which stands between presumption and despair, is the gift we ask of the Blessed Virgin as we begin the new Millennium. With her help, we shall conduct our lives on the assumption that 'to those who love God, all things work together for good.' One common obstacle to the growth of hope is excessive self-consciousness. All of us are too sensitive to the chance of failure. One who keeps looking in the mirror, will find good reason to become discouraged! One of the secrets of optimistic outlook is to fix the eyes of our minds on God.

MARY'S PROPHETIC ROLE

ROOT > The important role which the mother of Jesus holds in Christian tradition has been set forth in the New Testament. In the Gospel of Luke, Mary comes into full view. At the beginning of the Gospel, she it is who plays the leading role, with a genuine personality. At the birth of the Church, she takes part with disciples in the prayer in the upper room. In John's Gospel, at Cana as on Calvary, Jesus authoritatively defined the role of Mary, first as obedient disciple, then as the mother of the disciples. Thus, the very mystery of Jesus is inseparable from the woman of whom he was born.

> *"The Father chose her for a unique mission in the history of salvation: that of being the mother of the long-awaited Saviour. The Virgin Mary responded to God's call with complete openness" (John Paul II – TMA 54).*

FRUIT > Down through the centuries, Mary has filled a special prophetic role similar to that of the prophets in the Old Testament. At various times, the Lord sends Mary to appear on earth to alert, caution, and warn the people of God of some insidious dangers, threatening our relationship with him and weaning us away from his way of life. If these dangers have already have made inroads in our life or weakened our dedication to the Lord, Mary encourages us to repent and recommit ourselves to the Lord.

MARIAN YEAR

ROOT > The Marian Year (1987-1988) struck a resounding chord in all the believers. It was eagerly awaited and so profoundly experienced in the individual local churches, especially at the Marian Shrines around the world. Pope John Paul II's sixth encyclical *Mother of the Redeemer* was published during the Marian year, also in preparation for the celebration of the Millennium 2000. The documents elaborated on contemporary Marian themes such as the Mystery of Mary in the plan of salvation, Mary's role as the Model of the Church and Mary's mediation.

> *"The Marian Year was as it were an anticipation of the Jubilee, and contained much of what will find fuller expression in the year 2000" (John Paul II – TMA 42).*

FRUIT > As Marian Year emphasised: we will be fortified with courage in the new millennium, through the mediation of Mary. Fortitude is a moral virtue that enables us to overcome all difficulties in fulfilling the duties imposed on us by God's plan. It is free from rashness as from fear, ready to endure as to act, to defend itself against the attacks of spiritual foes as to assume the offensive. It follows the straight line of God's purpose. It shines in all its glory, when life is at stake in the cause of right, and therefore it is the special virtues of the martyrs.

MARY'S APPEARANCES

ROOT > Since the early days of the Church there have been many hundreds of reported visions and apparitions of Mary. The Church has always been cautious about the authenticity of supernatural phenomena and carefully investigates each claim. If, after examination, the Church does not find the claim to be harmful to the faithful, it may 'recognise' the apparition – which in no way binds Catholics to 'believe' in the appearance or any of the 'messages'. If the Church approves the apparition, it may grant permission for public devotions at the site, allowing Mary to be honoured there in a special way as in Fatima, Lourdes, Medjugorje, Guadalupe.

> *"The Blessed Virgin intoned the Magnificat, knowing that to accomplish the plan of salvation for all mankind, the Lord willed to bring her, a simple maiden of his people, into association with it" (John Paul II-Insegnamenti, 19 March 1982).*

FRUIT > Mary seems to seek out the simple and quiet people. We consider for a moment the various visionaries to whom Mary has appeared. The persons to whom Mary has appeared have been, for the most part, young, innocent people with a simple, trusting faith. In Israel these people would be classified as 'anawim'. These were humble, simple, prayerful people who were looking for the coming of Messiah. Their personal qualities give us an insight into the spiritual qualities Mary wants us to develop, that God may work in and through us.

LOURDES

ROOT > The most famous apparition of Mary occurred at Lourdes, France in 1858, to Bernadette Soubirous, a French peasant girl. It was in her last appearance at Lourdes that our Lady revealed her identity: "I am the Immaculate Conception". Millions of people come each year to honour Mary, to thank the Lord for his Mother and implore her powerful intercession. The countless healing of body, mind and soul that have taken place at Lourdes since 1858, are a powerful testimony to Mary's loving concern for the suffering and her healing power.

> *"The story of Lourdes is a poem of Mary's motherly love, always vigilant and concerned about her children, and it also sums up the history of so much suffering, which has become prayer, offering confident abandonment to God's will, drawing from it comfort and value for one's own suffering" (John Paul II – Audience, Rome, 11 Feb 1981).*

FRUIT > "I kept looking at her as hard as I could," said Bernadette, "and she kept looking steadily at me!" The thousands who flocked to the grotto at Lourdes that February day of 1858, saw nothing but Bernadette. So eager were they to touch the invisible that they asked, "Tell us, does the Lady look at anybody but yourself?" "Yes, indeed, she does," replied Bernadette, "she looks all around the crowd, and she stops at some as if they were old friends." As every beetle is a gazelle in the eye of its mother, so each of us, however low may be our standing in life, are dear to her, for we are all her children.

FATIMA

ROOT > World War I had been raging in Europe. Leaders of atheistic communism had a firm hold on Russia, and were determined to spread their ideology around the world. In the midst of this devastation, the Lord sent his Mother to bring hope and reassurance. In 1917 Mary appeared to three children, as they tended sheep in the countryside surrounding Fatima, Portugal. Mary identified herself as 'Our Lady of the Rosary', and urged prayers, especially Rosary, for the conversion of sinners and consecration of Russia to her immaculate heart.

> *"I have come on pilgrimage to Fatima, like most of you, dear pilgrims, with the rosary beads in my hand, the name of Mary on my lips and the song of the mercy of God in my heart" (John Paul II – Insegnamenti, 12 May 1982).*

FRUIT > Those who consecrate themselves to the Immaculate heart of Mary can at least do this: acknowledge sin as a reality. Sin is so devastating that as one leak could sink a ship, so one sin could destroy the sinner. What is sin? To put it simply: it is an attempt to be the author of one's own happiness, rather than to receive this happiness from God. And the greatest of modern sins is to be conscious of none. In our present age, even the grown-ups laugh at sin and at the idea of the fall of man from grace. And yet, sin is real and not artificial as many would think.

MEDJUGORJE

ROOT > One of the well-known apparitions of Mary began in the village of Medjugorje, Yugoslavia. Mary appeared to six children on 24 June 1981. Her appearances have continued to this day, making them the most frequent Marian apparitions in one place. Through the apparitions, the Madonna illuminates our path to a deeply committed Christian way of life, a way first outlined by her Son Jesus. Through her messages at Medjugorje, Mary invites us to live a deeper faith, more fervent prayer, personal renewal, sincere conversion, greater penance and genuine peace.

> *"May her maternal intercession accompany humanity toward the next millennium, in fidelity to him who 'is the same yesterday and today and for ever' (Heb. 13:8), Jesus Christ" (John Paul II – Centesimus Annus, 62).*

FRUIT > As a mother holds the wounded and frightened child, and with her breath, inspires trust, rekindles confidence and gives life back again, so Mary our Mother is with us, in times when we are blown down, too weak even to pray. She will hold us and breathe us back to life. Should we wither and fade, she will gather us up in her arms. She is ready to use our limbs, our heart beat, and our breath, as rhythms of God's own Spirit to bring comfort. Finally, when the tents which we are in now become burnt and ashes, she will hold us in peace for ever.

A RENEWAL PLAN

ROOT > Mary's appearances since her assumption emphasise the fact that, though she is physically absent, she is spiritually present with us, as a bright light guiding us in our present-day crisis in faith. She paves the way for us through her example, and through her messages in her apparitions, guides us on our way. She picks us up when we falter and fall in our efforts, to revitalise our spiritual lives and to bring others to a deeper appreciation of the Great Renewal in which we are involved.

> *"For every Christian, for every human being, Mary is the one who first 'believed,' and precisely with her faith as Spouse and Mother she wishes to act upon all those who entrust themselves to her as her children"* (RM 46).

FRUIT > By her assumption, Mary has not disappeared from us. She has only assumed a new and more powerful way of being present with us. Mary is more in the world now than any other woman. Cleopatra is remembered. Mary is addressed. She is the most closely present of all women. Because Mary is with us, we honour her with shrines. Hence we pray to her: "Draw us Mary after you and we shall run towards the fragrance of your perfumes."

August:

THE CHURCH

Week 1
Attributes

Week 2
Symbols

Week 3
Sacraments

Week 4
Vocation

ONE CHURCH

ROOT > The Church is one because of her source, which is the mystery of unity in the Holy Trinity, who is one God but three persons. The Church is one because of her founder Christ, who reconciled all people to God by the cross, restoring the unity of all in one body. The Church is one because of her 'soul', which is the Holy Spirit who indwells in every believer ruling over the entire Church. Therefore Jesus wanted his followers to be one in mind and heart, one in prayer and action, one in love and service.

> *"Baptism constitutes the foundation of communion among all Christians including those who are not yet in full communion with the Catholic Church. The emphasis on the centrality of Christ, of the Word of God and of faith ought to inspire interest among Christians of other denominations and meet with favourable response from them" (John Paul II – TMA 41).*

FRUIT > Jesus said, "I will build my Church." He did not say, "I will build my Churches." The Church is his Body. Christ cannot have many bodies. That would be a physical monstrosity. The existence of over 9,000 Christian denominations throughout the world, is an insult to Christ, a scandal to his Church and a hindrance to the spread of his Kingdom. We must all pray for unity, but union based on Christ himself and his teachings. A union which is not based on these two, is a conspiracy rather than a communion.

HOLY CHURCH

ROOT > The holiness of the Church comes from the abiding presence of Christ in it. He loved the Church as his bride, delivering himself up for her. This he did that he might sanctify her. Because the Church is the continuation of Christ, it brings his holiness, his salvation, his goodness to all people who come into contact with her. The sins and the failings of the individuals hinder the ability of the Church to sanctify all people. So, the Church and its members struggle on earth, to realise the holiness possible for them, because of their union with Christ.

> *"Although the Church is holy because of her incorporation into Christ, she does not tire of doing penance: before God and man she always acknowledges as her own her sinful sons and daughters" (John Paul II – TMA 33).*

FRUIT > The real need of the Church today is not for new methods of evangelism or increased activity, but for deep moral cleansing and a readjustment of heart and life, that will clear away barriers to fruitful communication of the Gospel. One of the chief reasons for the failure of the Church to have a great impact upon the life of people in the world today, is to the fact that its own life is not in order. We are producing Christian activities, faster than we are producing Christian experience of holiness.

CATHOLIC CHURCH

Root > The Catholic Church teaches that it is Catholic in two senses: First, because Christ is present in her. In her, subsists the fullness of Christ's body united with its head; this implies that she receives from him the fullness of means of salvation, which are correct, complete confession of faith, full sacramental life and ordained ministry in apostolic succession. The Church was, in this fundamental sense, Catholic on the day of Pentecost, and will always be so, until the day of Parousia. Secondly, the Church is Catholic, because she has been sent out by Christ on a mission to the whole of the human race.

> *"All men are called to this catholic unity of the People of God. And to it, in different ways, belong or are ordered: the Catholic faithful, others who believe in Christ, and finally all mankind, called by God's grace to salvation" (CCC 836).*

Fruit > The truth in the Catholic Church comes down from Christ. It is a truth so noble that when we begin to wander away from it, we lose our way. There is tremendous satisfaction in having a map. That is what the truth of Christ is like, in the Church. We may get off the road, by error or human frailty. But as long as we have that map, we can get back on the road. There are indeed some people who once get off the road, tear up the map. That is still a greater tragedy.

APOSTOLIC CHURCH

ROOT > It is the teaching of the Catholic Church that she is Apostolic, because she is founded on the apostles in three ways: First, she was and remains built on the Apostles, the witnesses chosen and sent on mission by Christ himself. Second, she has the indwelling Spirit helping her to hand on the teachings she had received from the Apostles. Third, she continues to be taught and guided by the Apostles, through their successors in pastoral office: the college of bishops, assisted by priests, in union with the successor of Peter.

> *"It was to the apostolic college alone, of which Peter is the head, that we believe that our Lord entrusted all the blessings of the New Covenant, in order to establish on earth the one Body of Christ into which all those should be fully incorporated who belong in any way to the People of God"* (UR 3).

FRUIT > The successor to Peter is the Pope. He is the head of the Church. It is surprising that those who admit with Scripture, that the Church is the mystical body of Christ, will not also admit a head. After Christ's ascension, how would people know his mystical body and where his life was to be found? He gave a sign, namely the head. Does not the unity of life manifests itself through the head? The head is the symbol, is it not, of the unity of life? Legs and arms can be amputated without destroying the unity of life. But cut of the head, it is the end of life.

CHURCH IS COMMUNION

ROOT > The Catholic Church is both a community and a communion. The word 'community' is generally used to refer to external union present among the members of the Church. When people strive to make their parish a loving, caring group of people, they demonstrate their sense of community. The word 'communion' refers to that special grace of inner union, that comes to those who are united to Christ. The Spirit becomes present to those who believe, making of them a communion that is one in heart and one in mind, much as they are in external action as a community.

> *"In the Universal Church and in the particular churches, is the 'communion' being strengthened? Does it leave room for charisms, ministries, and different forms of participation by the People of God?" (John Paul II – TMA 36).*

FRUIT > This is a Russian story: An angel came once to an old woman in hell and said to her, "If you can think of any one good thing you did in your life, I will let you go out of hell." The old lady said, "Well, I once gave a beggar a carrot." "Very well," said the angel, "I will let a carrot down into hell and you get hold of it, and I will pull you out." The old woman was being pulled out and of course thousands grabbed on to her, and she said, "Get off. This is for me." They all fell back down, including her, for true love implies solidarity and community.

SERVANT CHURCH

ROOT > In its role as the servant of the physical and spiritual needs of the people, the Church looks to Christ as the perfect example of total service. He healed, preached, taught and sanctified. While serving the physical, social and personal needs of the people in the world, the Church is aware of the secularised society in which she has to serve. Therefore, the servant Church best serves today, by reminding people of the Kingdom of God, and by calling them to live according to the Gospel values of justice, freedom, peace, charity, compassion and forgiveness.

> *"The Messiah's characteristics are revealed above all in the 'Servant Songs'. These songs proclaim the meaning of Jesus' passion, and show how he will pour out the Holy Spirit to give life to the many: not as an outsider, but by embracing our 'form as slave"(CCC 713).*

FRUIT > A Christian mystic from India, Sadhu Sundar Sing, wanted to go into Tibet to evangelise. He hired a Tibetan guide to take him over the Himalayas. They had gone but a short distance, when they became tired and sat on the snow and ice. Then Sing said, "I think I hear someone groaning in the abyss." The Tibetan said, "Well, what difference does it make? We are almost dead ourselves." Sing went down, found a man, and dragged him to the base of the Himalayas to a little village. Refreshed by his act of charity, he came back to find the Tibetan guide frozen to death on the ice. Those who serve others serve themselves!

RECONCILING CHURCH

ROOT > Jesus gave reconciliation and forgiveness of sins a very great importance in his earthly ministry. Jesus' death on the cross was intended to bring forgiveness, salvation, healing and eternal life to those who believe in him. Jesus' death effects a reconciliation and overcomes the sinfulness that stands between God and his human creatures. Jesus wants his Church and its ministers to carry on the work of forgiveness and reconciliation. The Sacrament of Reconciliation is one important way through which the Church offers forgiveness to the People of God.

> *"Among the sins that require a greater commitment to repentance and conversion should certainly be counted those which have been detrimental to the unity willed by God for his People" (John Paul II – TMA 34).*

FRUIT > Denominalism must go. We should be denominated by the name of Christ, as the wife is named by her husband's name. As long as the Church of Christ has to say, "My right arm is Catholic, my left arm is Anglican, my right foot is Baptist, and my left foot is Methodist," she is not yet truly married to Christ. She will be truly married, when she has washed out these divisive stains, when all her members have one Lord, and one faith and one baptism. If we all moved in one great mass to the attack of a certain evil, how much more easily might we prevail over the powers of evil!

THE MARTYR

Root > All Christians have the vocation to manifest the 'new man' which they have put on in baptism, by the example of their lives and the witness of their word wherever they live. At times, it may involve martyrdom, the shedding of blood bearing witness even unto death. Martyrs bear witness to Christ who died and rose. The Church has painstakingly collected the records of those who persevered to the end in witnessing to their faith. They form the archives of truth written in letters of blood, proclaiming for ever that the Church is a Church of martyrs.

> *"At the end of the second Millennium, the Church has once again become the church of martyrs. The persecution of believers – priests, religious and laity – has caused a great sowing of martyrdom in different parts of the world" (John Paul II – TMA 37).*

Fruit > It is unnatural for Christianity to be popular. If you are under any illusions about the attitude of this world towards Jesus Christ, try really living for him for a week and you will find out. The Word of God never yet prospered in the world without opposition. Let a person really dare to be a true Christian and take Christ seriously, beginning next Monday morning, and he or she will wake up to the fact that he or she is a sheep among wolves. Persecution is the legacy bequeathed by Christ to his followers.

BODY OF CHRIST

ROOT > Christians are united as one unit or one body, so that the actions of one Christian have an impact on other members of the Church. This unity comes from our union with Christ through faith, hearing of the Word and sharing in the one cup and one bread of the Lord. The most important element in the body is Christ, its head. Without the link to Christ, the Church would be like any other group of people organised for common human purpose. The presence of Christ as the head of the Church, fills it with holiness and unites it to God.

> *"Three aspects of the Church as the Body of Christ are to be specifically noted: the unity of all her members with each other as the result of their union with Christ; Christ as the head of the Body; and the Church as the Bride of Christ"* (CCC 789).

FRUIT > If we burn our face, doctors will graft skin from another part of the body to the face. If we are suffering from anaemia, doctors will transfuse blood from another member of society. Christians are members of the mystical body of Christ. If it is possible to transfuse blood in human body, it is possible to transfuse sacrifice in mystical body. If it is possible to graft skin in human body, it is possible to graft prayer in mystical body. The members of the mystical body are so interconnected, our prayers, our petitions, our sacrifices are transfused to our brothers and sisters in the body of Christ.

THE BRIDE OF CHRIST

ROOT > Christ is the Bridegroom and the Church is his Bride. The Church is betrothed to Christ to become one Spirit in him. As her Bridegroom, Christ gave himself up for her to sanctify her and joined her with himself in an everlasting covenant. He loves the Church with everlasting love, and never stops caring for her as his own body. He and the Church are no longer two but one; yet they remain two different persons as it happens in any conjugal union, that is, he remains as the head and she remains as his body.

> *"The Church is the Bride of Christ: he loved her and handed himself over to her. He has purified her by his blood and made her fruitful mother of all God's children" (CCC 808).*

FRUIT > Jesus wedded the Church as his Bride on the cross and after the resurrection he entered paradise bringing with him his Bride. The Bride of Christ can never be the individual faithful at prayer, but only the complete organism of all the faithful. The Church, like Blessed Virgin, conceives us as a virgin by the Spirit, bears us as a virgin without pain. Therefore, the Church of Christ is not an institution. It is a new life with Christ and in Christ. The Church, imitating Virgin Mary, daily gives birth to his members, and like her, remains a virgin.

THE HOLY REMNANT

ROOT > The Chosen People, disregarded God's Law and became unfaithful to the covenant and ended up in exile. Exile was apparently a failure of the promises, but it was also the mysterious fidelity of the saviour God, and the beginning of the promised restoration in the Spirit. Exile served the people as a period of purification, and hence the cross of Christ was pre-figured by this exile, and the remnant of Israel who returned from exile, prefigured the Church which Christ would build after his resurrection.

> *"Jesus said to them: 'You foolish men! So slow to believe all that the prophets have said! Was it not necessary that the Christ should suffer before entering into his glory?'" (Lk 24:25-26).*

FRUIT > The Church of today is the holy remnant of Israel. But we must note that it is called 'holy' remnant. Is it holy as God wants it to be holy? If the Church is long on membership but short on discipleship, if it is more anxious to gather statistics than to grow saints, it is not living up to its vocation to be holy. One wonders, whether one reason why the Church of God at this present moment has not much influence over the events of the world, might be, because the world has so much influence over the Church. The Church has a great need today to fall in love with holiness all over again.

A BUILDING

ROOT > The Church is called the building of God. Jesus once compared himself to the stone which the builders rejected, but which was made into a corner-stone. The apostles built this Church on this corner-stone; hence, it is Christ who gives the Church solidarity and unity. This building is sometimes called the house of God, in which God's children make their family with the Holy Spirit. In other words, the Church is the dwelling place of God among human beings.

> *"Christ is the centre of the People of God, his Body. Around this centre are grouped images taken from the life of the shepherds or from cultivation of the land, from the art of building or from family life or marriage" (CCC 753).*

FRUIT > Some say, "Well, I have given myself to the Lord, but I do not intend to give myself to the Church." Why not? "Because I can be a Christian without it." Are you sure? There is a brick. It is made for building a house. It is no use for that brick to tell me, that it is just as good a brick while it is kicking about on the ground, as it would be in the house. So too, we Christians who are like little stones after the manner of Christ, would be better off if we become part of the Church, of which Christ is the corner-stone.

THE TEMPLE

ROOT > Before Jesus came, the people worshipped God in a temple made of stone. But after his coming, the focus of worship shifted from temple to Christ himself. He, not the temple, now represents God's presence among his people. He is the house of God made flesh, and in him all the fullness of God dwells. Since Jesus embodies the meaning of the temple, and since the Church is his body, the Church is called the temple of God, being indwelt by the Spirit. The indwelling of the holy Spirit in the Church means that he indwells in every believer.

> *"Do you not realise that your body is the temple of the Holy Spirit, who is in you and whom you received from God?" (1 Cor 6:19).*

FRUIT > By our participation through Christ in divine life, we become the temples of God. That is why our body is sacred and we have reverence for it. The body is not a worm, something vile. It is God's temple and one day it will be glorified too. This is one of the reason for purity. If the human heart is pure, usually the human body will be pure also. A pure heart breathes out purity. As Luther said, "when God purifies the heart by faith, the market is sacred as well as the sanctuary." God does not demand a beautiful vessel, but he does demand a clean one.

A CULTIVATED FIELD

ROOT > The Church is a cultivated field, the vineyard of God planted by himself. The Chosen People of Israel were like olive trees, which had for their roots the prophets. The Church founded by Christ have us as olive trees, and our roots are the Apostles. It is in this filed reconciliation among all people takes place. Christ called himself the true vine in this vineyard of God, for it is he who gives life and fruitfulness to the branches. We are the branches, and we remain in Christ, the vine, through the Church. Apart from Christ, we can do nothing.

> *"After all, we do share in God's work; you are God's farm, God's building"* (1 Cor 3:9).

FRUIT > If the promises of God have to bear much fruit in our lives, we must cultivate our heart which is the field for God. We cultivate it by regularly withdrawing ourselves to retirement and prayer. If there is no withdrawal, there will be no gathering of forces. Athletic contests have the moments of respite. So in the military, momentary retreat can make for a strong offensive. Likewise, we have to withdraw spiritually, if we are to bear much fruits. The idea of saying that we are too busy to do anything else, to pray or commune with God, means that we remain spiritually uncultivated.

SHEEPFOLD

ROOT > Christ called himself the Good Shepherd and his followers the flock. He also called himself the gate and no one can enter the sheepfold except through him. It follows, then, that the Church which is the Mystical Body of Christ is the Sheepfold which Jesus referred to, and therefore is the one true way to holiness and salvation. It is in the Church, the saving power lies, and it is in that Body, the life of Christ is poured into the believers, who, through the sacraments, are united with him in a hidden but real manner.

> *"The Church is a Sheepfold, to which Christ is sole and necessary gateway. It is also the Flock of which God himself foretold that he would be the Shepherd, and whose sheep, even though governed by human shepherds, are unfailingly nourished and led by Christ himself"* (LG 6).

FRUIT > Suppose there was a great plague which affected a wide area of the world. Then some doctor in his laboratory found the remedy for this plague and made it available for everyone. There would be many who would seek the remedy. But there will be also some who would not, saying "How would I know he has the remedy? Why should I bother? I will cure myself." Jesus brought salvation to all, which is to be found in his Church, but there are those who doubt it, and keep out of his sheepfold.

MOTHER

ROOT > We refer to the Church as mother, because she brings forth in us new life from within her very being, and then nurturing and caring for that life. Church is said to be the mother for all people, because the Church corrects the evil brought about by Eve, the first woman of creation, on the entire human race. As Eve, through her sin, brought suffering and death to all children of the human race, so the Church, because of her intimate union with Christ, the universal Saviour, takes away that sin, and nurtures all back to God.

> *"Salvation comes from God alone; but because we receive the life of faith through the Church, she is our mother. We believe the Church as the mother of our new birth, and not in the Church, as if she is the author of our salvation"* (CCC 169).

FRUIT > Jesus was not crucified in the cathedral, between two candles, but in the world, on Calvary and openly for all to see. There were three languages written on the cross: Latin, Hebrew and Greek, but they could as well be English, Swahili and Tamil. It would make no difference. Jesus placed himself at the very centre of the world, in the midst of smut and thieves and soldiers and gamblers and he was there telling all, that he was the Saviour of all. His Church, the Mother Church, offers the same universal salvation of Christ to all.

BAPTISM

ROOT > By Baptism, a believer becomes truly incorporated into the crucified and glorified Christ, and is reborn to the sharing of the divine life. Baptism erases the effects of the original sin. At Baptism, our soul becomes the dwelling place of the Trinity. Through Baptism, we also receive the privilege of sharing in the prayers and blessings of the Church and of receiving other sacraments in due time. God may give divine life in ways other than Baptism to those who are unable to receive it. But Baptism is the ordinary way established by Christ for receiving the divine life.

> *"The commitment to make the mystery of salvation sacramentally present can lead to a renewed appreciation of Baptism as the basis of Christian living"* (John Paul II – TMA 41).

FRUIT > If a marble floor would suddenly begin to bloom, that would be an act which does not belong to the potencies and powers of a marble floor. Therefore, it would be supernatural. If the flowers on the altar suddenly begin to move from the shade and into the sunshine, that would be a supernatural act for flowers. Likewise, the privilege of becoming children of God by participating in his divine life through Baptism, no more belongs to our human nature, than blooming belongs to marble, or locomotion to flowers. It is a supernatural gift.

CONFIRMATION

ROOT > At Baptism, the Church takes us from the world into itself and into Christ, and makes us holy by giving us the divine life. At Confirmation, the Church sends us back into the world to draw others to Christ and to the Church. Therefore, through Confirmation, we receive the duty to be apostles for Christ and for the Church, and we receive also the power and strength through the gifts of the Holy Spirit, which we need to fulfil this duty.

> *"The primary task of the participation for the Jubilee includes a renewed appreciation of the presence and activity of the Spirit, who acts within the Church both in the sacraments, especially in Confirmation, and in the variety of Charisms, roles and ministries which he inspires for the good of the Church" (John Paul II – TMA 45).*

FRUIT > A lawyer in Berlin was a non-believer and he died. He had a Catholic law partner, and when his friend became ill, the Catholic lawyer visited him and said, "Now that you are about to die, do you not think it is time to make your peace with God?" The dying partner said to him, "If Christ and your Church have meant so little to you during your life, that you never once spoke to me about them, how can they mean anything to me at my death?" One serious malady of the Catholic Church is infantile paralysis – too many babies do not grow in the Spirit, even after Confirmation.

EUCHARIST

ROOT > Jesus instituted the eucharistic sacrifice of his body and blood. He did this in order to perpetuate the sacrifice of the cross until his second coming. He entrusted to his Church this memorial of his death and resurrection. The Eucharist is the sacrament of love, a sign of unity, a bond of charity, a paschal banquet in which we consume Christ. The result is that we are filled with grace, and a pledge of future glory is given to us. By receiving the Holy Communion, we become united, not only with the Lord but also through him to one another.

> *"The year 2000 will be immensely eucharistic: the Sacrament of the Eucharist. The Saviour, who took flesh in Mary's womb twenty centuries ago, continues to offer himself to humanity as the source of divine life" (John Paul II – TMA 55).*

FRUIT > Our whole problem with Mass where Eucharist is celebrated, is that we meet and go through the motions, and can't recognise the Lord who is there. Our young people are saying, "I don't want to go to Mass; I don't get anything out of it." Of course they don't. They don't bring anything to it. You don't get anything out of an opera, unless you know something about music. What are we teaching our young people? Doctrines, doctrines and doctrines, not discipline, not sacrifice, not charity. If we bring to Mass, a sacrifice, bring a commitment, bring a loving heart, we will certainly get something out of the Mass.

PENANCE

ROOT > If we turn away from God, deliberately choosing something which is against God's will, we commit a grave sin and we lose divine life in us and are left spiritually dead. However, God forgives our sins, normally through his Church, in the Sacrament called 'Penance'. By this Sacrament we are also reconciled with the Church which we have wounded by our sins. Even if we have no grave sin, it is good for us to receive this Sacrament, because in the Sacrament the Lord gives us special grace to steadily overcome even our small faults displeasing to God.

> *"The whole of the Christian life is like a great pilgrimage to the house of the Father, whose unconditional love for every human creature and in particular for the 'prodigal son' (Lk 15:11-32) we discover anew each day. The pilgrimage takes place in the heart of each person, extends to the believing community and then reaches out to the whole community"* (John Paul II – TMA49).

FRUIT > Today people are sick, not sinners. We go to a psychiatrist because we have committed adultery, to a mental therapist because we are homosexual, to a psychologist because we have been dishonest. There are no sinners; we are not responsible, we are not guilty. The worst thing in the world is not sin, but denial of it. If I am blind and deny that there is any such thing as light, shall I ever see? If I deny that there is any such thing as sin, how shall I ever be forgiven? It makes redemption impossible.

MARRIAGE

ROOT > Marriage which had its origin in God, was raised by Christ to a very high level, with a triple purpose: to be an imitation of the union between him and his Church, to be the means of increasing his Church and to be a sacrament, that is, to serve as a means of developing divine life in the spouses. Through this sacrament, Christ comes into the lives of the married couples. He abides with them thereafter, so that, just as he loved the church and handed himself over on her behalf, so the spouses may love each other with perpetual fidelity through mutual self-giving.

> *"Precisely because we are convinced of the abundant fruits of holiness in the married state, we need to find the most appropriate means of discerning them and proposing them to the whole Church as a model and encouragement for other Christian couples" (John Paul II – TMA 37).*

FRUIT > When husband and wife make love and nourish their love for each other, they nourish their union in love for God in Christ. But marriage has its downs as well as its ups. But even the downs of marriage are part of the on-going sacrament the couple share day-in and day-out. They encounter God's love in the painful times too, and when they are faithful to each other to the vows they had made, on the other side of the growing pains, they find even deeper joy which comes from God.

HOLY ORDERS

ROOT > The Sacrament of the Holy Orders is that action of the Church, by which bishops, priests and deacons are commissioned to serve the Church as its ministers, and receive from Christ the power and strength to perform their sacred duties. Those who receive these Orders, share in Christ's ministerial priesthood, so that when they exercise their priesthood, it is Christ who acts through them, in their pastoral care, especially: preaching the Word of God, offering the sacrifice of the Mass, administering the sacraments and counselling and assisting the faithful.

> *"Christ sent the Apostles just as he himself had been sent by the Father. Through these same Apostles he made their successors, the bishops, sharers in his consecration and mission. Their ministerial role has been handed down to priests in a limited degree" (PO 2).*

FRUIT > A priest is a servant of the servants of God. Nothing is more disappointing than a priest who is on an authority trip or an ego trip. There is a great joy, when a local community has a priest, who knows that to be a priest is not to be chiefly an administrator or financial planner. There is a great joy, in having a priest who is not an ecclesiastical legalist, cracking the moral whip over the bowed heads of the people. It is a joy, to have a priest who is a humble spiritual leader and guide, one who brings healing and forgiveness and listens more than lectures.

ANOINTING

ROOTS > When some member of the Church is sick, Christ and his Church come to the person's aid through the Sacrament of Anointing. It is the action of the Church through which Christ gives spiritual help to the believer who is ill. The purpose of the Sacrament is to restore or increase the divine life in the soul of the sick, giving strength to bear the sufferings and overcome the fear of death. Though the purpose of the Sacrament is to bring comfort to the soul, it will relieve bodily illness also, if this is beneficial to the soul.

> *"The Church exhorts the sick to contribute to the welfare of the whole People of God by associating themselves freely with the passion and death of Christ" (LG 11).*

FRUIT > We deeply sympathise with those who are sick. But I envy them too, for the great good they do to themselves and for the world by their suffering. I know a lady who has not for twenty years left her bed, and she has lived nearer to God than any of us, and has brought more glory to him than any of us. Many sick beds, I believe, are doing more for the spread of Christ's Kingdom on earth than our pulpits. What showers of blessings come down in answer to the prayers and tears of the invalids, whose weakness is their strength and whose sickness is their opportunity.

PEOPLE OF GOD

FRUIT > The Church is the People of God whom he acquired for himself from the time he chose Israel as his own, to be a royal priesthood and a holy nation. One becomes a member of this People by faith in Christ and Baptism. This People have Christ for their head and have the dignity and freedom of the children of God, bound by the new law of Christ: to love as Christ loved us. Their mission is to be the salt of the earth and the light of the world. Their destiny is finally the Kingdom of God.

> *"Jesus Christ is one whom the Father anointed with the Holy Spirit and established as priest, prophet and king. The whole People of God participates in these three offices of Christ and bears the responsibilities for mission and service that flow from them" (CCC 783).*

FRUIT > God wants all peoples on earth to become 'People of God.' and experience the salvation brought by Jesus. Hence, 'People of God' goes beyond the boundaries of the Catholic Church to include all peoples. While the fullness of the Church subsists in the Catholic Church, the notion of the People of God extends in a special way to all baptised Christians. Even people who have not formally heard about Jesus or the Church, can be considered a part of the People of God, because of their desire to know their Creator, do what is right and attain eternal happiness.

FAMILY OF GOD

ROOT > Those who are baptised, become members of the family of God which is his Church. Because through Baptism they become adopted children of God whom they can call 'Father', also have a right to call Jesus their 'brother'. All Christians, then, should bear a family spiritual resemblance to Jesus. Because they belong to this family, they are to be united with Christ and with one another as a family, even though they may be scattered all over the world and come from different cultural, ethnic and political backgrounds.

> *"At every time and in every place, God draws close to man. He calls man to seek him, to know him, to love him with all his strength. He calls together all men, scattered and divided by sin, into the unity of his family, the Church" (CCC 1).*

FRUIT > Tolstoy tells the story of a man who stopped to give alms to a beggar. To his dismay, he found that he had left his money at home. Stammering his explanation, he said, "I am sorry, brother, but I have nothing." "Never mind, brother," was the beggar's answer, "that too was a gift." The one word 'brother' meant more to him than money. The Church is a family. To be Church, to live as Church, means to live as a part of this family, aware that all of us are brothers and sisters in Christ.

PILGRIM CHURCH

Root > Christ is present in his Church but his reign is yet to be fulfilled with power and glory at his second coming. Till then, the Church marches on as a pilgrim. Christ's Passover has already defeated evil, but evil power goes on attacking Christ's reign. Hence, the pilgrim Church, armed with her sacraments and institution, will go on fighting against the powers of darkness. Thus, the pilgrim Church filled with the Spirit, is almost like an army in a spiritual struggle, wielding the living Word of God and delivering its people from the dominion of evil.

> *"The Church will receive her perfection only in the glory of heaven, at the time of Christ's glorious return. Until that day, the Church progresses on her pilgrimage amidst the world's persecutions and God's consolations" (CCC 769).*

Fruit > Suppose I am sick in bed and a friend gives me a canary to be my companion. If I told the bird, "You are in this tiny cage and you have wings, but this is the right place for you," I believe the bird would be depressed. If, however, I said to him, "You are in the wrong place, you have a gift of song that should mount to the heavens, and you have wings that should fly," the bird would then be happier. So we are unhappy, if we think we are locked in this little world which could be shattered by a bomb. But we have been told by Christ that our final home is heaven. So we march on together as happy pilgrims to our Father's house.

PRAYING CHURCH

ROOT > Without prayer a person cannot find God or salvation promised in Christ. While a person can learn to pray from the example of others, it is the Church as a praying community of believers that most clearly brings its believers into communion with the Lord. Prayer was essential to the life and ministry of Jesus. To bring people to God through prayer, is one of the chief functions of the Church. It carries this out especially through the prayerful celebration of the Mass and the sacraments. When we gather together to celebrate the Eucharist, we become a part of the praying Church.

> *"If the Christians are to live as true members of Christ and radiate the divine influence among the people with whom they are in contact, they will be obliged to develop a rich interior life of union with God" (Thomas Merton).*

FRUIT > We get tired when energy declines; but why does energy decline? Some say, that we have just a certain amount of it, like money in the bank. When it is spent, we are exhausted. Hypnotists say that by suggesting to a man by hypnotism that he is weak, he can lift a weight 40 percent less than normal and by suggesting to him that he is strong, he can lift 60 percent greater than normal. But my own experience is that when holiness declines, energy declines. When loving communion with God in prayer begins to peter out, I lose energy.

CHARISMATIC

ROOT > Charisms are graces of the Holy Spirit ordered to the Church's building up, to the good of people and to the needs of the world. The Church therefore has a duty to test all Charisms and to hold up to what is good, so that all diverse and complementary Charisms work together for common good. There are sacramental graces, gifts proper to the different sacraments. There are also special graces called Charisms.

> *"Charisms are a wonderfully rich grace for the apostolic vitality and for the holiness of the entire body of Christ, provided they really are genuine gifts of the Spirit and are used in full conformity with authentic promtings of this same Spirit" (CCC 800).*

FRUIT > What is the difference between a gift and a Charism? Gift makes us pleasing to God, and Charism, such as preaching, makes us helpful in relation to others. Since I preach about holy things, people say I am holy. Not necessarily. If there is any holiness in me, it is not because I exercise that particular Charism. As a matter of fact, there are hundreds of actors who could preach better than I do. If there is to be any holiness, it has to be before I come to the pulpit and after I leave it. There I am just exercising a talent that God gave. And he could take it away.

LAITY

ROOT > All the faithful, except those in Holy Orders and those who belong to a religious state approved by the Church, are called 'laity'. They are incorporated into Christ and integrated into the People of God by Baptism, and are made sharers in their particular way, in the priestly, prophetic and kingly office of Christ. The laity have their own part to play in the mission of the whole Christian people in the Church and in the world.

> *"It pertains to the laity in a special way so to illuminate and order all temporal things with which they are closely associated that these may always be effected and grow according to Christ and may be to the glory of the Creator and Redeemer" (CCC 898).*

FRUIT > The laity will be effective if they do the following: First, they have to be conscious of the fact that they are members of the people of God. Second, they must be theologically educated. Third, they must communicate with the world as Christians. It is necessary for them to guard against two extremes: to form a kind of ghetto, confining their religious activities to the church and keeping the commandments, or, to become so worldly that they can do nothing for it.

PASTORS

Root > Pastors are ordained ministers of grace in the Church. They are sent by the Lord to speak to the community in his name. They are authorised and empowered by Christ, for he is the source of ministry in the Church. The Word and the grace of which they are ministers, are not their own but are given to them by Christ for the sake of others. Chosen together, they are also sent out together and they place their fraternal unity among themselves, at the service of the fraternal communion of all the faithful.

> *"Christ the Lord set up in his Church a variety of offices. The holders of office, who are invested with sacred power, are, in fact, dedicated to promoting the interests of their brethren, so that all who belong to the People of God may attain to salvation" (LG 18).*

Fruit > In order to be pastorally effective, pastors have to strike a fine balance between their ego and God. Many pastors have been spiritually ruined by the modern philosophy of self-identity: I've got to be me. I've got to do my thing. Since when? Does not charity mean doing the other person's thing? Why this affirmation of the ego? Why do we have to act in a certain way to attract the attention of others to our human personality? As pastors, our human personality must take a back seat. Christ has to be in us at all times, acting through us, using us as his instrument.

THE CONSECRATED

ROOT > All the faithful are called to the perfection of charity. But the consecrated faithful freely commit themselves to a life with obligations of practising chastity in celibacy for the sake of the Kingdom, poverty and obedience. They profess these evangelical counsels within a permanent state of life recognised by the Church, a life that characterises life's consecration to God. The religious state is therefore one way of experiencing a more intimate consecration rooted in Baptism and totally dedicated to God.

> *"Religious life derives from the mystery of the Church. It is a gift she has received from the Lord, a gift she offers as a stable way of life to the faithful called by God to profess the counsels. Thus the Church can both show forth Christ and acknowledge herself to be the Saviour's bride" (CCC 926).*

FRUIT > The cumulative evil of this age is getting worse all the time. It is much similar to our atmosphere which is becoming more and more polluted with gases and exhaust fumes. The fear of one evil often leads you only into a greater evil. The belief in a supernatural source of evil is not necessary; human beings alone are quite capable of every evil. Just to mention a few: The evil of egotism. The evil of sexual permissiveness and the evil of greed. Therefore, our world needs some men and women to stand up against such evils, not just to condemn them orally, but to counter their effects by consecrating themselves to evangelical values of poverty, chastity and obedience.

September:

THE KINGDOM OF GOD

Week 1
Mysteries of the Kingdom

Week 2
Glad Tidings of the Kingdom

Week 3
Signs of the Kingdom

Week 4
Proclamation of the Kingdom

SOWER

ROOT > A seed has in it nitrogen, hydrogen and carbon in right proportions. You can make a seed in laboratory that will look exactly like the natural seed. But if you plant it, it will come to nothing. But if I plant the seed God made, it will become a plant, because it contains the mysterious principle which we call the 'life principle'. The Word of God in the Bible looks like other words. But planted in good soil, it shows that it has the life principle in it; it brings forth spiritual fruit. That is what Jesus wanted to convey through his parable of the sower.

> *"A sower went out to sow. As he sowed, some seeds fell on the edge of the path, and the birds came and ate them up. Others fell on patches of rock... not having any roots they withered away. Others fell among thorns, and the thorns grew up and choked them. Others fell on rich soil and produced their crop some a hundredfold"* (Mt 13:4-9).

FRUIT > Prayer is one of the best ways of letting the Word of God rain down upon us, work within us, change and transform us, so that God's loving purpose for all creation, can be fulfilled in us and through us. Let us bring to prayer our every day preoccupations and activities and let the Word of God fall upon them. We tend to regard these preoccupations as 'distraction' in prayer, and try to banish them from our minds. By doing so, we only keep God from interfering in our mundane lives. No, let us allow the Word of God to fall upon our earthiness as we bring it to our prayer.

MUSTARD SEED

ROOT > The mustard seed is very small and appears insignificant. Pliny the Elder, a contemporary of Jesus, wrote a great book called *Natural History*, in which he describes all the plants that were known in the Mediterranean world. He says only two things about the mustard plant: It is medicinal. So it did have some value. But he said not to plant it because it tends to take over the entire garden. It is a weed that cannot be stopped.

> *"The Kingdom of God is like a mustard seed which a man took and sowed in his field. It is the smallest of all the seeds, but when it has grown it is the biggest of shrubs and becomes a tree, so that the birds of the air can come and shelter in its branches" (Mt 13:31-32).*

FRUIT > Jesus was building on two images of the mustard seed to describe his Kingdom: Like the mustard seed, his Kingdom is therapeutic, but a weed. As therapeutic, it is life, it is healing, it is medicinal; as weed, it is like virus, that is, his Kingdom promotes 'stupid' things such as non-violence and simple life. But he has planted it and it is going to take over; we don't know when it is going to take over, but Jesus has planted his eternal truth in the world, and it is going to take over. Of course, it is going to grow with great difficulties, because there is going to be opposition; but it will prevail; it will eventually take over the whole garden.

YEAST

ROOT > Yeast is not the nice little package you buy at the grocery store. That is our modern, sanitised version of what people have known for centuries as leaven. Yeast actually evokes an image of corruption. You set sour dough in the corner until it gets bubbly and smelly. Then Jesus says that a woman took and hid this seemingly corrupt thing inside, and it was enough to leaven eventually the entire fifty pounds! Clearly, the three measures of flour is a deliberately large amount, in order to give us hope.

> *"The Kingdom of Heaven is like the yeast a woman took and mixed in with three measures of flour till it was leavened althrough" (Mt 13:33).*

FRUIT > The Church of Christ must be immersed in human reality. Believers are not to separate themselves from those who do not believe, for they are the yeast of the world. They are not to enclose themselves in their chapels or little communities or to spend all their energies working for 'their' church. They must be useful in the world together with all people of goodwill. Let us be yeast for the dough. The yeast transforms human history, not necessarily by bringing physically all people into the Church, but by infusing into human activity, the spirit which gives life to humankind.

HIDDEN TREASURE

ROOT > When a person finds by chance a treasure hidden in a field, just imagine the immense joy he or she will have! The joy will be so overwhelming that it will dominate all of one's feelings and thoughts. One will give up everything to obtain that treasure. This joy is so overwhelming that it seizes the person completely and penetrates one's inmost being. To secure this joy one will make any sacrifice; to possess that treasure, one will pay any price. This is the way it should be with the Kingdom of God, a hidden treasure after which we hunt.

> *"The Kingdom of Heaven is like a treasure hidden in a field which someone has found; he hides it again, goes off in his joy, sells everything he owns and buys the field"* (Mt 13:44).

FRUIT > If our discipleship is like the adventure of a treasure hunt, then why do we find it dull and tedious sometimes? Perhaps, we don't have enough faith to see the mystery and excitement that is there. If hearing the good news should overwhelm us with joy, then why are we so sad and serious sometimes? Perhaps, we don't have enough confidence in the power of God's word to generate joy. If following Christ fulfils our every expectation, then why are we so reluctant sometimes to make sacrifices for him? Perhaps, we don't have enough courage to take such risks for him.

PEARL

ROOT > In the parable of the 'treasure in the field' which Jesus told, the man who discovered it, stumbled upon it by accident but knew its value when he found it. In the parable of the pearl, the merchant was earnestly searching for the choice pearl, and when he found it, he sold everything he had to purchase it. In both cases, the treasure and the pearl were hidden, but became available. The 'pearl' in a certain sense, is Christ himself. He alone gives meaning to all the sacrifices of a Christian life. But he is hidden like a pearl, if we search for him, we will find him.

> *"The Kingdom of Heaven is like a merchant looking for fine pearls; when he finds one of great value he goes and sells everything he owns and buys it" (Mt 13:45).*

FRUIT > Like the pearl, the Kingdom is hidden and yet available. That is, the Kingdom is an open secret. Can we hold both of these words: 'hidden' and 'available, together? Yes, we can. For example, we have just flesh and blood people around us, but God is hidden in them. These are just flowers; this is just a table. Yet, God is working in them. In fact, the normal way we can see God is through what touches our senses. God is revealed in every one of our living moments. We are invited, therefore, to take this material world and human life seriously. Physical creation is both a hiding and revealing place for God.

NET

Root > By speaking of the net, Jesus reminds us that the first activity of the Church is mission to bring people into the net. But in a net, all kinds of fish are found. This means, that not all who are in the visible Kingdom can necessarily be truly the children of God. In other words, Churches and Christian organisations are not synonymous with the true people of God, who are believers living in true faith and uprightness. It is true that the Church has given the Kingdom to those who entered, but some of those who belong to the visible family of God, may not be having the spirit of the Kingdom and hence, be in actual fact outside it.

> *"The Kingdom of Heaven is like a dragnet that is cast in the sea and brings in a haul of all kinds of fish" (Mt 13:47).*

Fruit > We are to follow God's desires and tell others about his grace and goodness, but we are not to say who is part of the Kingdom of Heaven and who is not. This sorting will be done at the last judgement, by him who is more infinitely qualified than we. How we would like to have a Church made of only upright persons, in which each would discover the gifts of God! However, Christ did not want to have a Church like that, nor is that the way for the Church to serve the world.

VINEYARD

ROOT > It is the parable of the workers who received the same wages, even though some worked shorter hours. But the employer did nothing illegal. If the employees sued him, they would be laughed out of court. Jesus told the parable to the Jewish people. They were the ones who had struggled through the ages bearing the burden of serving God, the vineyard owner. Now Jesus was telling them, that at the final Judgement, the wages of salvation were to be given to the late comers as well. This is God's mercy overtaking justice, which can offend our legalistic sense of justice.

> *"In the evening, the owner of the vineyard said to his bailiff, 'Call the workers and pay them their wages, starting with the last arrivals and ending with the first'" (Mt 20:8).*

FRUIT > Through the image of the vineyard owner who gave work to the unemployed, and gave the same wage also to the latecomers out of mercy and charity, Christ is asking us to have charitable social concern for the needy in society. Should not we hear Christ saying: "I was ignorant and you became a teacher. I was hungry and you became a farmer. I was downtrodden and you became a politician who cared. I was homeless and you became a builder of houses which the poor could afford. I was a street kid and you opened a hospice?"

MARRIAGE FEAST

ROOT > Jesus goes to great trouble to convince us of God's unconditional self-giving. One of the central parables he uses for this purpose is that of the wedding feast. All and sundry are invited for the feast. The feast is a symbol of God's sharing himself with us. Some reject the invitation to be part of God's people and so miss out on eternal life. Others accept the invitation first, but then refuse to live as God asks, and their loss is just as great. It is not God who withdraws the gift, but their selfish lifestyle prevents them from accepting it.

> *"The Kingdom of Heaven may be compared to a king who gave a feast for his son's wedding" (Mt 22:2).*

FRUIT > In spite of all appearances to the contrary, God has a plan for this bankrupt world. He is not running an antique shop. He knows what he is doing to make of this world. His plan is to take us all to that Kingdom, which will be a banquet of fellowship with all nations in peace, unity and joy. But God's plan for our humanity requires that we respond to his call to accept the Good News his Son proclaimed, and endeavour to live by it. Great plans need landing gears as well as wings. It is not enough that we know about God's banquet, but we must choose to come to it.

THE POOR IN SPIRIT

Root > The Greek word which Mathew and Luke use for the 'poor', literally means the very empty ones, those who are crouching, the little nobodies of this world who have nothing left. It is inner emptiness. Of course if you are poor in spirit, it won't be long before you accept material poverty, too. In other words, you won't waste the rest of your life trying to get rich because you will know better. It is these God chooses to be rich in faith and to be heirs to the Kingdom. They already possess the Kingdom for they are the free ones now, without anything to protect or anything they need to prove their worth.

> *"How blessed are the poor in spirit: the Kingdom of Heaven is theirs"* (Mt 5:3).

Fruit > If we are poor in spirit, we know the universe does not revolve around us. We know that, while acknowledging our own needs, the needs and concerns of others also important. If we are poor in spirit, we learn how to be of service to others, not saving the world, but making a difference where we can. If we are poor in spirit, we don't compartmentalise life and religion. We take the time to see how spirituality can't be separated from any human life. If the love of things makes our vision blurry, the love of others and God puts everything in clearer focus. We see ourselves better, others better and God better.

THE GENTLE

ROOT > If there was one hated group in Palestine of Jesus' day, it was landlords, those who possessed the land usually by violence, by oppression, by holding onto it and making all the little peasants pay a portion of their harvest. Jesus was turning that around and saying no; he said to the peasants that it is they the little ones who are finally going to possess the land. It is said with sarcasm, with irony, but with hope. Jesus was redefining the meaning of land, as something which only God possessed.

> *"Blessed are the gentle: they shall have the earth as inheritance" (Mt. 5:4).*

FRUIT > Private property forces us behind fences, boundaries and walls. We actually think that we 'own' the land, because there is a deed down at the court-house. Is not that strange? People closer to the earth know that only God possesses the earth, that we are all stewards, pilgrims and strangers on earth. Possession is an illusion, in the light of the Kingdom. What do you possess? Wait a few years – we will see how much you possess when you are six feet under. The gentle St Francis told us, not to own anything so that you can be open to everything.

THE MOURNING

ROOT > It is impossible to get through life without feeling pain, without feeling disappointment and without feeling grief. We are all fragile and we are all vulnerable. In many ways, we are not in control of our lives, and our best laid plans in an instant can turn to dust. Therefore, to those who argue that it is senseless to believe in God when there is so much suffering in the world, the *Beatitude* answers, that without a God so much suffering would make no sense. It says that those who mourn have the opportunity, the ability to more clearly see reality, to more surely head towards our loving Creator.

> *"Blessed are those who mourn: they shall be comforted"* (Mt 5:5).

FRUIT > Doctors say that weeping is therapeutic. We speak of salt in tears. And now there is evidence of washed-out toxins. Theology says that weeping perhaps will allow you to know God much better than ideas. In this *Beatitude*, Jesus praises the weeping class, those who can enter into solidarity with the pain of the world, and not try to extract themselves from it. That is why Jesus says that the rich man cannot see the Kingdom. The rich one spends life trying to make tears unnecessary, and ultimately impossible. Tears over our sins and sins of the world, are like God's own tears which are always for everybody.

HUNGER AND THIRST

ROOT > Jesus says that those who hunger and thirst for justice or uprightness are blessed. To live a just life in this world is to have identified with the longings and hungers of the poor, the meek and those who weep. This identification and solidarity is already a profound form of social justice. But who can thirst and hunger for justice of this kind, if they don't hunger and thirst for God? As it is impossible to have a genuine love for our neighbour without loving God, it is also not possible to thirst for justice without thirsting for God.

> *"Blessed are those who hunger and thirst for uprightness: they shall have their fill" (Mt 5:6).*

FRUIT > Hungering and thirsting for more and more material goods, leaves one incapable of hungering for God, and consequently thirsting for his justice. One must accept at least late in life, that those who long and thirst for material goods are never satisfied any way. Even the wealthiest person is never satisfied. The very character of greed is that it is insatiable. It needs ever-higher dose to achieve the old satisfaction. Jesus would say, "Why not go the exact opposite direction? Directly and positively, choose emptiness, until it looses its terror."

THE MERCIFUL

ROOT > Mercy and forgiveness are unearned, undeserved, not owed. When we think that someone has to earn mercy, we have lost the mystery of mercy and forgiveness. The experience of mercy or forgiveness is the experience of a magnanimous God. God's mercy is not patient, benevolent tolerance, a kind of grudging forgiveness. Mercy of God is a loving allowing, a willing breaking of the rules by the One who made the rules, a firm and joyful taking of our hand, while we clutch at our sins. Jesus asks us to show similar mercy and forgiveness towards others.

> *"Blessed are the merciful: they shall have mercy shown them"*
> *(Mt 5:7).*

FRUIT > Shall we look at the times when we have withheld forgiveness? It is always our final attempt to hold a claim over the one we won't forgive. It is our secret way of holding on to power over another person. In effect we say, "I will hold you in unforgiveness, and you are going to know it just by my coldness, by my not looking over there, by my refusal to smile, or whatever." We often do it subtly, to maintain our sense of superiority. Non-forgiveness is a form of power to manipulate, shame, control and diminish another. Jesus refuses to acknowledge all such power.

PURE OF HEART

ROOT > When the heart is right, seeing will be right. All we need do is to keep the lens clean. That is what Jesus says in another *Beatitude*. If your heart is cold, your vision is distorted. Perhaps you don't like someone; you want to hurt her because she hurt you. You want to make him feel bad and let him know that he hurt you. If there is coldness and unforgiveness or the desire to violence verbally, or just to avert your loving gaze so that another person will feel your rejection, you will not be able to see clearly. The heart is not pure.

"Blessed are the pure in heart: they shall see God" (Mt 5:8).

FRUIT > A great many people are distressed by sensual defilement, and very frequently, they fail to make progress with them for one reason, namely, that while they are anxious to get rid only of this sensual defilement, they are not trying after goodness in every area. They dislike impurity of life and heart. It weighs upon their conscience and destroys their self-respect. But thy have no similar horror of pride or uncharity. People very often say, that it is impossible to lead a 'pure' life. It will be true, if a person will not try to be religious in every area, to be Christ-like altogether.

PEACEMAKERS

ROOT > Jesus called peace makers blessed. A peacemaker literally is the one who reconciles quarrels. Hence, Jesus is not on the side of violence but on the side of the non-violent. Jesus connects his peace with justice and self sacrifice. The one who works for Christ's peace does so by sacrificing the false self of power, prestige and possession. Such peacemakers will not be popular. In fact, such peacemakers will not be admired inside the system, for they will look dangerous. Therefore, the followers of Jesus are doomed to perennial minority status, but to God they are his dear children.

> *"Blessed are the peacemakers: they shall be recognised as children of God" (Mt 5:9).*

FRUIT > If you are truly pro-life, your very means have to be non-violent, and you have to be consistently pro-life, from womb to tomb. Some Christians today retain the right to decide when, where, and with whom they will be pro-life peacemakers. At the extreme end, if the others can be determined to be wrong in any way, it is apparently acceptable to kill them. That entirely misses the ethical point that Jesus is making: We are never the sole arbiters of life or death, because life is created by God and carries the divine image.

THE PERSECUTED

ROOT > Persecutions happened in the first centuries after Christ. How we are indebted to those martyrs! We are today reaping the harvest planted by the seeds of their blood. The seeds continue to be planted. There are those today, like Archbishop Romero, who are tortured and killed for the cause of Christ. They continue to plant seeds of Christian faith, the seed of liberty and a sign of hope. Because they continue to live the Gospel and because they refuse to live a life that does not seek justice for every one, especially the weakest, poorest in society, they are persecuted.

"Blessed are those who are persecuted in the cause of uprightness: the Kingdom of Heaven is theirs" (Mt 5:10).

FRUIT > Some otherwise pious believers try to remove the cross from their creed. The head of Christ was crowned with thorns, and do we think to be crowned with roses? Never did the Church so much prosper and so truly thrive, as when she was baptised in blood. The ship of the Church never sails so gloriously along, as when the bloody spray of her martyrs falls on her deck. We must suffer and even be ready to die, if we are ever to conquer this world for Christ. But, the weight of glory awaiting us, makes persecution light.

THE BLIND SEE

ROOT > Our hearts go out to those whom we see physically handicapped, especially the blind, the deaf, the dumb, the lame. But I have always seen on their faces a special joy. It cannot but be a spiritual joy, springing from their hearts, hearts which must be experiencing the riches of God's Kingdom within them. They may be blind, but through their dark colour, perhaps they see the wonderful colours of God's love and perhaps they prefer it, to the multiple colours of atrocities the world is offering.

> *"Are you the one who is to come, or are we to expect someone else?" Jesus answered, "Go back and tell John what you hear and see; the blind see again" (Mt 11:4-5).*

FRUIT > Two thousand years have gone by, since Jesus Christ came. Are we still spiritually blind? With the eyes of faith open, we should be able to see whether there is Kingdom of God within each of us, or we belong to someone else; whether Jesus is the Lord in our families, our parishes, and our Church; whether we are truthful followers of Christ, with burning hearts to seek justice and peace for all people. If our eyes of faith are open, we should be able to see the suffering of God in the homosexuals, the prostitutes, the divorced, the single parents, the AID sufferers and reach out to them in compassion and mercy.

THE LAME WALK

ROOT > The prophets foretold that when the Messiah comes, people could see signs such as the blind seeing and the lame walking. These signs were really something new, because in the past, God usually manifested himself as a powerful saviour. These healings pointed to the liberation that Jesus was bringing: not punishment of sinners, which was a great part of John the Baptist's preaching; But the Messiah was proclaiming, through these signs, that he has brought to the world, above all else, a reconciliation suited to healing a world of sinners, of violent and resentful people.

"the lame walk" (Mt 11:5).

FRUIT > Are we spiritually lame or handicapped? We are spiritually lame, if we do not put into practice what we believe. Practice is incarnation of faith. Faith without works is a body without clothes; no warmth. Wherever there is genuine faith, it must blossom into works. If you believe that there is a God who hears our prayer, why do you not pray? If you know that you must be born again, how is it you are content without the new birth in the Spirit? A life of faith involves hard work, courage and discipline. You may as well separate weight from lead or heat from fire, as action from faith.

THE DEAF HEAR

ROOT > Our ears may be like a taxi cab with both doors open, but if the Word of God is just buzzing in our ears, it is not going to take us across the vale of tears. "Today", said Jesus after speaking in the Synagogue, "this Scripture passage is fulfilled in your hearing" (Lk 4:21). Do we hear God's Word with our minds alone? Many people have made a tragedy of their lives because they could not make up their minds! Therefore, we are to hear God's Word with our hearts. Only the ear of the heart, is like the lover's ear, that will hear even the lowest sound, when God speaks.

"the deaf hear" (Mt 11: 5).

FRUIT > Are we spiritually deaf? If we really hear the Word of God, it will make its home in our hearts. Some make the mistake of going from one preacher to another. A raven may fly from cage to cage, but it is not thereby changed into a dove. Go from room to room of the royal feast, but mere sight of the tables will never satisfy your hunger. You have to eat the meal. Likewise, the main thing is to have and hold the truth of Christ and hold it personally and inwardly. It is a pity that the bulk of hearers of Christ are hearers only. More is wanted than just hearing.

THE POOR HEAR THE GOOD NEWS

Root > The higher up you are in society, the more trapped you are. But, the more you are outside the powerful circles in society, the freer you are. For every promotion or recognition you accept, is there not a price to be paid, for example, more adherence to party line? That is true of business and almost any organisation. The problem is that when you are high up in anything, you are expected to represent it, hold it together and affirm it. So Jesus says that those who are low and poor in society, are freer to hear the Word of God and do it.

"The good news is proclaimed to the poor" (Mt 11:5).

Fruit > By implication, Jesus is warning of the dangers the rich face. The rich tend to be content with their present comfortable existence and in their self-sufficiency, they tend to forget who their Master really is; and hence, they find it extremely difficult to listen to what the Master wants to say about their true destiny in life. Some of the rich even refuse to accept that there is resurrection of the body, with the result they tend to denigrate their own body by pampering it with too much material comforts. If there is no resurrection, then surely blessed are the rich, more blessed are the full, and most blessed are those who laugh now.

THE DEAD ARE RAISED

Root > Jesus had been preaching in the villages beyond the Jordan, when he received the news of Lazarus' sickness. Jesus did not leave immediately, but waited two days until Lazarus died, before returning to Judea. When he arrived in Bethany, Jesus raised Lazarus from the dead. Jesus raised also others from the dead, including Jairus' daughter and a widow's son. Jesus has power over life and death, as well as power to forgive sins. This is because he is the Creator of life. He who is life, can surely restore it when it is lost.

"the dead are raised to life" (Mt 11:5).

Fruit > Lazarus came back to life. But Lazarus had to die again. Hence, the raising of the dead by Jesus had an ulterior purpose. It foretells the true resurrection which, does not just prolong life but transforms our entire being. This resurrection which Jesus offers is spiritual. It begins when faith moves a person to give up wrong ways of living, and become open to receiving God's life. That is, one who lives in submission to Christ, has already passed from death to life, and because of this, he or she will never die. Hence, eternal life can begin for us here and now.

THE SICK ARE HEALED

ROOT > Jesus was frequently moved to pity at the sight of suffering, and cured hundreds of people with all kinds of diseases, both of mind and body, as reported chiefly in the Gospel of Luke (Lk 4:40-41). Usually, Jesus just spoke a few words and touched the sick person and he or she was cured immediately. These wonderful cures were witnessed by thousands of people, many of whom were alive when the Gospel was written, and many more who heard it preached by the Apostles after Christ's death, could testify that what was written was true.

> *"those suffering from virulent skin-diseases are cleansed"* (Mt 11:5).

FRUIT > Christ's healing miracles are powerful signs of what he can do for us, on a deeper spiritual level. They are parables of sacramental experience. There is no difference between those who were originally healed by him and ourselves, in terms of our ability to experience the Lord's healing and transforming power. The deathless Christ becomes part of us in the Eucharist. We can draw strength, power and vitality from his risen presence in the Eucharist and be healed. Our life here, is not a dress rehearsal for eternity. We can even now begin to enjoy spiritually that eternal life, where there will be no sickness at all.

EVIL SPIRITS FLEE

ROOT > One of the truths about Jesus' ministry is that Jesus was an exorcist. He drove out devils. For some reason, the existence of the Devil and his angels, is not universally accepted today within Christianity; while ironically, the opposite is true among many non-believers, who show great interest in witchcraft and the occult. In the New Testament, evil spirits emerge as the cause of possession and illness, again and again. Also, they reveal themselves as ones who are in a state of continuous combat with Jesus and his disciples.

> *"Jesus rebuked (the unclean spirit) saying, 'Be quiet! Come out of him!' And the unclean spirit threw the man into convulsions and with a loud cry went out of him" (Mk 1:25-26).*

FRUIT > The deeper meaning behind Jesus' exorcism is, that the Kingdom of Satan, which enslaved people since Adam's sin, is now giving way to the Kingdom of God. If Jesus inaugurated the Kingdom of God more than 2000 years ago, why is evil still widespread today? The answer is that the coming of God's Kingdom is not an instant happening. It is a gradual process. Jesus put the plant – the Kingdom – in the soil. But he left to us the job of cultivating it. It is our job to see to it that the Kingdom bears the fruit, God intended it to bear.

ALL CAN ENTER

ROOT > Jesus gives eternal life to all those who belong to his Kingdom and he alone can offer it, for it is he who 'comes down from heaven and gives life to the world' (Jn 6:33). Everyone is called to enter the Kingdom. First announced to the children of Israel, this Messianic Kingdom is intended to accept people of all nations. To enter it, one must accept Jesus' word which is compared to a seed which is sown in a field. Those who hear it with faith and are numbered among the flock of Christ, have truly entered the Kingdom. Then by its own power, the seed sprouts and grows until the harvest.

> *"Whoever believes in Jesus and enters into communion with him has eternal life, because he hears from Jesus the only words which reveal and communicate to his existence the fullness of life" (John Paul II – EV 37).*

FRUIT> In Kiltegan in Africa, there is a beautiful carving which symbolises the bond between the members of the human family. Each individual in the ebony carving, is connected either by hand or foot, as a sign that each is a part of the whole and depends on the others. Everybody has a place, including the sick, the old and the weak, even the dead. While another person may look at such a tree and perhaps see only firewood, when I look at it, I feel that this is the Kingdom of universal fellowship that Jesus came to offer, and he is calling all people to enter into it.

TO THE POOR AND LOWLY

ROOT > In our world, it is considered bad form to show weakness, to be poor and lowly. But Jesus castigated those who despise children and the little ones of this world, for it is to them his Kingdom belongs. To be poor and lowly is to accept our inner poverty for we, both the rich and the poor, depend on God for our existence. Anytime we deny our limits and refuse to acknowledge our dependence on God, we violate inner poverty. This admission of inner poverty hurts our pride, but without it we cannot become the citizens of God's Kingdom.

> *"The Kingdom belongs to the poor and lowly, which means those who have accepted it with humble hearts. Jesus is sent to 'preach the good news to the poor'; he declares them blessed, 'for theirs is the Kingdom of God'" (CCC 544).*

FRUIT > Poverty of the spirit in the poor and the lowly, offers a suitable soil for many Kingdom-values to flourish, for example, patience. The poor in spirit are patient, not only with others but also with themselves, for they are wise to realise the rewards of such patience. Patience with oneself breeds considerateness and softness of manner towards others. It disinclines us to censoriousness, because of the abiding sense of our own imperfections. It quickens our perception of utter dependence on God and grace, and produces at the same time evenness of temper.

SINNERS INVITED

ROOT > Whatever you may say of sin; you may call it a thorn in the side of justice, a stab at the heart of truth; you may castigate sin as the mother and nurse of all evil, the egg of all mischief, the fountain of bitterness and the root of misery. Yet, all sins are forgiven by Christ, and all repentant sinners are invited to his Kingdom. Repentance is part of salvation, and when Christ saves us he saves us by making us repentant. To God, repentance is like the cry of a new-born babe, which indicates that the child is alive and God will not kill a life, meant for his Kingdom.

> *"Jesus invites sinners to the table of the Kingdom: 'I came not to call the righteous, but sinners.' He invites them to that conversion without which one cannot enter the Kingdom, but shows them in word and deed his Father's boundless mercy for them" (CCC 545).*

FRUIT > Have you seen the two famous seas of Israel? The Sea of Galilee receives constant replenishment from the Jordan, teems with life and provides food for all who live close by. By contrast, the Dead Sea has only desultory inlets and no outlets. It has no movement, it is heavy and lifeless. You can see the sun sparkling on the surface, yet it is deceptive in its deadness. What does it show? It shows that we must be constantly challenged to move on, lest we become stunted. Moving on from the deserts of our past life, into the green pastures of the Kingdom, is conversion.

EVANGELIZATION

ROOT > The Church evangelises and keeps on proclaiming Christ as the Way, the Truth, and the Life. The Church is human and therefore is weak, yes; but still, it never tires of proclaiming Christ. If the world is not Catholic by denominational point of view, it is nonetheless deeply permeated by the Gospel. We can even say that the mystery of the Church is in some way invisibly present in the world. Hence, we need not lose hope. The Church may have suffered losses, and yet the future is bright. Such hope is the sign of the power of the Spirit.

> *"As the year 2000 approaches, our world feels an urgent need for the Gospel. Perhaps we feel this need precisely because the world seems to be distancing itself from the Gospel, or rather because the world has not yet drawn near to the Gospel" (John Paul II – CTH p.114).*

FRUIT > The majority of Catholics, these days, are not strongly inclined towards evangelization. One reason may be that the Catholic Church is highly institutional, sacramental, and hierarchical in its structures. Another reason could be that too many Catholics of our day seem never to have encountered Christ. They know something about him from the teaching of the Church, but they lack direct personal familiarity. Whatever may be the reason, we cannot forget that the Church is a means of drawing the whole world into union with God through Jesus Christ.

NEW EVANGELIZATION

Root > The new evangelization does not consist in a 'new gospel,' which would be equivalent to a human invention, which can't offer salvation. The new evangelization begins with the premise, that the riches in Christ are unsearchable which no culture, no age can exhaust, for these riches are Christ himself. All human beings can approach Christ through faith and through incorporation into his Church, and find answers to the mystery of human existence. The new evangelization undertakes to proclaim this Gospel, with new ardour, with solid faith and intense pastoral charity.

> *"There exists today the clear need for a new evangelization. There is the need for a proclamation of the Gospel capable of accompanying man on his pilgrim way, capable of walking alongside the younger generation" (John Paul II – CTH p. 117).*

Fruit > A good part of the new-evangelization is actually the re-evangelization of the baptised. When speaking of the danger of political and social ideologies that point to a false salvation in purely temporal terms, Pope John Paul II, told the bishops of Latin America in 1992: 'What will free us from these signs of death? Experience in the world today increasingly shows that ideologies are unable to defeat that evil which keeps people enslaved. Christ is the only one who can free us from this evil. It makes the task that the Church is facing more urgent: to rekindle in the heart of all the baptised the grace they received.'

NEW PENTECOST

ROOT > It is the Holy Spirit who brings God who is far away, near to us, and the Christ of the past history, into today's faith experience. Without him, the Gospel will remain a dead letter, the Church simply an organisation. Without him, authority is domination, not service, mission a matter of propaganda, the liturgy no more than an evocation and Christian living a moral slavery. The world itself that groans with the birth-pangs of the Kingdom, requires a New Pentecost to usher in the Kingdom.

> *"Just as the people of the new covenant received life through the Holy Spirit at Pentecost, only the Holy Spirit can now raise up a people capable of giving birth to men and women who are renewed and free, and conscious of their dignity"* (John Paul II – AHM 3).

FRUIT > All the baptised are called to fan into flame the gift of the Holy Spirit which we received at our Baptism. We received it free from God, but for the Holy Spirit to become active in us, we need to personally respond to the Lord's call to conversion. We need to open our hearts and minds to the transforming power of the Spirit in our daily lives. Only with the help of the Holy Spirit, the Church can adequately respond to its pastoral needs and those of the world.

FOR A NEW WORLD

root > With the development of science and technology we can now solve long standing problems of hunger, ignorance and disease. A dense network of relationships draws the multitude together. We are marching towards personal freedom and of united human race. And yet, new forms of oppression bear down upon us. Technology plunders the world's natural resources, exploitation pollutes the environment, and the dignity of the person is more publicised than respected. Does our common human enterprise have any meaning? It does, because the Holy Spirit is also working in the world for the dawn of the New Kingdom in Christ.

> *"To accept the Gospel's demands means to affirm all of our humanity, to see in it the beauty desired by God, while at the same time recognising, in the light of the power of God himself, our weaknesses: 'What is impossible for men is possible for God' (Lk 18:27)" (John Paul II – CTH p. 223).*

Fruit > A father reading his Sunday paper and wishing not to be disturbed by his little girl, cut up a map of the world, gave it to her, and told her to put it together. After awhile she returned with it, and every place was in its place. The father was very much surprised and said: "Why, how did you do it, darling? You don't know anything about geography." The little one replied, "There was a picture of Jesus on the other side, and I knew, when I had Jesus in the right place, the whole world would be all right."

October:

THE CRISIS OF CIVILISATION

Week 1
The Crisis

Week 2
Religious Indifference

Week 3
Loss of Higher Values

Week 4
The Return

SECULARISM

ROOT > This is a secularised society we live in. There is so
much to enjoy in our world, and we have the time to get
into it. We all have time, money and leisure to find ways of
fulfilling ourselves, without getting mixed up with religion.
Secularism drives people to become insensitive to eternal
things. It also leads to a consumer mentality which craves
for earthly goods. A thoroughly secularised individual makes
himself or herself the exclusive measure of all things without
referring to God, from whom all things come and to whom
all things return, and thus they become slaves to their own
finite state.

> *"Unbelief and secularisation pose challenges which ought
> to be taken up by all believers, for they are called to witness
> together to God's primacy in all things" (John Paul II –
> AHM 4).*

FRUIT > There are twelve steps that the members of the
'Alcoholic Anonymous' have to take to help them come to
terms with their problem. The first step, is that they have
to admit that they are powerless to help themselves. The
second, is that they must believe in a power greater than
their own, God, who alone can help them. The third, is that
they have to turn their lives over to God. These steps
suppose that there can be no renewal in our lives, unless we
are able to see and admit to our own utter weakness as
finite beings, and accept God's primacy in all things.

MATERIALISM

ROOT > Materialists believe that what there is, is only matter. All that matters is mater. Reality is to be understood in purely material terms. Because all that there is only matter, there is therefore no reality in religion, or morality or aesthetics. There is no real mind, soul or feeling. All these have no actual existence. All these things can be reduced to matter without remainder. For example, love is just a chemical reaction. Since those who understand matter are scientists, if you want to understand what things really are, ask the scientist.

> *"Today an invasive materialism is imposing its dominion on us in many different forms and with an aggressiveness sparing nó one. Human beings cannot be reduced to the sphere of their material needs. Progress cannot be reduced to material values alone. The human being's spiritual dimensions must have its rightful place" (John Paul II – AHM 5).*

FRUIT > Materialists waste their energy in unrewarding efforts. Setting all their affections on material things, they try them all in turn, before they dream of trying God from whom all things proceed. It is however a practical impossibility, to make such a trial of all other things, before we turn to God. Life is too short, our strength is too limited, the number of competitors for this world's goods too great; so long a journey and such unfruitful toil, would wear us out. We would be much wiser to seek God first.

HUMANISM

ROOT > Humanists hold that human beings are self-sufficient. They need nothing else. Human beings are autonomous, in the sense of being free to make their own laws. They believe that humanity can find all the answers for itself, because these are only answers people can understand, and certainly the only ones they can live with. Humanity is free. Human beings can do all things if they exercise their will. In short, humanity is the standard of everything. Human beings create God, morality and everything else.

> *"Humanisation of human being is putting the human being in the place of God, thus 'deifying' humanity. It is a temptation to confer the Creator's divinity on human beings (made in God's image and likeness) to take God's place with the 'divinisation' of humanity against God or without God"* (John Paul II – AHM 6).

FRUIT > Those who think and live as if they are self-sufficient, become interiorly divided and drained of their spiritual strengths. Their soul is darkened and alien spirits take possession of it. The flowering of humanity is possible only so long as the human persons are not cut off altogether from their divine roots. The persons who have lost God give themselves up to something inhuman, prostrate themselves before material necessity. What humanism sets free is not the human person, but those dark spirits from the deep, which beat upon human person, like waves from every side.

EXISTENTIALISM

ROOT > The existentialists say they are overwhelmed by a feeling of anxiety and dread. According to them, there are two particular areas of life which tend to lead people to the experience of anxiety and dread and to commit suicide. Those areas are: the experience of pointless suffering and the lack of any sense and meaning in existence. However, one can retort them saying that if everything is really meaningless, then what they think and say about human existence, is also meaningless!

> *"Christ is the image of the unseen God, the first-born of all creation, for in him were created all things in heaven or on earth: everything visible and everything invisible, thrones, ruling forces, sovereignties and powers, all things were created through him and for him" (Col 1:15-16).*

FRUIT > Why should I not commit suicide? Because God made me. Because God entered into human existence. Because Jesus, the God-man, died for me. Because his resurrection ensures that death is not an end, but there is victory over the grave. Because that same Jesus summons me to follow in his footsteps and to be conformed to his likeness. As he summons me, I am called upon to choose Jesus Christ. Therefore, there is meaning and purpose in life. That meaning stems from a living relationship with the eternal God.

RELATIVISM

Root > Relativism turns many people into sceptics. Objective moral values and reference-points are hardly acknowledged. Individualism and subjectivism become the dominant factors in ethical thought and decision, making certain types of behaviour as normal and morally acceptable, just because they are common to vast number of people. Many have concluded that there is no such thing as absolute truth, because we all see things differently in the end. The result is a kind of despair. Everyone puts together his or her personal world-view and it is no one else's business.

> *"To what extent have the People of God been shaped by the climate of secularism and ethical relativism? And what responsibility do they bear, in view of the increasing lack of religion, for not having shown the true face of God, having failed in their religious, moral, or social life?" (John Paul II – TMA 36).*

Fruit > There are two big problems with the conclusion that there is no absolute truth. The first, is that we all have self-fulfilment at the top of our list of things, that are true for ourselves personally. Therefore we now live in a society full of people whose top priority is themselves. The second is that our inability to find truth does not actually mean that truth does not exist at all; it only means that we can't find it because we are fallen, and hence we need help. And the help came in Jesus who said that he is the Way, the Truth, and the Life.

ANARCHISM

ROOT > All anarchists are committed to the utmost freedom. They reject authority. To be precise and fair, the anarchists claim to be rejecting authoritarianism, but in the end, it seems to reduce to an attack on authority itself. The word 'anarchy' literally means 'no rule' or 'absence of rules.' Many anarchists are professional demonstrators and agitators who take up a worthwhile cause, not for its own sake, but as a means of creating disorder and destructions, and as a direct challenge to the power of those who are in authority. It is crass embodiment of disharmony.

> *"Everyone is to obey the governing authorities, because there is no authority except from God and so whatever authorities exist, have been appointed by God. So anyone who disobeys an authority is rebelling against God's ordinance" (Rom 13:1-2).*

FRUIT > During the time people live without common authority to preserve order, they are in that condition which is called war, one person against another. I think, most people, after a little freedom, have preferred authority, for they realise obedience to authority makes them truly free, because all legitimate authority derives its power from God. Therefore, obedience to authority is not only the touchstone of all progress, but it is the only safe course. God uses broken soil to produce plants, and broken clouds to produce rain. He wants our stubbornness broken too, into humble obedience to produce peace.

NATIONALISM

ROOT > Christians are called to live for God and Christ by following the honourable customs of their nation and as good citizens, to practise true and effective patriotism. At the same time, they are expected to avoid racial prejudice and bitter nationalism, fostering instead universal love for all people. Citizens need to develop a generous and loyal devotion to their country but without any narrowing of mind. That is, we are always to look simultaneously to the welfare of our nation and of the human family.

> *"In the countries of the former Eastern block, after the fall of communism, there appears the serious threat of exaggerated nationalism. This obliges us to make a serious examination of conscience and to acknowledge faults and errors, both economic and political" (John Paul II – TMA 27).*

FRUIT > Fanatical or bitter nationalism is like a silly cock crowing on its own dunghill. Bitter nationalism is a form of incest, idolatry and insanity. Bitter nationalists have broad hatred and narrow love towards people of other nations. Where there is the lowest degree of culture, you find fanatical nationalists. The efficiency of a truly national leader, consists primarily in preventing one's own nation from being alienated from the rest of the humankind. If I wish the greatness of my own country only, soon I begin to wish evil to neighbouring nations.

INNER EMPTINESS

ROOT > While wonderful in its continued conquests, technology often has impoverished people in their essential human life, for it deprives of their inner, spiritual dimension, stifling their sense of true and higher values. The primacy of the spiritual is being questioned. We can notice this in modern trends of opinions, fashions, and social communication media. They often excuse everything which leads to unbounded permissiveness. As a result the only point of reference seems to be what is conducive to the well-being of the individual.

> *"The crisis of civilisation has become apparent especially in the West which is highly developed from the standpoint of technology but is interiorly impoverished by its tendency to forget God and to keep him at a distance"* (John Paul II – TMA 52).

FRUIT > More and more people are suffering from inner emptiness. This is true as much for those within the Church, as for those outside its walls. This may sound surprising, when we have experienced major Church renewal movements which have focused on new life in the Spirit. The reason could be that much of the renewal movements has not produced a depth of spirituality, a passion for God's Kingdom of justice and mercy, and a prayer life which expresses itself in costly discipleship and servanthood. Has 'life in the Spirit' become a comfortable self-seeking and 'me-centred' form of spirituality?

FAITH UNDER PRESSURE

ROOT > Imagine a goldfish in a tank. As long as the water is reasonably pure, it will survive and thrive. But if we introduce tiny quantities of toxic waste, the fish will eventually die. We are in the same situation. We are surrounded by an atmosphere of unbelief. Without knowing, we are breathing its toxins. As a result, we are all under some pressure to give up faith. We are struggling to believe. But Jesus tells us to persevere in the struggle, because it is not so hopeless and the fight can be won.

> *"As for the part in the rich soil, this people with a noble and generous heart who have heard the Word, and take it to themselves and yield a harvest through their perseverance"* (Lk 8:15).

FRUIT > When we feel that our faith is under pressure, we can do two things. First, persevere despite the pressures on your faith, because there will come a time when they will lessen and you will have won. The second, is to be willing to listen to God in the Scriptures, and act on what he says, because faith thrives when we listen to God's word. While spinning above the fatal abyss, a solo climber has a choice: can he believe the voice or not? It all depends whether he can trust what he hears. Likewise, if you are moving on the edge of unbelief, the safest thing is to listen, and trust the voice you hear in the Scriptures.

DOUBTS

ROOT > Many accept that there are reasons to believe in God; but as many have maintained that there are also reasons to doubt, or even deny his existence. They ask: Why does not he reveal himself more clearly? Why does not he give everyone more tangible and accessible proof of his existence? The answer is that through our own wisdom which God has shared with us we can know him, for he has revealed himself in some manner in creation, though he has not revealed all of his mystery. But definitively, God's self-revelation has come about, by his becoming man in Christ.

> *"How can we remain silent about the religious indifference which causes many people today to live as if God did not exist, or to be content with a vague religiosity, incapable of coming into grips with the question of truth"* (John Paul II – TMA 36).

FRUIT > If we do not clear our doubt about God at its initial stage, it will drive us to edge of unbelief step by step. The first is spiritual indifference; you feel unconcerned about religion, and cold in worship and you stop reading the Bible. In the second step, it takes you beyond coldness in worship, to cynicism about other Christians; you wonder how they can be so fervent when you cannot, and conclude that they are all fooling themselves. In the third stage, you start envying people who are not Christians, for you think that they are free to enjoy themselves, while you are shackled with irrelevant rules.

ATHEISM

ROOT > Atheism is one of the most serious problems of our time. It rejects and denies the existence of God. It refuses to accept human being's dependence on God. It has many forms: One is practical materialism which restricts human needs to material things. Another is atheistic humanism, which considers human beings as an end to themselves, with supreme control of one's own history. Another form looks for the liberation of human beings solely through economic and social liberation.

> *"Materialistic ideologies on the one hand and moral permissiveness on the other have led many people to believe that it is possible to build a new and better society while excluding God. However experience shows us all too clearly that without God, society is dehumanised and the human person is deprived of his or her greatest riches"* (John Paul II – AHM 7).

FRUIT > One of the reasons why people keep God at arm's length, is their subconscious fear of his judgement and condemnation. But the true image of God that we see in the Scriptures is different. "If you will not listen, my soul will weep in secret for your pride; my eyes will weep bitterly and run down with tears, because the Lord's flock has been taken captive" (Jer 13:17). Such passages give us the true image of God. Time and again, we get glimpses of how God feels, when we refuse to let him love us and to provide for us.

AGNOSTICISM

ROOT > Agnostics ask: "Why is not there more concrete proof of God's existence? Why does he seem to hide himself, almost playing with his creation? Should it not all be much simpler? Should not his existence be obvious?" Agnosticism is not systematic atheism. Instead of denying God, it postulates the existence of a transcendent being, which cannot reveal itself, and about which we can say nothing. Agnostics in general do not pass any judgement on the existence of God, but declare that it is impossible to affirm or deny.

> *"Agnosticism can sometime include a certain search for God, but it can equally express indifferentism, a flight from the ultimate question of existence, and a sluggish moral conscience. Agnosticism is all too often equivalent to practical atheism"* (CCC 2128).

FRUIT > Doubts and fears are like toothache, nothing more painful, but never fatal. There is only one creature that God has made, that ever doubts him. The sparrows don't doubt. They sweetly sing at night as they go to their roosts, though they know not where tomorrow's meal will be found. The very cattle trust him, and even in days of drought you have seen them how they pant for thirst expecting water. But it was left for human being, the most favoured of all creatures, to doubt his God.

RATIONALISM

ROOT > Rationalists want to live by reason alone, as if God does not exist. For them, God is not necessary, because his existence as Creator or his Providence, is in no way helpful to science. If God exists, he is not interested in the world, and hence it is necessary to act as if God did not exist. If some rationalists accept a God outside of the world, it is primarily because he is an unverifiable hypothesis. Therefore, such a God must be expelled from the world, according to them.

> *"Only those who accept their intellectual and moral limitations and recognise their need for salvation, can make themselves open to faith, and in faith encounter, in Christ, their Redeemer"* (John Paul II – AHM 8).

FRUIT > The existence of God can be known by natural reason, but our knowledge is often obscured by error; hence, faith comes to enlighten reason in the correct understanding of the truth. Beyond the natural knowledge that every person can have of the Creator, God progressively revealed himself to humanity, but you need faith to accept this self-revelation of God. Faith often outreaches reason, but it does not outrage it, for both are God's gifts, one supernatural and the other natural. The grace of faith opens the eyes of my heart, whereas the gift of reason opens the eyes of my mind. God never contradicts reason, he transcends it.

THE LAST THINGS

ROOT > The Church believes in the existence of heaven as the dwelling place of God, the place of the saints, and of angels who surround God. It affirms the existence of hell and its eternity. Immediately after death the souls of those who die in a state of mortal sin descend into hell, where they suffer the punishment of hell for all eternity. The chief punishment of hell is eternal separation from God. The resurrection of all the dead of both the just and unjust, will precede the Last Judgement, which will come when Christ returns in glory.

> *"People of our time have become insensitive to the Last Things. On the one hand, secularisation and secularism promote this insensitivity; on the other hand, the 'hells on earth' created in this century have also constituted to this insensitivity" (John Paul II – CTH p. 183).*

FRUIT > First, the doctrine of heaven, hell and judgement, reminds us we are given desperately important choices. It matters whether we decide to follow Christ or not. Secondly, this doctrine reminds us that our choice for God is not once and for all. It is a daily decision. Thirdly, it is a doctrine of hope. We know that no one will go to hell unless, in a sense, they have decided that is what they want. A person who truly wants to love God and to be with God for ever, will be given the grace and help, to fulfil that best of all desires.

CATHOLIC UNBELIEF

ROOT > In many Catholics, a remarkable weakening of faith in God as a person, is noticeable. The result is that their faith in Jesus Christ as the Son of God is also being eroded. They find it difficult to accept the Church as a Sacrament. As a consequence of all these, they tend to equate spirituality with philanthropy and social action, and give not much importance to prayer life. Not only lay people but also some male and female religious, are getting involved in more and more social action, equating it to missionary work.

> *"Faith already put to test by the challenge of our times, is sometimes disoriented by erroneous theological views, the spread of which is abetted by the crisis of obedience vis-à-vis the Church's Magisterioum" (John Paul II – TMA 36).*

FRUIT > When we decide that God is getting in the way of what we want to do, unbelief follows sooner or later, and our doubts can give us a convenient smokescreen to hide our selfishness. In Jesus' story about the field of corn, the birds, weeds and desert heat, each represents the forces at work to 'squeeze the faith out of us.' Some of us who responds to God's Word, are drawn away by what Jesus called 'life's worries, riches and pleasures'. In other words, the world is full of things that compete with God for control of our lives.

HUMAN LIFE

ROOT > Human life is not an egoistic possession, but a gift to welcome with gratitude, not an arbitrary game but a project of love, not a meaningless accident but a vocation to be realised, not a problem hard to solve but a mystery to wonder. In a world that seems to despise, reject, humiliate, and kill life, the Christians are called to accept the Good News which welcomes, defends, protects and gives life. We are called to have an attitude of compassion towards the neediest, in order to oppose a culture that increasingly promotes war, tension, hatred, violence, division and death.

> *"Human life is sacred because, from its origin it implies the creative action of God and remains for ever in a special relationship with the Creator, its one and only purpose" (CDF 5).*

FRUIT > We must support any woman with a problem pregnancy, both during the pregnancy and afterwards. We should have compassion for those who have recourse to abortion – they are victims of our selfish society and need help. But abortion is killing of human life in the womb. From the very first century onwards, the killing of the unborn and the newly born child was forbidden. And yet, respect for life is now so eroded that abortion can happen where the sex of the child is not what the parents wanted.

HUMAN PERSON

ROOT > Every human person is created in the image of God and is endowed with a rational soul. Each has been redeemed by the sacrifice of Christ and has been called to participate in the same divine beatitude. This is human dignity. All are equal, as they have the same nature and origin, from which the inalienable human rights flow. Hence, every form of social or cultural discrimination in basic human rights, must be curbed, for that would be incompatible with God's design.

> *"The laity are called to contribute to the promotion of the person, for this is particularly necessary and urgent today. It is a question of saving – and often re-establishing – the central value of the human being who, precisely because of being a person, can never be treated as an object to be used, or as a means or as a thing" (John Paul II – ChL 37).*

FRUIT > A person convinced of the dignity of another human being, can take this practical resolution: "Brother, sister I am beside you; I will be Christ to you; I pray for the grace to let you be as Christ to me. I will listen when you are speaking. I will grow to accept that your ideas too are valid. I will think about the meaning which you are trying to convey. I will share your problems with you; I will help you to face oppression. I will always remember that God made you and I will not take that dignity away."

HUMAN RIGHTS

ROOT > Human rights is a consequence of human dignity, which flows from the fact that the human person is created in the image of God, gifted with freedom, redeemed by Christ and destined to be with God for ever. When the Son of God took on human nature, and paid the supreme price for us all, he confirmed the human rights simply by restoring us to our dignity, as created in the image and likeness of God. The Gospel of Christ is the fullest confirmation of all human rights, when it commands us to love one another as Christ has loved us.

> *"The commandment of love is not limited to excluding all behaviour that reduces the person to mere object of pleasure. It requires more; it requires the affirmation of the person as a person" (John Paul II – CTH p. 201).*

FRUIT > Injustices are committed worldwide against human rights. In 1997 *Amnesty International* ran a refugee campaign highlighting an estimated 15 million refugees worldwide fleeing violence and a further 20 million people forced out of their homes but not out of their country. A refugee is produced every 21 seconds. World figures for 1980s show that 80% of war dead are unarmed civilians. However appalling may be the situation of injustice in the world, it is our Christian hope that one day justice will triumph, and human rights be restored.

HUMAN BODY

ROOT > Human body shares in the dignity of the image of God in which a person is created. It is animated by a spiritual soul. It is someone, in the sense that it is the manifestation of the person, a means of being present to other people. It is the whole human person that is intended to become, in the body of Christ, a temple of the Spirit. Therefore, we owe respect and love for our body, and cannot despise our bodily life. Rather, we are obliged to regard our body as good and to hold it in honour, since God who created it, will also raise it up on the last day.

> *"Have great respect for your own bodies and for those of others! Let your body be at the service of your inner self! Control of the body! Yes! Transfiguration of the body! Even more so!" (John Paul II – AHM 9).*

FRUIT > If anything is sacred, human body is sacred, but we have a soul too. There are two things that a master commits to his servant's care: the child and the child's clothes. It would be a poor excuse for the servant to say at his master's return, "Sir, here are all the child's clothes, neat and clean, but the child is lost!" Would it be the same way, with the account many of us will give to God of our souls and bodies at the last day? "Lord, here is my body. I neglected nothing that belonged to its content and welfare. But as for my soul, that is lost. I took little care of it."

SEX

ROOT > Sexuality belongs to the original plan of the Creator, and hence it needs to be held in high esteem and respected in its deepest nature. Sexuality is not mere instinct, rather, it is a specific language in the service of love. It has to be controlled by intelligent and free human beings. It is directed either to fellowship between man and woman or to the birth of new persons. This truth is evident, even to the light of reason and therefore, free love, homosexuality, and contraception are morally unacceptable.

> *"Sexuality affects all aspects of the human person in the unity of his body and soul. It especially concerns affectivity, the capacity to love and to procreate, and in a more general way the aptitude for forming bonds of communion with others" (CCC 2332).*

FRUIT > In society today, there is an increasing approval of pre-marital sex. Dating for many has become a time for exploring each other's bodies, instead of each other's mind, feelings, beliefs, values and expectations. Love is reduced to sex and there is a de-emphasis on respect, responsibility and care. What is assumed to be sexual freedom really is increasing bondage to one's physiological drives. By ignoring the divine standards that free us for maximum life fulfilment, many have cast away their freedom and settled for a biological enslavement.

MARRIAGE

ROOT > Marriage is a vocation which calls the couple to learn marital love day by day, a love according to soul and body. When the soul is taken away from marital love, husband and wife, especially the wife, is changed from subject into object, and all of love's great content is reduced to enjoyment. Marriage is the place for begetting and bringing up of children. In begetting children, husband and wife collaborate with their Creator's love. In family planning, husband and wife are called to responsible parenthood, which respects the ethical norms and criteria.

> *"The materialistic, consumerist civilisation penetrated this marvellous whole of conjugal, fatherly and motherly love, robbing it of that deeply humane content, which since the beginning of the world has been pervaded by a mark and reflection of the divine" (John Paul II – AHM 10).*

FRUIT > The joy of marriage cannot be identified with the pleasures of the marriage bed. True joy comes from couple's experience, that when they make love something bigger than the two happens. This most physical way to express their love for each other, is the most spiritual way too. This is because we are not just bodies with souls rattling around inside us some place. The body is not just the temporary home for the soul. We are embodied spirits. Anything that affects the body affects the soul. Hence sex in marriage is a spiritual exercise.

COMMUNITY

ROOT > Every one of us necessarily lives in two worlds. We live within the four walls of the place that we call home, and where our companions are the members of our own family. This is our private world. But equally, we have to go out of our house and home, and have to live in a public world. I am not only a member of a family; I am also a member of a community, a state, a world. I am not only a private person; I am a public citizen. Hence we have duties and responsibilities, both to our private home and to the community at large.

> *"I am not asking you to remove them from the world, but to protect them from the Evil One"* (Jn 17:15).

FRUIT > While being a citizen of the world-community, we have to keep in mind that, though we live our life in the world fully, what gives this world a value and significance, is the end which is beyond this world. Hence, as Christians, we need to have an attitude to the world which combines involvement and detachment. We are involved in the world and its life as Jesus was; but at the same time, to him the world is not everything. It is the threshold to a larger and a wider life which begins when this life ends.

MORALS

ROOT > God has given to every human being moral or natural laws engraved in the soul of each person. This law enables us to discern by reason the good and the evil, the truth and the lie. Its principle precepts are expressed in the Ten Commandments. This law is nothing other than the light of understanding. Through it, we know what we must do and what we must avoid. This law, present in the heart of each one and established by reason, is universal in its application, and extends its authority to all people.

> *"But this command of the human reason would not have the force of law if it were not the voice of and interpreter of a higher reason to which our spirit and freedom must be submitted" (Leo XIII).*

FRUIT > Morality is not the custom of one's country, and the current feeling of one's peers. It comes from God, and hence it is the same everywhere. Morals is not an acquirement like music, but each person is born with it. Morality is practical, not a gesture, worse still a complicated gesture, learnt from books. It is a way of living, and those who live it will instinctively feel good and powerful. But we must never delude ourselves into thinking that physical power is a substitute to moral power. A breakdown in moral order leads to a breakdown in civil order. Without civic morality, communities perish, and without personal morality their survival has no value.

TURNING FROM EVIL

ROOT > To come out unscathed from the crisis of civilisation, and start living a fuller human life, what is required is conversion, a turning away from evil, a radical re-orientation of our whole life to God with all our heart. Repentance is the beginning of conversion, and true repentance entails the desire and resolution to change one's life, with hope in God's mercy and trust in the help of his grace. The movement of return to God entails also sorrow for our wayward life, and a firm purpose of amendment in the future.

> *"Authentic conversion includes both a 'negative' aspect, that of liberation from sin, and a 'positive' aspect, that of choosing good, accepting the ethical values expressed in the natural law, which is confirmed and defended by Gospel" (John Paul II – TMA 50).*

FRUIT> Repentance and conversion are not that easy. Take just one example: our human relationship. There may be many people with whom I am not still at peace, for no matter how well we try, we don't arrive at a happy solution. We have gone to admit our faults and sought forgiveness, but disharmony continues to linger. And sometimes, the harder we try to make things right, the worse it gets. Frequently the difficulty is, that we do not quite know what is really amiss. We are aware of the symptoms, but the ability to speak heart to heart is wanting. At such times, we need to ask God for help.

TRUSTING IN GOD'S MERCY

ROOT > God is our Father. He did not put us on earth to collect merits and rewards, but that we may discover that we are his children. We are born frail; from the start of our life, we tend to be led by our feelings, and the bad example of society in which we have been raised. God is not surprised at our weakness, since in creating us free, he accepted the risk that we might fall. But he is with all of us, in our experience of good and evil, until he can call us his sons and daughters, thanks to his Son Jesus.

> *"The Incarnation of the Son of God attests that God goes in search of man. If God goes in search of man, he does so because he loves him eternally in the Word, and wishes to raise him in Christ to the dignity of adoptive son" (John Paul II – TMA 7).*

FRUIT > After having resolutely turned to God and have begun walking on his way, we may still find ourselves on the way, enveloped by darkness. Have you seen nature, when the dawn begins to break through: a blackened sky with a faint light in the distance suddenly begins to spread, first creating an eerie of half light producing shadows, then breaking out into a radiant and dominating light that banishes all shadows and darkness, and makes everything visible? Similarly, for those who trust in God, even when dark shadows surround them, a sunrise is a promise.

CONFIDENT IN GOD'S GRACE

Root > Grace is favour, the free and undeserved help, that God gives us to respond to his call to become his children, and partakers of his divine nature. Grace being a participation in the life of God, it introduces us into intimate relationship with the Holy Trinity. This grace of Christ is infused by the Holy Spirit into our soul at our Baptism, to cleanse it from sin and sanctify it. Therefore, the grace of God is in us, as the source of strength to return to God. Hence, confident in the power of that grace, we must make every effort to repent and return to God.

> *"The divine initiative in the work of grace, prepares and elicits the free response of man. Grace responds to the deepest yearnings of human freedom, calls freedom to co-operate with it and perfects freedom"* (CCC 2022).

Fruit > Be confident in the power of God's grace, as you walk towards him. The grace of God can work in marvellous ways, even through electronic channels. A young man had been for some time under a sense of guilt, longing to find mercy; but he could not reach it. He was a telegraph clerk, and being in the office one morning, he had to receive and transmit a telegram. To his great surprise, he spelled out these words: "Behold the lamb of God who takes away the sin of the world." A gentleman out for a holiday, was telegraphing a message, in answer to a letter from a friend who was in trouble of soul. It was meant for another, but he who transmitted it received life, as the words came flashing into his soul.

TOWARDS GOD

ROOT > When the human heart has distanced itself from God, it feels heavy and requires almost a new heart to begin anew the journey towards God, but God can give a new heart. The grace of God which already indwells a believer provides this new heart, enabling us to return to him pleading, in the words of the Scripture: "Restore us to thyself, O Lord, that we may be restored" (Lam 5:21). As the heart resolutely turns towards God, it begins to discover the greatness of God's love, begins to fear offending God and being separated from him.

> *"The sense of being on a journey to the Father, should encourage everyone to undertake, by holding fast to Christ the Redeemer of man, a journey of authentic conversion" (John Paul II – TMA 50).*

FRUIT > Turning our hearts to God is the first step on our journey, towards full life of happiness. But turning alone is not enough. We much choose God, preferring him to all other things, such as wealth, power, position, self-seeking, pride and the rest. Choosing is willing. Our will is ever free to follow our inclinations. It is simply the engine in the car. It can't steer. It is the person who has to steer it. So, with all the strengths of our will, we must choose God's will above all other things in life. The more one enters into the will of God, the closer the person is with the life of God.

REPENTANT CHRISTIANS

Root > Christ's call to conversion continues to resound in the lives of Christians. We can call it, 'the second conversion' which is an uninterrupted task for the whole Church. Christians are called to repent for the responsibilities they too have for the evils of today, especially for the grave forms of injustice and discrimination that exist in society. In this respect, we must repent for our failure to put into practice the principles of the Church's social doctrine. It is necessary to ask God's forgiveness, also for the part we have played for the disunity in the Church.

> *"Among the sins which require greater commitment to repentance and conversion should certainly be counted those which have been detrimental to unity willed by God for his people. Even more than in the first millennium, ecclesial communion has been painfully wounded"* (John Paul II – TMA 34).

Fruit > The vision of God for the human race as one people and one world, will be realised. But visions are funny things. They never work unless you do. God's vision of united world and Christ's own death to make it come true, will become a reality, if we make his vision our own and practise today the vision of tomorrow, especially, by working for unity among Christians themselves. Our work for unity may be small and insignificant. But it is needed. As from little fountains large streams flow, and as from little acorns tall oaks grow, so our little actions will mould the world of tomorrow.

REPENTANT CATHOLICS

Root > The Catholic Church, the bride of Christ, the light of salvation, should become more than any other Christian Churches, fully conscious of the sinfulness of her children. Her children have in the past departed from the spirit of Christ and his Gospel. She has failed to offer the world the witness of life, inspired by the values of faith. She has instead indulged in acts of counter witness. The Church must also repent for the part she has played, in the break up of Christian unity.

> *"For the Church, acknowledging the weakness of the past is an act of honesty and courage which helps us to strengthen our faith, which alerts us to take today's temptations and challenges and prepares us to meet them"* (John Paul II – TMA 33).

Fruit > Once I was at the General Post Office. I had bought some stamps, went to the high table on the other side of the hall, and was sticking the stamps on. Next to me two ladies were talking to each other. I did not want to listen in, but I could not help it for they were so loud. I don't know their complete conversation; I only heard one say, "You know, they are Catholics, of course, they think they have the truth, the way and the life, they have no time for us." "Yes", I heard the other answer, "Silly, isn't it?", and after that I heard nothing more. We Catholics need to repent for our share in the break up of Christian unity.

RECONCILIATION

ROOT > For the first time, we experience God's forgiveness at our Baptism. But there is a necessity in every Christian life, to experience this forgiveness again and again, for we are living in a world trapped in moral crisis, in which conscience seems to have eclipsed. Without a healthy awareness of our human frailty, it is not also possible to experience God's redeeming love in Christ. Only God's grace can really heal the conflict, which human frailty causes in human heart. And this grace of God is available in the Sacrament of Reconciliation.

> *"Purify your hearts in the Sacrament of Reconciliation. Sacramental Confession is not repression but liberation; it does not revive feelings of guilt, but wipes guilt out; it cancels the evil committed and bestows the grace of forgiveness"* (John Paul II – AHM 11).

FRUIT > Millions of Hindus, covered with sacred ash plunge into the river Ganges in Northern India on a particular day during the 15-week long *Kumb Mela* or pitcher festival, held every 12 years in the city of Hardwar. They believe that the freezing water from the Himalayas will wash away their sins, and help them achieve *nirvana* or freedom from the cycle of death and rebirth, in a century old ritual. The line of bathers stretches for miles across 30 bridges built for them across the Ganges in the city of Hardwar. Christian faith affirms that only Christ can forgive sins, and the Catholic Church believes that he washes away our sins normally at the Sacrament of Reconciliation.

A CULTURE OF HOPE

Root > Unjust wars, divisions among people, the almost irreversible poverty of some continents, eroding of solidarity with the needy, growing unemployment, violent interference with nature, contagious diseases spread in perverse ways, widespread use of drug, all such things have plunged the world into anguish and fear for the future. But as Christians we believe that there is someone who holds us in his hands, and the destiny of the passing world. We pitch our hope in Christ, who can't allow humankind to dissolve into nothingness, but will take us into an existence full of happiness in God.

> *"Have no fear of that which you yourselves have created, have no fear of all that man has produced, and that everyday is becoming more dangerous for him! Finally, have no fear of yourselves" (John Paul II – CTH, 219).*

Fruit > John Paul II, lists some of the things which are signs of hope for our world today: In civil society, the progress made by science, technology and medicine, the keener sense of responsibility towards environment, the efforts to establish peace and justice, the resolute desire for reconciliation and solidarity among peoples. In the Church, a more attentive listening to the voice of the Spirit, intense devotion to the cause of Christian unity and attempts made to dialogue with non-Christian religions and contemporary culture. Yes, in times of trouble we must not turn away our face from hope, for the soft marrow abides in the hard bone.

November:

BACK TO BASICS

Week 1
Faith

Week 2
Scriptures

Week 3
Prayer

Week 4
Family

FAITH IN GOD

ROOT > God is the beginning and end of all things. God is the Father, the first divine Person of the Holy Trinity. Creation is the foundation of all God's works. God is one in nature, substance and essence. God revealed himself progressively to his people under the name, 'I AM', which means he is always present to his people to save them. God is merciful and gracious. He is truth which is wisdom by which who governs the whole created order. He is love and his love for his people is stronger than a mother's for her children. His love is everlasting.

> *"The Jubilee celebration should confirm the Christians of today in their faith in God who has revealed himself in Christ, sustain their hope which reaches out in expectation of eternal life, and rekindle their charity in active service to their brothers and sisters" (John Paul II – TMA 26).*

FRUIT > Faith is to our soul what a main spring is to a watch. It is the identifying mark of a Christian. It means coming to know God's greatness and majesty. It means living in thanksgiving. It means knowing the unity and true dignity of all human beings, for everyone is made in the likeness of God. It means making good use of created things, in so far as they bring us closer to him. It means trusting God in every circumstance. Faith is not shelter against difficulties, but trust in the face of all difficulties.

FAITH IN CHRIST

ROOT > Christian belief in God is inseparable from belief in Jesus Christ, his 'beloved Son' in whom the Father is 'well pleased' and to whom the Father asks us to 'listen' (Mk 1:11). The Lord Jesus himself told his disciples: "You believe in God, believe also in me" (Jn 14:1). We believe in Jesus Christ because he himself is God, the Word made flesh. "No one has ever seen God; it is the only Son who is close to the Father's heart, who has made him known" (Jn 1:18). Jesus is the only one who knows God and one who can reveal him.

> *"Christ is the centre of the Christian faith. Jesus reveals the Father's love to us. But the Truth is Jesus Christ. Love the Truth! Live in the Truth! Carry the Truth to the world! Be witnesses to the Truth! Jesus is the Truth that saves us. He is the whole Truth to which the Spirit of Truth will lead us" (John Paul II – AHM 12).*

FRUIT > The Truth of Christ is light to the world, and we are called to be like little stars, that shed Christ's light in the world. A star is concentrated energy. It does not simply twinkle in the sky but burns with an incredible intensity. Even after it has expired, after all that matter has been burned away, the light it produced continues on, through the darkness of the cosmos. In the same way, the good we do, the peace we make, can travel distances we can't even imagine. It can inspire others to look for the light of Truth. And even after we are dead, the example we set, the life we lived, can be like the light from a star that no longer exists.

ECCLESIAL FAITH

ROOT > 'Believing' for a Christian, is an ecclesial act. The Church's faith precedes our faith. It is the Church that believes first and nourishes and sustains our faith. She, the pillar of truth, guards our faith as she guards the memory of Christ's words. Having received the faith from the Apostles and their disciples, from generation to generation she hands on the faith. She teaches us the language of faith, in order to introduce us to the understanding and the life of faith. The Church is the mother of all believers.

> *"I urge you to preserve intact your faith in Jesus the Saviour. Listen carefully to his Gospel which the Church continues preaching to you with unchanging fidelity to what has been taught from the beginning"* (John Paul II – AHM 13).

FRUIT > "My conversion to the Catholic Church," said Malcolm Maggaridge, "in a sense, is a homecoming; of picking up the threads of a lost life; of responding to a bell that has long been ringing; of finding a place at a table that has long been vacant." The Church helps us to keep a sky in our life, and to look up, to keep our hand in God's, and hold on to him; to see the eternal values above the material, to lift our life above self to the service of Christ; to test the motive of life and choose the best; to do what is just, to love mercy and to walk humbly.

FAITH AND REASON

ROOT > It is God who reveals mysteries and infuses faith. He has also bestowed reason to human beings. But, God who is truth cannot contradict himself. In other words, there can be no conflict between faith and reason. It follows, then, all branches of scientific research, as long as they are carried out in true scientific manner, and do not override moral laws, can never contradict faith. On the contrary, God who is the author of both the things of the world and the things of the reason, leads by hand a humble and conscientious researcher, into discovering and understanding truth.

"Reason is finite and cannot do everything of itself. However, the 'learned and the clever' believe they know all there is to know about God, that they have the final answer, that they have nothing more to learn. And that is why they reject the Good News" (John Paul II – AHM 14).

FRUIT > All science is essentially the ceaseless seeking of something nearer to the truth. So, science cannot start from a definite God. Religion, on the other hand, begins with a full affirmation of God; it is certain of Christ and certain of the Church. It is a gift from above downwards, not a groping from below upwards. It is not like science a coral-leaf. It is more like a golden shower from above. If we assimilate religion to science, we have levelled it down to something which has taken from religion its entire force and good. We have shorn Samson of his locks, with a vengeance.

LIFE OF FAITH

ROOT > A life of Christian faith calls us to dare to be different, if need be, from other members of our social group, and to understand faith as a precious opportunity in life. A life of faith transcends the view and manner of our secularised society. If we live by our faith, we feel enriched in our life-experience. We gain steady strength to be steadfast in the struggle for life, to successfully resist attacks of every kind of pessimism and despair, and to commit ourselves to furthering justice and peace in the world. A living faith consoles us in sorrow and cheers us to live our lives more fully and deeply.

> *"Certainly, the human race is going through a difficult patch, and we often have a painful impression that the forces of evil, in many manifestations of social life, have got the upper hand. And yet, we are called to overcome the world by faith"* (John Paul II – AHM 15).

FRUIT > Faith is a great saviour in a life of troubled existence. Whenever things happen in our life and we can't make any sense out of them, we yearn to see some meaning in our life. Whenever we are troubled about the past and its mistakes, the present and its problems, and about the future and its darkness, we long to see a way out of the trouble. Whenever we are washed in the afflictions of grief, loss, pain and death, we cry out to God to be able to see some purpose in them. Jesus says: "Put your faith in me and you will see."

NOURISHING FAITH

ROOT > We nourish the gift of faith by putting even the little faith we have, into action. We can't be like the man who had ten bushels of wheat, and was waiting till more grew, before he would sow what he had. We must sow it now, and we will have a hundredfold. By keeping it, we will not get anymore, but the rats will eat up even what we have. We must also nourish it by other spiritual means. Have we forgotten the importance of frequent participation in the Eucharist? Have we ever taken seriously the need to pray daily with the Scriptures? These two sources of spiritual nourishment never go out of style.

> *"The Apostles said to the Lord, 'Increase our faith.' The Lord replied, 'If you had faith like a mustard seed, you could say to this mulberry tree, 'Be uprooted and planted in the sea,' and it would obey you'"* (Lk 17:5-6).

FRUIT > If we desire increase of faith, we must consent to its testing. Our faith is never perfect; we are partly unbelievers. Unless our faith be now and then raised up through sacraments, it will lie prostrate. Unless it is warmed through praying for it, it will be frozen. Mature faith does not grow by answers to our prayers, but by prayer itself. Unless it be aroused by good works, it will grow torpid. Since the secret of power in our lives is to know God, the larger the God we know, the larger will be our faith.

OBEDIENT FAITH

ROOT > Faith is more than praying in humble solemn tone; it is wanting God's will to be done. Faith is more than trusting when weary and alone, it is accepting weariness and loneliness from God's hand. Faith is more than believing, it is well-ordered life according to Christ's way of life. Faith is more than victory over sin and death, it is pleasing God in every detail of life. Faith is more than planting the seed under the soil, it is sharing the fruits as God has intended. Faith is daily walking hand in hand with God.

> *"By faith, man completely submits his intellect and his will to God. With his whole being man gives his assent to God the revealer. Sacred Scripture calls this human response to God, the author of revelation, 'the obedience of faith'" (CCC 143).*

FRUIT > Only he who believes is obedient and he who is obedient believes. Faith obeys Christ's commandments, especially that of love. In fact, faith and love must be inseparable companions. There is a necessary connection between them. Faith without love is no living grace and love without faith is no saving grace. Faith obeys God's will, even if it brings sufferings. In fact, we don't know what faith we have, until it is tested. Faith is such a vital matter that it needs to be put to test, in order to prove that it is genuine, and to purge and strengthen it.

THE WORD OF GOD

ROOT > God is the author of the Sacred Scriptures. Whatever have been put down in the Scriptures are divinely revealed realities, for they have been written down under the inspiration of the Holy Spirit. It is he who inspired the human authors. He acted in them and by means of them. Thus, the Scriptures teach us God's saving truths without error. The interpretation of the Scriptures must take into serious consideration, what God wants to reveal through the sacred authors.

> *"In the revealed text it is the heavenly Father himself who comes to us in love and who dwells with us disclosing to us the nature of his only begotten Son and his plan of salvation to humanity" (John Paul II – TMA 5).*

FRUIT > Everything in the railway service depends upon the accuracy of the signals. When these are wrong, life will be sacrificed. On the road to our Father's house, we need unerring signals or the catastrophes will be far more terrible. The Bible is this unerring signal, because it is inspired by God. If I did not believe in the inspiration of the Bible, I would rather be without it. If I am to judge the Bible, it is no judge of me. If I am to sift it, and lay *this* aside and accept only *that*, according to my own judgement, then I have no guidance whatever.

THE OLD TESTAMENT

ROOT > The Old Testament is a library of different books, but one thing binds them together: God speaks through them his truths. It is the story of God's People before Christ, but looking towards Christ. It is the foundation for God's self-revelation in the living Word made flesh, Jesus Christ. The books of the Old Testament attain and show forth their full meaning in the New Testament. The Old Testament contains matters imperfect and provisional, but nevertheless shows us authentic divine teaching.

> *"The Old Testament is an indispensable part of Sacred Scripture. Its books are divinely inspired and retain a permanent value, for the Old Covenant has never been revoked" (CCC 121).*

FRUIT > Ingersoll held up a copy of the Bible and said, "In fifteen years I'll have this book in the morgue." Fifteen years rolled by, Ingersoll was in the morgue, and the Bible lives on. Voltaire said that in one hundred years, the Bible could be an outmoded and forgotten book, to be found only in museums. When the one hundred years were up, Voltaire's house was owned and used by the Geneva Bible Society. And recently ninety-two volumes of Voltaire's works – a part of the Earl of Derby's library – was sold for two dollars!

THE NEW TESTAMENT

ROOT > The central object of the New Testament is Jesus Christ: his acts, teachings, passion, and glorification, and his Church's beginnings under the Spirit's guidance. The story of Jesus is told by his Apostles. If we take into account the findings of historians and archaeologists confirming the accuracy of social, geographical and political information in the Gospels, we realise that they were written down by people who had a passion for getting the story absolutely right. On this basis, we can entrust our life to the Son of God who lived then and lives now.

> *"The New Testament writings, although documents of faith are, no less reliable as historical testimonies, if we consider their references as a whole" (John Paul II – TMA 5).*

FRUIT > Have you never noticed that some people who are ill and are ordered to take pills are foolish enough to chew them? That is a very nauseous thing to do, though I have done it myself. The right way to take medicine of such a kind is to swallow it at once. In a sense, the teachings of Christ in the New Testament are undoubtedly true, and many of them have to be swallowed at once by an effort of faith, and must not be chewed by perpetual questioning.

BREAD OF LIFE

Root > The Scriptures are venerated in the Church as the Eucharist, the body of the Lord, since both are bread of life, which nourish and govern the whole Christian life. As the psalmist says: the Word of God is 'lamp to my feet and a light to my path' (Ps 119:105). Since it is the Word of God and not of man, we find in it strength for our on-going pilgrimage to the Father's House. Spiritual nourishment that the Scriptures offer, is due to the fact that in them the Father who is in heaven comes lovingly to meet his children and talk with them.

> *"We should turn with renewed interest to the Bible, whether it be through the liturgy, rich in divine Word or through devotional reading, or through instructions suitable for the purpose and other aids" (John Paul II – TMA 5).*

Fruit > I am told by a reliable source that a bird can go nine days without food. A man twelve days. A dog twenty days. A turtle five hundred days. A snake eight hundred days. A fish one thousand days. Insects twelve hundred days. But food is necessary for all of God's creatures. Are there some 'turtle' Christians, who go five hundred days without much real Bible meat? Are there 'bird' Christians who go more than nine days without Bible food? Are there at least few 'fish' Christians, who go one thousand days without eating much of the bread of life?

A TREASURY OF TRUTHS

ROOT > It is not possible to comprehend the extent of
what is to be discovered in a single utterance of Christ. For
we leave behind in it, far more than we take from it, like
thirsty people drinking from fountain. The facets of his Word
is more numerous than the faces of those who learn from it.
God has hidden within his Word all sorts of treasures, so that
each of us can be enriched by it, from whatever aspect we
meditate on. God's Word is the tree of life, which proffers to
you on all sides blessed fruits.

> *"Since therefore all that the inspired authors or sacred
> writers affirm should be regarded as affirmed by the Holy
> Spirit, we must acknowledge that the books of Scripture
> firmly, faithfully, and without error teach that truth which
> God, for the sake of our salvation, wished to see confided
> to the Sacred Scriptures" (CCC 107).*

FRUIT > A thirsty person rejoices because he has drunk.
He is not grieved because he is incapable of drinking the
fountain dry. Likewise, if the reader is incapable of finding
more in what he or she reads in the Bible, there is no need
to grieve that something has been left over. We must allow
the fountain of Scripture vanquish our spiritual thirst, but
our thirst will not vanquish the fountain. And it cannot,
for the Scripture is like a window in this prison-world,
through which we are looking into eternity.

THE STUDY OF THE SCRIPTURES

ROOT >In the Scriptures, truth is proposed and expressed in a variety of ways, depending on whether a text is history of one kind or another, or whether its form is that of prophecy, poetry, or some other type of speech. The study of Scripture investigates into the meaning that the sacred writer intended to express in a particular literary form. The purpose of the study is also to find out what eternal truths are revealed, what deeds are narrated, what future events are foretold and what commands or counsels are given.

> *"The Church forcefully and specifically exhorts all the Christian faithful to learn 'the surpassing knowledge of Jesus Christ' by frequent reading of the divine Scriptures. Ignorance of the Scriptures is ignorance of Christ" (CCC 133).*

FRUIT > Everything that we read in the Scriptures, shines and glitters even in the outer shell, but the marrow is sweeter. If we desire to eat the kernel, we must first break open the shell, that is called study. Bible study is the metal that makes a Christian. This is the strong meat on which holy people are nourished. We must consult lexicons and commentaries to see the literal meaning of the words and their relation to one another. But when we have done all that, we shall still find that our greatest help will come from prayer!

PRAYING THE SCRIPTURE

ROOT > The action of a mill is driven by the circling pressure of water. The mill has to go on operating, as long as the water goes on turning the wheel. It is for the person operating, to decide what sort of grain to grind. In the same way, our minds are under constant pressure with a constant stream of distracting thoughts to divert it from lasting values. But we can decide which of these thoughts can be allowed and processed. If we regularly read and pray over the Scriptures, we can keep in our minds the things of the Spirit, which will lead us to a peaceful life and future blessedness.

> *"Let them remember that prayer should accompany the reading of sacred Scripture, so that a dialogue takes place between God and man. For we speak to him when we pray; we listen to him when we read the oracles" (CCC 2653).*

FRUIT > A young lady, asked by her friend to explain what is meant by praying the Scripture, she gave this answer: "Yesterday morning I received a letter from one to whom I had given my heart, and devoted my life. I freely confess that I have read that letter five times, not because I did not understand it at the first reading, nor because it was my duty, but it was simply one of pleasure. I read it because I am devoted to the one who wrote it." Similarly, when we read and re-read the Scripture because they are words of our beloved heavenly father, we can say that we pray the Scripture.

WHAT IS PRAYER?

ROOT > Prayer, in a sense, is to reflect upon God's kindness and to love and praise him for it. Prayer is letting our mind rest in the awareness of God in his naked existence, and to love and praise him for what he is in himself. Theresa of Child Jesus said: For me, prayer means launching out of the heart towards God; it means lifting up one's eyes, quite simply, to Heaven, a cry of grateful love from the crest of joy or the trough of despair; it is a vast, supernatural force which opens out my heart, and binds me close to Jesus.

> *"Prayer is, before all else, is an act of intelligence, a feeling of humility and thankfulness, an attitude of trust and surrender to him who has lovingly given us life. Prayer is a mysterious but nonetheless a real dialogue with God, a dialogue of confidence and love" (John Paul II – AHM 16).*

FRUIT > Prayer is more than asking God to give us this or that. If prayer is a dialogue between me and God, my prayer must lead me into ever closer relationship with God, and 'asking' cannot be the be-all and end-all of a relationship. If there is no more to human relationship than what each can get from the other, then the relationship is barely personal at all. Hence, at the centre of a genuine relationship with God, ought to be an openness between God and me. This makes possible a process of sharing between us, of giving and receiving. Persons share because they care.

HOW TO PRAY?

ROOT > Pray where you are; God is present everywhere and ready to listen. Pray, when possible, in a quiet place where you can be alone. Pray to God simply and naturally, as to a Father. Tell him what is on your mind. Pray, remembering the good things God has done for you. Pray for God's forgiveness, for the unworthy things that you may have done. Pray for the things you need, especially for those that will make your life finer and more Christlike. Pray for others; Pray for the world in need. And pray, above everything, that God's will may be done.

> *"Pray in faith. Faith is a filial adherence to God beyond what we feel and understand. It is possible because the beloved Son gives us access to the Father. He can ask us to seek, and to knock, since he himself is the door and the way"* (CCC 2609).

FRUIT > As many as are the flowers of summer, so many are the varieties of prayer. Prayer may be salted with confession or perfumed with thanksgiving. It may be sung to music or wept out with groanings. We can draw near to God even though we cannot say a word. A prayer may be crystallised in a tear. A tear is enough water to float a desire to God. But let us remember this: whatever the form of prayer, only that prayer which comes from our heart can get to God's heart.

PRAYING ALWAYS

Root > If the essence of prayer is the movement of the
heart and will towards God, there is a sense in which we
can pray always. When there is co-ordination in our life,
we can turn all daily activities into an exercise of a single
master-drive. If a person is a whole, and the wholeness
consists in the fact that the person is trying to love God
with all heart, soul and strength, then the current that gives
the power to all the activities, is his or her love for God. To
the extent to which that is true, the person is seeking God
always, therefore praying always.

> *"We are to pray without ceasing. This tireless fervour can
> come only from love. Against our dullness and laziness the
> battle of prayer is that of humble, trusting and persevering
> love. This love opens our heart to God enabling us to pray
> always" (CCC 2742).*

Fruit > One will not be able to pray always, unless there
are regular periods of deep recollection devoted to explicit
or formal prayer, with the attempt to put God in the centre
of one's consciousness. Both explicit prayer and Christian
living, are the affirmation of Christ, by which we say 'yes' to
his loving demands; but we will not say, 'yes' consistently in
our lives, unless we say that 'yes' formally in our prayers. To
work is to pray, if regularly we pray without working. The
enrichment of our inner life through formal prayer, is not
an option extra. It is life itself.

ITS NECESSITY

ROOT > Without prayer, what are the Church's agencies, but the stretching out of a dead man's arm, or the lifting up of the lid of a blind man's eyes? Teresa of Avila said: "Souls without prayer are like people whose bodies or limbs are paralysed; they possess feet and hands but they cannot control them." In the same way, there are souls so infirm and so accustomed to busying themselves with outside affairs, that they seem incapable of entering into themselves at all. Hence we Christians should work, as if all depended on us, and pray as if all depended on God.

> *"We should pray because we are believers. For prayer is the recognition of our limitations and of our dependence; from God we come, to God we belong, to God we shall return"* *(John Paul II – AHM 17).*

FRUIT > Dryness is perhaps the most common difficulty in prayer. Yet, if it is understood correctly, dryness can be a special time of grace. Sometimes, our failure to experience God in a sensible manner, comes through no fault of our own, but is a normal stage in God's purification of our desire to serve and follow him. When we experience his presence in a satisfying way, our feeling may well become the motive for our love of him. But love will not mature unless it reaffirms its choice of the beloved, when the consolation is not there.

ITS EFFICACY

Root > God the Holy Spirit writes our prayer, God the Son presents our prayer, and God the Father accepts our prayer. And with the whole Trinity to help us in it, what prayer cannot achieve? All our perils are nothing, so long as we have prayer. As the moon influences the tides of the sea, even so does prayer, for it influences the tides of God's providence in favour of us. There are powers in the universe such as electricity, attraction, gravitation and the like. But my experience is that prayer has more omnipotent force than all these powers.

> *"Prayer gives us strength for high ideals and keeping the Faith. Prayer gives us the courage to rise above indifference or above guilt. Prayer gives us the light to see and consider events in our personal lives in the salvific perspective of God and eternity" (John Paul II – AHM 18).*

Fruit > Imagine a whole nation kneeling to pray. This spectacle of a nation at prayer, is more awe-inspiring than the explosion of an atomic bomb. The force of prayer is greater than any possible combination of human-made or human-controlled powers, because prayer is human beings' greatest means of tapping the infinite resources of God. Invoking by prayer the mercy and might of God, is a very efficacius means of guaranteeing peace and security of the harassed and helpless people of the earth.

PRAYING IN CHRIST'S NAME

ROOT > There is no way of obtaining any favour from God, but through the mediation of Jesus Christ, for he is the sole mediator between God and humankind. Jesus is God made flesh. He is God and he is human being, hence he is in the most privileged position to speak to God on our behalf. During his earthly life, Christ called his disciples to live in him: "Abide in me and I in you" (Jn 15:4). Anyone who lives in Christ cannot but pray in Christ. Jesus said: "I am the Way." Hence our prayer's surest way to the Father is through Jesus.

> *"The name of Jesus is at the heart of Christian prayer. All liturgical prayers conclude with the words 'through our Lord Jesus Christ'. The Hail Mary reaches its high point in the words 'blessed is the fruit of thy womb, Jesus'" (CCC 435).*

FRUIT > Heavenly Father answers all our prayers made in Christ, but at times, he answers in strange ways. You pray for strength to do greater things, but you are given infirmity that you might do better things. You ask for riches that you might be happy, but you are given poverty that you might be wise. You ask for power that people may praise you, but you are given weakness that you might feel the need of God. Thus, you may receive nothing you asked for; and your prayer may seem unanswered, and yet, you will be very blessed.

THE OUR FATHER

ROOT > Christ gave the 'Our Father' to the disciples as the pattern for our prayers, expressing as it does, the order in which the requests should be made: we praise God, pray for his work in the world, pray for our daily needs, and pray for help in our daily struggles. No matter how holy we become, we can never outgrow this prayer. And no matter how ignorant we think we are of theology or religion, we can still say the 'Our Father' with meaning, as our Lord's own prayer.

> *"For everything one can and should say to the Father is contained in those seven petitions which we all know by heart. In them is such simplicity that even a child can learn them; but at the same time there is such depth that one might spend a lifetime reflecting on their meaning" (John Paul II – AHM 19).*

FRUIT > While journeying on horseback one day, St Bernard met a peasant walking along the road. "You have got an easy job," said the peasant. "Why don't I become a man of prayer? Then I too would be travelling on horseback." "You think praying is easy," replied the saint. "If you can say one *Our Father* without any distraction, you can have this horse." "It's a bargain," said the surprised peasant. Closing his eyes and folding his hands he began to say the *Our Father* aloud: "Our father, who art in heaven, hallowed be thy name, thy Kingdom come..." Suddenly he stopped and looked up, "Shall I get the saddle and bridle too?"

PRAYER, ALWAYS ANSWERED

ROOT > The ancient Greeks had two words for time, *Chronos* and *Kairos*. *Chronos* means time in quantitative sense. It is a kind of time we can count and divide into minutes, days and years. It is the kind we expect God to respond to. *Kairos* means time in a qualitative sense. It is the time that is characterised by what happens in it, by its appropriateness. *Kairos* is more important than *Chronos*, because it usually affects our lives the most, and means that something is happening inside us. God normally answers our prayers in *Kairos* time.

> *"So I say to you: Ask, and it will be given to you; search, and you will find; knock, and the door will be opened to you" (Lk 11:9).*

FRUIT > We pray to be healed of an illness or to get rid of a problem, and we expect it to be accomplished today or tomorrow at the latest. But perhaps we are not ready, in *Chronos-time*, for what we are expecting from God. Perhaps God knows that much more crucial good comes to us by waiting, struggling, asking, until the right *Kairos-time* comes. We get impatient when things don't happen when we think they ought to. Such times are excellent opportunities to remember, that God may not come when we want, but God will always be right on time.

GOD, FAMILY'S ORIGIN

ROOT > Family was instituted by God. After creating man 'in his image' (Gen 1:27), God was deeply concerned about Adam's loneliness. So he took something, may be a rib, out of man, and that became Eve. Adam felt one with Eve. He owned her as his very own. God blessed them saying, "Be fruitful and multiply and fill the earth and subdue it" (Gen 1:28). They were encouraged to cling to each other. They were one and not two. That is God's calculation in arithmetic, regarding married ones.

> *"In creating man and woman, God instituted the human family and endowed it with its fundamental constitution. Its members are persons equal in dignity. For the common good of its members and of society, the family necessarily has manifold responsibilities, rights and duties" (CCC 2203).*

FRUIT > God is not just a noun but also a verb, that is, God is not just a person but also a certain flow of life, between three divine persons of the Trinity. Inside God, there is a kind of family life going on. So he created human beings as he is, as a family. When within family, we give and receive from each other, when within the family, we break open our lives and hearts and joys and frustrations and egos and finances and share them with each other, we are letting the life of God flow through us, and we are giving skin to the inner life of the Trinity. In that sense, family life is a sacrament.

THE UNIT OF SOCIETY

ROOT > The family is the basic cell of society, because it is the cradle of life and love, the place in which the individual person is born and grows; because all that is accomplished by the family in favour of the person, is also a service rendered to society, and all that is done in favour of society redounds to the benefit of the person; and because, the inherent social dimension of the human person that calls the individual to communion with others and to the giving of self to others, is best cultivated in a family.

> *"The family is a fellowship of life and love. It trains and guides its members towards full human maturity and serves for the good of all, along life's road. The future of the world and the Church thus pass through the family" (John Paul II – AHM 20).*

FRUIT > Every human being is unique. It follows that every human being has some unique gift to give to his or her family and then to one's country and to the world. The small world of human home is built up of the gifts of each member of it; the larger world is built up, in the same way, of various gifts, economic, political, cultural, religious, of its individual citizens. If we are Christians, we dismiss once and for all the idea that our business in the world is to serve ourselves and nobody else, to become holy ourselves and pay no attention to anyone else.

MARITAL COVENANT

ROOT > The marriage originates in a marital communion which is a 'covenant' in which man and woman give themselves to each other. "So they are no longer two but one flesh." (Mt 19:6). The family is brought about in the full and specific sense, when the conjugal covenant opens the spouses to a lasting communion of love and of life, through procreation of children. The children born to them are expected to consolidate their parents' conjugal covenant, by enriching and deepening the communion of their father and mother. When this does not happen, it is possible that selfishness dominates marital love.

> *"From the outset the spouses need to have their hearts and thoughts turned towards the God from whom every family is named, so that their fatherhood and motherhood will draw from that source the power to be continually renewed in love" (John Paul II – LF 7).*

FRUIT > There will be times in family life when profound crises can threaten marital love which naturally tends towards fatherhood and motherhood. At such moments, marriage-counselling centres offer great help. However, marriage being a sacrament and a covenant of persons in love, this love can be deepened and preserved chiefly by God's love. Therefore, the spouses who face such marital problems must beg the Holy Spirit to activate that Love, which has already been poured into their hearts at Baptism.

SELF-GIFT

ROOT > Human beings find their fulfilment in love, and love means to give and receive something freely and mutually. When a man and woman in marriage, mutually give and receive each other in the unity of 'one flesh', the sincere gift of self becomes a part of their life. Without this, marriage would be empty, but with this, it becomes a communion of persons. When they transmit life to the child, a new human being becomes a part of their horizon. The newborn child is a gift, for it gives itself to its parents, by the very fact of its coming into existence.

> *"In the newborn child is realised the common good of the family. Just as the common good of the spouses is fulfilled in conjugal love, ever ready to give and receive new life, so too the common good of the family is fulfilled through the same spousal love, as embodied in the newborn child" (John Paul II – LF 11).*

FRUIT > It is true that the birth of the child means more work, new financial burdens and further inconveniences. Does this mean that the child is not a gift? First of all, every human being is the 'glory of God' who creates the child for itself, not just as a part of humanity, but as this 'individual' with unique human dignity. Secondly, every child is a particle of the common good, without which human communities risk extinction. Thirdly, the child becomes a gift to its entire family, by sharing in their life and contributing to their common good.

THE CULTURE OF 'USE'

ROOT > The Church teaches that abortion is an abominable crime. The law of God is univocal and categorical with respect to human life. God commands, "You shall not kill" (Ex 20:13). It no less applies to the embryo, than to people who have already been born. Human reason also supports this. Science of today attests to human character of embryo. It assures that from the moment of its conception, it is an original and biologically autonomous being, endowed with an internal programme which will keep operating until it has developed to maturity.

> *"If an individual is exclusively concerned with 'use', he can reach the point of killing love by killing the fruit of love. For the culture of 'use', the 'blessed fruit of your womb' (Lk 1:42) becomes in a certain sense an 'accursed fruit'"* (John Paul II – LF 21).

FRUIT > Respect for life is now so being eroded that in some countries an abortion can happen where the sex of the child is not what the parents wanted. Laws are passed by some States that fail to respect the right to life from the moment of conception. Nevertheless, in the last few decades, some consoling signs of reawakening of conscience have appeared. There is a new and growing sense of respect for life; 'Pro-Life' movements are beginning to spread. This is a leaven of hope for the future of family and of all humanity.

PARENTHOOD

ROOT > Parenthood is not just procreation of children; it also means proper upbringing of them. It is the duty of Christian parents to regard their off-springs as children of God, and respect them as human persons, to provide for their growth in every respect, to create a home suited for education in virtues, to teach them to give priority to spiritual values, to initiate them into solidarity and communal responsibilities, to introduce them at an early age, into the mysteries of faith, and to associate them with the life of the Church.

> *"Married people should regard it as their proper mission to transmit human life, and to educate their children; they should realise that they are thereby co-operating with the love of God the Creator and are, in a certain sense, its interpreters"* *(CCC 2367).*

FRUIT > Parents are prone to give their children everything except the two things they need most: time and good example. First: Time for listening, time for understanding, time for helping, and time for guiding. It sounds simple, but in reality it is the most difficult, and the most sacrificial task of parenthood. Good example: Every word and deed of a parent is a fibre woven into the character of a child, which ultimately determines how that child fits into the fabric of society.

CHILDREN

ROOT > Children are to show filial respect to their parents and filial respect means true docility and obedience. As long as the children live at home with their parents, they should obey their parents in all they ask of them, for their good and that of the family. Children should also obey the reasonable directions of their teachers. As they grow up, they should continue to respect their parents. As much as they can, they must give their parents material and moral support in old age and in times of illness or loneliness, recalling their duty of gratitude.

> *"Honour your father and mother, because they are the ones who introduced you to human existence in a particular family line, nation and culture. After God they are your first benefactors" (John Paul II – LF 15).*

FRUIT > Children must have trust in the guidance of their parents, for a mother's heart is a child's schoolroom, and one father is more than a hundred school masters. Children must respect their parents' authority over them. Pity the home where everyone is the head. Children owe gratitude to parents and show it especially in their old age. We never know the love of our parents till we have become parents. The fourth commandment, "Honour your father and mother," cannot be discarded like the clothes and toys of childhood, once we have become independent adults.

FAMILY PRAYER

ROOT > Daily family prayer will send you forth to your daily task with cheerful heart. It will give you strength to meet the discouragements. It will make you conscious throughout the day, of the attending presence of the unseen One. It will sweeten home life and enrich home relationships; It will solve all the misunderstandings. It will exert hallowed influence on those who come to you as guests. It will furnish an example and stimulus to other homes, for the same kind of life and service and devotion to God.

> *"The Christian family is the first place of education in prayer. Based on the sacrament of Marriage, the family is the 'domestic church' where God's children learn to pray 'as the Church', and to persevere in prayer" (CCC 2685).*

FRUIT > Teen-aged Rodney got up late and had just time enough to gulp down some hot chocolate and a piece of toast before rushing off to school. He arose from the table hastily. "Where are you going, son?" "To school, of course." "No, my boy; you do not go to school without first looking up to God. Sit down for family prayer." Rodney did so with resentment. But as he was riding his bicycle at top speed to school, some thoughts were crystallising underneath his resentment: "Dad is right. God is managing our lives, and we should always commit ourselves and our day to him."

December:

CIVILISATION OF LOVE

Week 1
Love

Week 2
Solidarity

Week 3
Liberty

Week 4
Peace

LOVE

ROOT > Christian love is to see the image and likeness of God in another person, whom God decides to introduce into my life, not for an exercise of human pity, but for relating myself to the root of that being, which is truly the part of God in him or her. God loves every human being, for he alone knows the priceless and unique treasure called 'person', which he gave every human being. Christian love is our participation in that divine knowledge. When I love a person in this way, I discover in that person that which is loveable in him or her, namely, that which is from God.

> *"Love is the constructive force for humanity's every positive road. The future does not gather hopes from violence, from hatred, from the intrusiveness of individual or collective selfishness" (John Paul II – AHM 21).*

FRUIT > Christian love is inclusive love, which cherishes the lame and the blind. It is providential love, which quenches thirst and smoothes the road. It is liberating love, which rescues the oppressed and restores their identity. It is all embracing love, which gathers a people and guards a flock. It is generous love, which satisfies need with food in abundance. And it is comforting love, which turns mourning into joy and sorrow into gladness. It is always spring time in the heart that loves, for love is a constructive force.

LOVE RISKS

ROOT > Love has its risks, for to be able to love properly, I have to detach myself from many things, above all from myself. I must be ready to give freely and to the end. True love requires stripping of oneself, which is a laborious and long job. Besides, when we are prepared to rescue others from their genuine needs, we will be faced with some people who seek help from us, without first trying to help themselves. Even then, true love goes to help them, thinking beyond the moment and hoping for a life-time of growth for that person. This can be a tough love.

> *"Love is essentially a giving of oneself to others. Far from being an instinctive inclination, love is a conscious decision of the will to go out to others" (John Paul II – AHM 22).*

FRUIT > To love is to be vulnerable. Love anything and your heart may be broken. If I don't risk that, then I must give my heart to no one. But then, I will end up wrapping my heart carefully with hobbies, pets and little luxuries, which, I am afraid, is equivalent to locking it safe in the coffin of my selfishness. And if I don't dare to unlock it for fear of loving human beings, my heart thus locked in the dark, motionless and airless, will soon freeze, become unbearable, impenetrable and irredeemable.

NON-LOVE

Root > All sufferings are signs of non-love. An ugly girl is neglected at a dance, and a woman whose husband does not kiss her any more. A child is left at home because he is a nuisance, and a grandfather is made fun of because he is too old. A worried man is not able to confide in anyone. An adolescent is troubled because his worries have been ridiculed. A man who, wants to work but is unemployed, and a worker ruins his health for a ridiculous wage. A father has to pile his family into a single room, next to an empty house. These are some modern signs of non-love.

> *"Deprived of love, we fall victim to an insidious spiral for ever contracting the horizons of brotherhood while prompting each of us to make ourselves, our own ego and our own pleasure, the only criterion of judgement"* (John Paul II – AHM 23).

Fruit > The energy of love does not develop as quickly as the energy of the mind. For example, thousands of centuries were necessary for human being to rise above the level of the savage, while only a few centuries were necessary to produce an Einstein. We shudder to think of man's destiny: What if, as we become more and more intellectual and more and more attracted to the world, we become less and less able to achieve unity through love? An old house may be torn down and replaced by a splendid new one, but our society can be reborn in a new and better form, only if there is an increase of love.

LOVE FOR GOD

ROOT > God loves us as our Father. Hence, his love is a strong and faithful love. It is full of compassion, offering us the grace of conversion when we have sinned. The supreme revelation of God's love took place on the cross, where God's Son died overcoming sin and death for our sake. God loves us with an everlasting and unconditional love in Jesus Christ. He loves us all. He loves us in adversity as well as in prosperity. It is therefore but right, that our hearts should be on God when the heart of God is so much on us.

> *"This is how God loved the world: he gave his only Son, so that everyone who believes in him may not perish but may have eternal life" (Jn 3:16).*

FRUIT > Some of us may doubt about our strength of love for God, and wonder whether we can be faithful in our love to the end of our journey. A way out of this fear is to make sure, that we love God just minute by minute, not bothering about the future. As the saying goes, "Take care of the minute and the hours will take care of themselves." The present moment is all that we have to handle now. It is not fair to burden one moment with the weight of the next. If we have to walk a hundred miles, we would still have to take but one step at a time.

LOVING OTHERS

ROOT > No lofty reasoning about God and about his relations to us will do away with the obstinate fact that if we love God, not in our reveries alone, we must love our neighbour not in theory alone. Human being is the culmination-point of an eternal love which issues from God. That is the reason why human being is worth loving, not by reason of what he or she is for oneself, but by reason of what they are for God. We will never reach a human being by starting from the earth; we must first reach heaven to find our neighbour through God.

> *"I believe that poverty does not consist of being hungry for bread, but rather it is tremendous hunger for human dignity. We need to love and to be somebody for someone else. This is where we make our mistake and shove people aside"* (Mother Teresa).

FRUIT > There seem to be three kinds of love. The first is, 'if-love'. This kind of love is ego-centred, and offered only in exchange for something our neighbour wants from us. The second is, 'because-love'. With this love a person loves the other, because of a quality the other possesses, something she or he has, or something she or he does. This kind of love seems a little better than 'if-love' at first, but after a while it, too, becomes a burden. The third kind of love is 'in spite of love'. It is unconditional love, for we are loved 'in spite of', not 'because of'. This is the way we are to love others.

FORGIVING LOVE

ROOT > Forgiveness is the highest point of love because it is the absolute proof that love is unconditional. Often we love only those who love us and are good to us. But the Lord asked us to love even our enemies, those who do us harm. By forgiving such people, we are not approving what they have done, but we refuse to judge them and enclose them for ever in their frailty. By forgiving our enemies, we are not sunbathing to them, which is weakness. No, it is a sign of strength, because love always conquers in the end.

> *"But I say this to you, love your enemies and pray for those who persecute you; so that you may be children of your Father in heaven" (Mt 5:44-45).*

FRUIT > We hurt only ourselves by hating our enemies. Hating people is like burning down your own house to get rid of a rat. The fire of hate compressed within our heart would soon burn fiercer and break in flames, consuming not only our own selves but also engulfing the world. Some say that the world will end in fire, others say in ice, but after knowing what hate has done so far between races, nations and communities, we can also say that the world could end by hate. We hurt ourselves by contemplating on revenge, because by doing so, we keep our wounds open which otherwise could heal.

LOVE OF THE POOR

ROOT > We all long for heaven where God is, but we have it in our power to be in heaven with him, right now. But being happy with him now, means loving the poor as he loves, helping them as he helps, giving them as he gives, rescuing them as he rescues. The poor are God's distressing disguise. On the last day, we will be judged by how we have treated the poor: "I was hungry, naked, homeless. And whatever you did to the least of my brethren, you did it to me." Yes, the poor are the hope of humanity.

> *"If we recall that Jesus came to 'preach the Good News to the poor' how can we fail to lay greater emphasis on the Church's preferential option for the poor and the outcast?" (John Paul II – TMA 51).*

FRUIT > We are being challenged to see the Millennium as a Jubilee. We are at a key moment in history, and as Church we need to decide what kind of world we want to build together. The alternatives are stark and clear. We can go along with globalisation and the marked values, that bring an ever-increasing gap between those who contribute to the economy and those excluded, because they are not productive. Or, we can insist on the worth of human beings wherever they are, and seek to live by Jubilee values: love, justice and peace.

LOVE IN ACTION

ROOT > If we want to be open to God, so that he can use us, we must put love into action. We can begin this action with our family, with our closest neighbours. We must try to discover the poor in our own setting because only if we know them, we will be able to offer them our love. It is easy to love those who live far away. It is not always easy to love those who live right next to us. It is easier to offer a loaf of bread to meet the hunger of a needy person, than to comfort the loneliness and the anguish of someone in our own home who does not feel loved.

> *"It is not anyone who says to me, 'Lord, Lord,' who will enter the Kingdom of Heaven, but the person who does the will of my Father in heaven" (Mt 7:21).*

FRUIT > One day there was a workman aboard a trolley car, and he noticed that every time the door was pushed open it squeaked. Rising from his seat, he took a little can from his pocket, and dropped oil on the offending spot. He sat down again quietly remarking, "I always carry an oilcan in my pocket, for there are so many squeaky things that a drop of oil will correct." Love is the oil which, when put into action, can make everyday life in home, business and society harmonious. Knowing is not enough, we must apply. Willing is not enough, we must do. Loving is not enough, we must act on it.

ONE FATHER

Root > Human beings are often very good at drawing dividing lines that cannot be crossed, saying: "On this side is good, on that side is evil; truth is on this side and error is on the other." That is bad enough, but even worse is when God is claimed for one camp or the other. How often that has happened in history! Two armies are drawn up against each other, ready to fight to the death, claiming the same God for themselves and call on him to support them in their just war. Surely, we ought to go to God himself to find out that he is the Father of all.

> *"Our awareness of the common fatherhood of God, must bring to our vision of the world a new criterion for interpreting it. Beyond human and natural bonds, already so close and strong, there is discerned in the light of faith a new model of unity of the human race, which must ultimately inspire our solidarity" (John Paul II – AHM 24).*

Fruit > In our world of loneliness and despair, professional helpers abound: psychiatrists, social workers, therapists and others. Each plays a specialised role. However, people don't always need specialist help. They may need companionship, care, affirmation and love, that is, they may need to know that God's love is unconditional which embraces them, forgives them for what they are, since he is their Father. If they experience his love themselves, they can be signpost of hope for others too, provided they acknowledge that God is Father of all people.

SOLIDARITY IS PRESENCE

ROOT > God in the person of his Son, came to earth to enter into and to assume the totality of human nature. He came in the body of a man, with a heart of a man, to live a human life. God, because he became man in Jesus, took to himself, by virtue of that humanity, all people of every time and every place. Jesus willingly accepts the bond which unites him to us. He came through love and it is through love he unites himself to us and among ourselves. Hence, 'God made flesh,' is more than God's presence with us. It is solidarity in the truest sense.

> *"The Church must become part of peoples for the same motive which led Christ to bind himself in virtue of his Incarnation, to the definite social and cultural conditions of the human beings among whom he dwelt" (AG 10).*

FRUIT > Christian solidarity is first presence. What does it mean in concrete term? Suppose, an individual or a group of Christians are sent to a village to evangelise. They know that through them the Church is supposed to be present among the villagers. Their first preoccupation ought not to be to preach but to become one with the people, to be integrated into the community. As long as they appear to be outsiders or foreigners or pressure group, they have not started their mission nor are they fit for it. Everything should be done from within.

WORKING TOGETHER

ROOT > Solidarity is not a presence as an observer, however sympathetic and well-intentioned that be, nor even as reformers and benefactors, however much they may be needed, but a presence of fellow travellers and co-citizens, brothers and sisters. It is not a Christian presence that pretends to superiority but equality. It is sharing the local people's fields of action, their problems, their joys and hopes, their tragedies and triumphs. It is working together with the people and for the people.

> *"The Church through her children, is one with men of every condition, but especially with the poor and the afflicted. On their behalf she gladly spends herself" (AG 12).*

FRUIT > Gardeners go down to the pond and dipping their water pots, carry the refreshing liquid to the flowers. A child comes into the garden and wishes to help, and yonder is a little pot for him. The little water pot, though it does not hold so much, yet carries the same water to the plants. And it does not make any difference to the flowers that receive that water. So too, in working for a better world, Christians need to work with all other good-willed people, respecting their contribution, however small that may be. We are all equal, at least in doing good to make a better world.

FELLOWSHIP

Root > Christianity is not first of all and essentially a philosophy, a code of ethics, a doctrinal system. It is, above all, a life of relationship and fellowship among persons: with God and with one another, animated by charity. The relationship of love with others, is a sign and proof of our relationship with God in love. If the love we bear towards others flows from the very love that God has poured into our hearts through the Holy Spirit, we will love all human beings, and foster fellowship among Christians.

> *"The presence of the Christian faithful among other people in the world should be animated by that charity with which God has loved us and with which he wills that we should love one another" (AG 12).*

Fruit > Christian fellowship born of charity and respect, will not just tolerate fellow human beings. Toleration is often exalted as a virtue, but who on earth yearns to be 'tolerated'? Does the heavenly Father merely tolerate us all? I tolerate without much thought, the motorway at dawn, stale air in city streets, siren and motor horn. We tolerate an icy wind, and the daily grind. Should we likewise just tolerate other human beings? People do not want to be tolerated. They want to be loved, welcomed and understood.

DIALOGUE

Root > The relation between God and human beings in the course of salvation history has been one of dialogue. Dialogue is an eloquent proof of our solidarity with fellow human beings and a necessary means of knowing them. Thus, dialogue becomes a condition and a form of service. Through dialogue with others, one can learn what treasures, a bountiful God has distributed among the nations of the earth. The object of this dialogue may be human problems and situations, values and aspirations whether human, religious or Christian. All the three are important, one leading to the other.

> *"Just as Christ himself searched the hearts of men and led them to divine light through truly human conversation, so also his disciples, profoundly penetrated by the Spirit of Christ, should know the people among whom they live and should establish contact with them" (AG 11).*

Fruit > A world-community can exist only with world-communication, which means something more than extensive short wave facilities scattered about the globe. It means common understanding, a common tradition, common ideas, and common ideals which can come only through dialogue. How should a dialogue be? Shakespeare said, "Dialogue should be pleasant without scrutiny, free without indecency, learned without conceitedness, novel without falsehood." In dialogue, we must listen to the other person's story, to the other person's full story, to the other person's full story first.

COLLABORATION

ROOT > Dialogue is not restricted to mere mutual knowledge and understanding, social and cultural contacts, exchange of ideas and experiences. It can take the form of collaboration in various activities. In fact, such a collaboration serves as the best way of dialoguing. Some of the needs where collaboration is needed are: education, concerted efforts to eradicate famine and disease, projects for socio-economic development and better way of life, promotion of social justice, moral values and freedom, and the cause of international concord.

> *"In this activity the faithful should be eager to offer their prudent aid to projects sponsored by public and private organisations by Government, by international agencies, by various Christian communities and even by non-Christian religions" (AG 12).*

FRUIT > Collaboration is a form of service, but service is not always doing things for others; rather, the true character of service consist in doing things with others. We find it easier to do things for others. We can then be our quick and efficient self. We can then set the terms and conditions. We can then be available or withdraw when it suits us. Such service makes us feel good, but it frequently disempowers the other person. True service is one that joins with the other. It is companionship, collaboration, and walking a common road for a period of time.

THE SPIRIT OF SERVICE

ROOT > Solidarity is presence, fellowship, dialogue and collaboration; but all these need to be carried out in a spirit of service, in humility and self-effacement. The Church must be and appear to be as existing for the world and therefore always at its disposal. However, service has to be relevant and relevance is determined by the needs, requests, and desires of those whom we want to serve. Sometimes, religion as well as serving people may not be aware of people's real needs, in which case it is incumbent on the Church to bring about this awareness.

> *"Christians have to raise their voice on behalf of all the poor of the world, proposing the Jubilee as an appropriate time to give thought to reducing substantially, if not cancelling outright, the international debt which seriously threaten the future of many nations" (John Paul II – TMA 51).*

FRUIT >One of the relevant needs where service is needed today is the need for cancellation of international debts. The late Cardinal Basil Hume wrote: "No one wants to see debt relief squandered on arms or dissipated through corruption, instead of helping the poorest people. But some highly indebted poor countries would be willing and able to spend the money saved on properly managed poverty-alleviation and development programmes. They should be given far more generous debt relief now."

CARING AND SHARING

Root > The English word *care* goes back to a Gothic root, *kara*, meaning, 'to lament, weep with, grieve.' So, caring should mean that we become aware of the other person in ways that stir deep feelings; then, out of these feelings, resolve to care for them in appropriate ways. In the New Testament, the Greek noun *koinonia* simply means 'sharing'. It is translated variously as, 'communion,' 'communication,' 'community,' 'fellowship,' 'partaking,' and 'contribution.' An ancient inscription put up by a husband in memory of his wife said: "I shared all life with you."

> *"The close proximity of luxury and extreme poverty accentuates the sense of frustration in the disinherited. We can all do something, in ourselves and around us. Is it not possibly true that the most deprived areas are often the places where solidarity evokes gestures of outstanding generosity?"* (John Paul II – AHM 25).

Fruit > An Irish tenant farmer died long ago leaving a widow and three little children. The man who owned the farm needed the house, so this poor widow was literally turned out to the roads, and no one came to help her. After four days of no food and sleeping out doors, one morning the youngest child woke up with a burning fever. By noon, all three children were sick, and before the sun went down, the neglected family was the centre of an epidemic of diphtheria that spread the whole town. This woman's plight ought to have been the concern of the larger community.

TRUE LIBERTY

Root > Human liberty is a gift from God. True liberty consists in freely obeying the divine law, inscribed in our conscience and received as an impulse of the Holy Spirit, and thus gain mastery over ourselves, and become a child of God which is our royal vocation. But our liberty is finite and fallible. Our desire may be drawn to a false good; and if we choose a false good we fail in our vocation to liberty, for by our free will, which makes us masters of our own life, we harm ourselves.

> *"God willed that man should be left in the hand of his own counsel, so that he might of his own accord seek his Creator and freely attain his full and blessed perfection by cleaving to him" (CCC 1730).*

Fruit > Bishop St John Fisher refused to recognise the validity of the divorce of King Henry from Catharine, because it was against the teachings of Christ as taught by the Church on marriage. When he was in prison, some of his friends came to his cell to plead with him to reconsider, in order to save his life. The bishop told his friends to come after a week and he would give his answer. At the end of the week they approached him, and the prisoner asked them this question: "What benefit is it to anyone to win the whole world and forfeit or lose his very self?" (Lk 9:25). Sadly, they walked away, as the bishop gladly went to his death, a truly free man.

LIBERTY IN CHRIST

ROOT > The words of Jesus: "The truth will make you free"
(Jn 8:32), is to enlighten and guide our faith life. Full truth
which comes from God has its centre in Jesus Christ, for he
is 'the way, and the truth and the life' (Jn 14:6). Through his
Incarnation and Redemption, Christ has brought our
redemption, which is liberation in the strongest sense of the
word, since it has freed us from the most radical evil, namely
sin and the power of death. Hence, by uniting ourselves with
Christ, we lay for ourselves the foundation and the measure
of all liberating action.

> *"If you make my word your home, you will indeed be my*
> *disciples; you will come to know the truth, and the truth*
> *shall set you free" (Jn 8:31-32).*

FRUIT > At times, the truth can be cruel, but it can still be
loved, for it makes free those who have accepted it. For
example, you are in a great painful situation for no fault of
yours but due to unavoidable circumstances or cruelty of
others. Suppose, in a situation such as this, you say to
yourself, "I accept it, for it is God's plan for me", or say,
"I forgive those who have caused this pain". You will
experience true freedom, that is, in the midst of evil you
will be at peace within. This is because you are following
the teachings of Christ on how to react to such situations.
Thus the truth of Christ frees you.

HOW FREE?

ROOT > Freedom is complete obedience, to the purpose for which we were designed. It is complete obedience to the pursuit of truth, not the truth of facts or of science, but truth about what we are for. Freedom is complete obedience, to the calls and demands of love that has been poured into each of us to spent out on others. Freedom is complete obedience, to the special elements for which we were designed. For some, the element is listening or caring. For others, of being a bridge-builder or a community catalyst. For others, gardening, or writing or teaching or pasturing. Obedience to the specific purpose, is the entrance to freedom.

> "Do you want to be healed?" (Jn 5;6). "What do you want me to do?" (Mk 10:51).

FRUIT > How far do we want to go into freedom? Jesus asked, those who were seeking help from him this question many times in different words. His parables and stories also posed this question: do you want to go as far as the good Samaritan? Are you more serious than the brother of the prodigal son? Can you take lessons from the flowers of the field and the birds of the air? Do you want to go as far as praying for your enemies? And what about the undeserved insults and weight of the cross? Is your desire for freedom that wide and deep?

THE LIBERTY OF THE LITTLE ONES

ROOT > The reality of the depth of freedom which can be found in any true believer, is especially found among the little ones and the poor. In their faith, these little ones know that they are the object of God's infinite love. Whatever the forms of poverty, injustice and affliction they endure, they offer up their supplications in the Psalms. They endure persecution, martyrdom and death; but they live in hope of deliverance. They trust in God to whom they commend their cause. The 'poor of Yahweh' know, that communion with God is the most precious treasure and one in which human beings can find their true freedom.

> *"My soul proclaims the greatness of the Lord and my spirit rejoices in God my Saviour; because he has looked upon the humiliation of his servant" (Lk 1:46-48).*

FRUIT > One of the principle errors that has seriously burdened the process of liberation of human beings, comes from the widely held conviction that material prosperity should serve as a basis for achieving freedom. But our actual experience is different. Increasing prosperity has not made people more friendly toward one another. They are better off; but the new found wealth has not resulted in a new sense of community. There is more competitiveness, more envy, more unrest and more anxiety. There is less opportunity to relax, to get together informally, and enjoy the little things in life. Success has isolated a lot of people and made them lonely.

RULES OF LIBERTY

ROOT > Freedom is not the liberty to do anything whatever. It is the freedom to do good, and in this alone happiness is to be found. The good is thus the goal of freedom. In consequence, we become free to the extent that we come to the knowledge of the truth, and to the extent that this truth – and not any other forces – guides our will. Liberation for the sake of a knowledge of the truth which alone directs the will towards good, is the necessary condition for freedom worthy of the name.

> *"Human freedom is a force for growth and maturity in truth and goodness; it attains its perfection when directed toward God, our beatitude" (CCC 1731).*

FRUIT > Liberty not oriented toward truth and goodness, leads to worship strange cults and suffer its consequences. Already threatened by environmental disasters, falling of social values, a general atmosphere of insecurity, and the growing ache of dissatisfaction, people with disoriented freedom, become more vulnerable to the influence of occult cults and the consequences are unimaginable: young people are brainwashed, families are split, idols are venerated and worshipped. In our own times, we have witnessed some horrible results of such cults, such as the mass-suicide of hundreds of men, women and children in South America.

ABUSE OF LIBERTY

ROOT > A line runs through society. It is an extremely important line, for it creates a moral climate in which we live. On one side of the line, is what we consider ethical and appropriate behaviour; on the other side of the line, is what we consider immoral and destructive behaviour. On one side is what we deem sacred, valuable, and beautiful, on the other side what is vulgar, base, and demeaning. It is a movable line and actually is moved by the people of society for they are free to move it. The more we push the line back, the more we abuse our freedom and hurt ourselves in the process.

> *"From its outset, human history attests to the wretchedness and oppression born of the human heart in consequence of the abuse of freedom"* (CCC 1739).

FRUIT > Freedom is the ability to do what we ought; licence is the ability to do whatever we want. Sometimes, what we ought to do and what we want to do are two very different things. I may like some of the nice things you own and want to take a few for myself, but I ought not to do so because they are your property. Those oblivious to this distinction, find it hard to accept any curbs on the human ego and behaviour. The result is wild liberty, which feeds iron conscience. To know how to free oneself is nothing; the arduous thing is to know what to do with one's freedom.

AUTHENTIC LIBERATION

ROOT > The very core of the liberation accomplished by Christ, our Redeemer, is that we have been delivered from sin, the most radical evil. He thus restored freedom to itself and showed it the right path, which is marked out by the supreme commandment of love. Love permeates authentic freedom, moving people thus freed, to a liberating task in the world, that is, to work for truth, justice and peace, until a civilisation of love becomes the sole civilisation for all humankind.

> *"In the exercise of their rights, individual men and social groups are bound by the moral law to have respect both for the rights of others and for their own duties toward others and for the common welfare of all" (DH 7).*

FRUIT > Our failures to love, which is the sole path to authentic freedom, cause people to lose their direction, placing them outside the plan of the Father which is to unite all things in love. There are, in effect, only two great forces in the world. One, is the force of expansion toward God and toward others; and that force is called love. The other, is the force of withdrawal into oneself; and that force is called selfishness, pride, and all the other names which signify that egocentric regression.

PEACE OF CHRIST

ROOT > Everybody loves to talk about calm and peace, whether in a family, national or international context; but without inner peace, how can we make real peace? It is the inner peace Christ came to offer humankind. World peace through hatred and force is impossible. Even in the case of individuals, there is no possibility to feel happiness through anger. If in a difficult situation, one becomes disturbed internally, then external things will not help at all. However, if despite of external difficulties, internally one's attitude is love, warmth and kindness, then problems can be faced and accepted easily.

> *"The crisis of civilisation must be countered by the civilisation of love, founded on the universal values of peace, solidarity, justice and liberty, which find their full attainment in Christ" (John Paul II – TMA 52).*

FRUIT > Many people ask: "If the Lord truly bequeathed us peace, why there is so much violence around us, and in some countries, warfare is actually raging?" The answer to this question may be another question: "What have we done with the Lord's gift of peace, with his precious legacy?" Perhaps we have preferred the kind of peace that the world gives: a peace that consists in the silence of the oppressed, in the helplessness of the conquered, and in the humiliation of those whose rights trampled underfoot.

PEACE WITH GOD

ROOT > The Greeks thought that one had only to follow one's nose and he or she would arrive at blessedness. But the Greeks had forgotten that every human being has a broken nose. What I mean is that human beings destined for blessedness are twisted in their nature, since the original fall from God's grace. God formed the first pair of human beings holy, innocent and perfect. But they were not able to sustain so great a glory without falling into pride. They wanted to make themselves their own centre and independent of his help, thus withdrawing themselves from his rule.

> *"Talking about peace in merely earthly terms and taking no account of our relationship with our Creator produces scant and frail results" (John Paul II – AHM 26).*

FRUIT > Just go to a three-lane motorway in the rush hour. All the drivers recognise the right of central government to decide how they should drive, with the result the road is quite safe as long as no body makes a mistake. Now, what if all the drivers decided that they had a right to choose what rules were right for them as individuals? There will be confusion, chaos and deaths. Likewise, our rebellion against God destroys our lives sooner or later, for it is the rejection of God's plan for us. Human rebellion against God is an aberration of self, a moral twist which screws up all we have, all we do and all we are. Hence the need to make peace with God.

NON-VIOLENCE

ROOT > *Ahimsa* or non-violence is a powerful idea that Mahatma Gandhi made familiar throughout the world. Non-violence is not just accepting violence on oneself. It is something more positive and more meaningful than that. The true expression of non-violence is compassion. Some people seem to think that compassion is just a passive emotional response, instead of a rational stimulus to action. To experience genuine compassion is to develop a feeling of closeness to others, combined with a sense of responsibility for their welfare.

> *"Blessed are the gentle: they shall have the earth as inheritance" (Mt 5:4).*

FRUIT > Basic human nature is not violent, as some people think it is. Examine different mammals, say, those animals such as tigers or lions. They very much depend on others' lives for their basic survival, and so they have long teeth and long nails. But look at the peaceful animals such as deer. They are completely herbivorous, and so their teeth and nails are completely different – more gentle. Likewise, we the human beings belong to the gentle category. Our teeth or nails are very gentle. So, human beings have a non-violent nature. We are called to live according our gentle nature.

PEACEMAKERS

ROOT > Everyone says peace, but when things are related to self-interest, nobody bothers about war, killing and stealing. Although we may talk of achieving global demilitarisation, to begin with, some kind of inner disarmament is necessary. The key to genuine world peace is a sense of understanding and respect for each other as human beings, based on compassion and love. It is worthwhile and important to make an individual effort to stop, or at least minimise, the danger of war. To begin, of course, we must control the anger and the hatred in ourselves.

> *"As disciples of Christ we are called in a special way to be peacemakers; we are called to overcome injustices, to renounce the use of force, to be ready to understand and also to forgive one another" (John Paul II – AHM 27).*

FRUIT > One day, a young man was dying; but strange to say, he could not die. A Sister of Mother Teresa asked him: "What is it?" "What is it?" And he said: "Sister, I cannot die until I ask my father to forgive me." So the Sister found out where the father was, and called him. And something extraordinary happened. The father embraced his son and cried, "My son, my beloved son!" And the son begged the father, "Forgive me! Forgive me!" And the two of them clung to each other tenderly. Two hours later the young man died.

PEACE AND JUSTICE

ROOT > Justice is fairness or rightness. A just person tries to treat everyone fairly and expects to be treated that way, too. Justice is an essential element in relationships and society. If justice is present to a significant degree in society, it promotes security, peace, and trust. If it is not present, the well-being of a community begins to disintegrate, people feel unsure, and fear and distrust escalate. Personal safety becomes the ultimate concern. A vague feeling grows that life is not right, and we feel powerless to change things.

> *"The Church is always aware of her duty to act decisively to promote and defend the basic values of peace and justice in the face of contrary tendencies in our time" (John Paul II – TMA 22).*

FRUIT > God dreamt of the world as one family, although we still seem to be having two families: the Haves and the Have-nots. The earth is essentially a common inheritance, the fruit of which should be for the benefit of all. It is unjust for a privileged few to go on accumulating superfluous possessions by squandering available resources, while multitude of people live in conditions of misery, at the lowest level of subsistence. Economic injustices grind the faces of the poor; but the triumph of justice is the only peace.

PEACE AND HUMAN RIGHTS

ROOT > Promotion of peace is closely linked with the promotion of human rights. Human rights flow from the spiritual and transcendental dimensions of the person. It is crucial to understand that human rights are also the rights of God, since anything that affects the human dignity is an offence to God the Father, who by creating us in his own image, gave us his own dignity as a gift and a treasure. Therefore, when someone acts against another person's rights, that person is hurting his or her own dignity and is offending God.

> *"In all my ministry as pastor of the universal Church, I have tried to draw particular attention to the safeguarding and the promotion of the dignity of the person and of his rights, at all stages of his life, and in every political, social, economic and cultural situation"* (John Paul II – AHM 28).

FRUIT > Respect for fundamental human rights cannot remain an ideal to be achieved, but a requisite foundation for a peaceful society. When we demand the rights and freedoms we so cherish, we should also be aware of our responsibilities. If we accept that others have an equal right to peace and happiness as ourselves, do we not have a responsibility to help them to procure it? Respect for human rights is as important to the people of Africa and Asia, as it is to those in Europe or the Americas.

A THREAT TO PEACE

ROOT > The earth has never produced so much, and yet there are more poor people now than ever before. The fruits of world development are not shared out evenly. Mounting poverty makes the poor grow more numerous and poorer. It creates marginalisation, cultural deprivation, racism, and break-up of families. Very often, street demonstrations, climate of suspicion and the sights to which the media and the press give voice, are expressions of world's poor people's dissatisfaction and their powerlessness over basic necessities, which are disregarded by society as a whole.

> *"A covert but real threat to peace is extreme poverty. By eating away at human dignity, it constitutes a serious attack on the value of life and strikes the peaceful development of society at heart" (John Paul II – AHM 29).*

FRUIT > Are not the sharing out of the goods of the earth, a just distribution of profits, a healthy resistance to excessive consumerism and protection of natural and human environment, the urgent duties of all those who are in public office, and who have special responsibility for world peace? We can confidently say that, as long as the individual is not sufficiently respected and not taken into consideration, not loved for what he or she is, there will be injustice, inequality and threat to peace.

THE YEARNING FOR PEACE

ROOT > On the human level, nobody actually wants war, because it brings unspeakable suffering. Everyone wants peace. But we need a genuine peace founded on mutual trust and the realisation that as brothers and sisters we must all live together without trying to destroy each other. We can no longer invoke the national, racial or ideological barriers that separate us, without destructive repercussions. In the context of our new interdependence, considering the interest of others is the best form of self-interest. Interdependence, in fact, is a fundamental law of nature.

> *"Never before in the history of mankind has peace been so much talked about and so ardently desired as in our day. The growing interdependence of peoples and nations make almost everyone subscribe to the ideal of universal brotherhood" (John Paul II – AHM 30).*

FRUIT > Responsibility for world peace does not lie only with the leaders of our countries. It lies with each of us individually. Peace, for example, starts within each of us. When we have inner peace, we can be at peace with those around us. When our community is in a state of peace, it can share that peace with neighbouring communities, and so on. Wars arise basically from a failure to understand one another's humanness. Hence, instead of summit meetings, why not have our families meet for a picnic and get to know each other, while the children play together?